CREATIVE POSITIONS IN ADULT MENTAL HEALTH

For my dearest friend Ellie,
we've had so much fun
together in various odd
parts of the world — I so
value your friendship
with much love
Sue.

Systemic Thinking and Practice Series

Charlotte Burck and Gwyn Daniel (Series Editors)

This influential series was co-founded in 1989 by series editors David Campbell and Ros Draper to promote innovative applications of systemic theory to psychotherapy, teaching, supervision, and organisational consultation. In 2011, Charlotte Burck and Gwyn Daniel became series editors, and aim to present new theoretical developments and pioneering practice, to make links with other theoretical approaches, and to promote the relevance of systemic theory to contemporary social and psychological questions.

Other titles in the Series include

(For a full listing, see our website www.karnacbooks.com)

Perspectives on Supervision
  Edited by David Campbell and Barry Mason

Self in Relationships: Perspectives on Family Therapy from Developmental Psychology
  Astri Johnsen and Vigdis Wie Tortsteinsson

Dialogical Meetings in Social Networks
  Jaakko Seikkula and Tom Eirk Arnkil

Intellectual Disabilities: A Systemic Approach
  Edited by Sandra Baum and Henrik Lynggaard

Innovations in the Reflecting Process
  Edited by Harlene Anderson and Per Jensen

The Performance of Practice:

Enhancing the Repertoire of Therapy with Children and Families
  Jim Wilson

The Dialogical Therapist: Dialogue in Systemic Practice
  Paolo Bertrando

Systems and Psychoanalysis: Contemporary Integrations in Family Therapy
  Carmel Flaskas and David Pocock

Intimate Warfare: Regarding the Fragility of Family Relations
  Martine Groen and Justine Van Lawick

Being with Older People: A Systemic Approach
  Edited by Glenda Fredman, Eleanor Anderson, and Joshua Stott

Mirrors and Reflections: Processes of Systemic Supervision
  Edited by Charlotte Burck and Gwyn Daniel

Race and Culture: Tools, Techniques and Trainings: A Manual for Professionals
  Reenee Singh and Sumita Dutta

The Vibrant Relationship: A Handbook for Couples and Therapists
  Kirsten Seidenfaden and Piet Draiby

The Vibrant Family: A Handbook for Parents and Professionals
  Kirsten Seidenfaden, Piet Draiby, Susanne Søborg Christensen, and Vibeke Hejgaard

Culture and Reflexivity in Systemic Psychotherapy: Mutual Perspectives
  Edited by Inga-Britt Krause

Positions and Polarities in Contemporary Systemic Practice:
The Legacy of David Campbell
  Edited by Charlotte Burck, Sara Barratt, and Ellie Kavner

CREATIVE POSITIONS IN ADULT MENTAL HEALTH

Outside In–Inside Out

Edited by

Sue McNab and Karen Partridge

KARNAC

First published in 2014 by
Karnac Books Ltd
118 Finchley Road, London NW3 5HT

British Library Cataloguing in Publication Data

A C.I.P. for this book is available from the British Library

  ISBN 978 1 78049 192 9

Edited, designed and produced by The Studio Publishing Services Ltd
www.publishingservicesuk.co.uk
e-mail: studio@publishingservicesuk.co.uk

Printed in Great Britain

www.karnacbooks.com

CONTENTS

ACKNOWLEDGEMENTS   ix

ABOUT THE EDITORS AND CONTRIBUTORS   xi

SERIES EDITORS' FOREWORD   xix

FOREWORD by Bebe Speed   xxiii

PREFACE by Louise and Rob   xxix

PREFACE: The Moving on Group by Sue McNab   xxxiii

INTRODUCTION: "The soul within the symptoms"   xxxvii
by Sue McNab

SECTION ONE
OUTSIDE IN: A STANCE TOWARDS THEORY

PART I: DECONSTRUCTING THEORETICAL POSITIONS

CHAPTER ONE
Psychiatric diagnosis and its dilemmas   5
  David Harper

CHAPTER TWO
Missing the point: the shy story of disappointment   25
  Duncan Moss

CHAPTER THREE
Dancing between discourses   43
  Sue McNab

        PART II: CONSTRUCTING ALTERNATIVE POSITIONS

CHAPTER FOUR
Coming to reasonable terms with our histories: 67
narrative ideas, memory, and mental health
  David Denborough

CHAPTER FIVE
"Where the hell is everybody?" Leanna's resistance   87
to armed robbery and negative social responses
  Allan Wade

CHAPTER SIX
Psychiatry, emotion, and the family: 109
from expressed emotion to dialogical selves
  Paolo Bertrando

                    SECTION TWO
        INSIDE OUT: AN APPRECIATION OF PRACTICE
              PART I: SPACE IN TIGHT CORNERS:
                 PRACTICE-BASED EXAMPLES

CHAPTER SEVEN
Open dialogues mobilise the resources of   131
the family and the patient
  Jaakko Seikkula and Birgitta Alakare

CHAPTER EIGHT
Narrative psychiatry   151
  SuEllen Hamkins

CHAPTER NINE
Family needs, family solutions: developing family   167
therapy in adult mental health services
  Roger Stanbridge and Frank Burbach

CHAPTER TEN
The significance of dialogue to wellbeing: 187
learning from social constructionist couple therapy
  Taiwo Afaupe

PART II: PRIVILEGING THE VOICE OF
THE CLIENT AND THERAPIST

CHAPTER ELEVEN
Narrative therapy with children of parents   205
experiencing mental health difficulties
  Ruth Pluznick and Natasha Kis-Sines

CHAPTER TWELVE
Hearing Voices: creating theatre from stories told   227
by mental health service users
  Clare Summerskill

CHAPTER THIRTEEN
Beyond the spoken word   241
  Gail Simon

CHAPTER FOURTEEN
Voices from the frontline: "keeping on keeping on"—   259
what matters to staff working in adult mental health
services?
  Iona Cook

AFTERWORD: Reflections from trainee therapists   273
  Shona Reed-Purvis and Paul Flecknoe

AFTERWORD: The Moving on Group   279
  Jo and Kevin

INDEX   283

ACKNOWLEDGEMENTS

With grateful thanks to Bebe Speed and Alec McNab for their editorial support and to the many individual and families who have so openly shared their stories with us. With thanks to Hermann, Marius, and Leonie Maier for their boundless love and support through challenging times.

Thanks to Rebecca Dyer Szabo for permission to use her photographs for the cover: front cover photograph: "Interior detail, 8 Ferri Pavillion, Ex-psychiatric hospital of Volterra, Italy"; back cover photograph: "Exterior, 14 Ferri Pavillion, Ex-psychiatric hospital of Volterra, Italy". These photographs were taken by Rebecca Dyer Szabo when she documented what remains of the former psychiatric hospital in Volterra. This hospital survived many political regimes and its history is a reflection of the uses and abuses of psychiatric institutions in Italy and elsewhere. In 1904, a state law was passed which decreed that any person causing harm or scandal to himself or others be forcibly held in the psychiatric hospital. During the Fascist regime of Benito Mussolini, political prisoners were held there as well. Treatments included medically induced fevers (malaria therapy, pyretic therapy) insulin-induced comas, ergotherapy, electro-convulsive therapy, and, beginning in the 1960s, psychopharmacological therapy. In 1978,

Law 180, also knows as the Bersaglia Law, was passed in Italy, requiring that all state-run psychiatric institutions cease to admit new patients and that the facilities be closed within five years. The established patients were gradually released to their families, or turned out on the streets, except for a few who were transferred to psychiatric wards within the local general hospital. Law 180 was part of a trend, especially in Western Europe, which prompted the closure of most psychiatric hospitals in favour of what was considered a more humane and effective treatment focusing on community-based care.

In Chapter Two, excerpts from "The Love Song of J. Alfred Prufrock" are taken from *Collected Poems 1909–1962*, by T. S. Eliot. Copyright © 1936 by Houghton Mifflin Harcourt Publishing Company. Copyright © renewed 1964 by T. S. Eliot. Reprinted by permission of Houghton Mifflin Harcourt Publishing Company in the United States and by Faber and Faber Ltd throughout the rest of the world. All rights reserved.

We thank the copyright holders for their permission to reproduce these lines.

Taiwo Afuape is employed as a systemic psychotherapist at an adult mental health psychology and psychotherapy department for Central and North West London Foundation Trust, where she sees couples and families for therapy, and as a lead clinical psychologist and systemic psychotherapist for the Tavistock an Portman Foundation Trust in South Camden Community CAMHS. Her work in CAMHS supporting children and young people involves working with systems such as parents, families, schools, social care and health systems, and community agencies.

Birgitta Alakare is a psychiatrist and family therapist in Länsi-Pohja Health Care District, Western Lapland, Finland, where she has worked since 1982. She has been a member of the team developing family and social network based practices and the open dialogue approach in psychiatry. She is interested in the treatment of psychotic and other severe crises and in the use of medication. She has also been a member of the research team looking at the treatment outcomes of acute psychosis. She currently works in public psychiatry and is instrumental in making this a more open and respectful service for patients and their families.

Paolo Bertrando, MD, PhD, graduated in medicine and specialised in psychiatry in Milan, where he also attended the Milan school of systemic therapy directed by Luigi Boscolo and Gianfranco Cecchin. He works in private practice as a systemic psychotherapist at the Studio il Dialogo in Milan, as well as a teacher in the Turin branch of the Milan School. He has published several articles and books on systemic therapy, including *The Times of Time* (1993); *Systemic Therapy with Individuals* (1996), both co-written with Boscolo; and *The Dialogical Therapist* (2007).

Frank Burbach is a consultant clinical psychologist with the Somerset Partnership NHS Foundation Trust. He is Head of Psychology (Adults and Young People) and lead for early intervention in psychosis services. He has a Diploma in Marital and Family Therapy (Exeter University) and is also a registered cognitive–behavioural psychotherapist. He is a member of the "triangle of care" national steering group, chairs the Family Interventions Network within the Division of Clinical Psychology Psychosis and Complex Mental Health Faculty, is joint IRIS South West Early Intervention Lead, and is also a member of the Editorial Board of the *Journal of Family Therapy*.

Iona Cook is a systemic psychotherapist working in Newham Talking Therapies. Her previous professional background is in psychiatric nursing. At the time of writing her dissertation, she worked in a role supporting carers and families of people with severe and enduring mental health difficulties within a community mental health team. At that time, she was also working as a trainee systemic psychotherapist in Bexley Child and Adolescent Mental Health Service. She is passionate about social justice and social change. She loves to walk and immerse herself in the countryside, and also loves to read.

David Denborough works as a teacher and writer/editor for Dulwich Centre and a community practitioner for the Dulwich Centre Foundation. His publications include: *Collective Narrative Practice: Responding to Individuals, Groups, and Communities Who Have Experienced Trauma*; *Family Therapy: Exploring the Field's Past, Present And Possible Futures*; *Trauma: Narrative Responses to Traumatic Experience*. Recent teaching/ community assignments have included Bosnia, Rwanda, Uganda, Canada, Brazil, Argentina, Chile, South Africa, and a number of

Aboriginal Australian communities. David's songs in response to current social issues have received airplay throughout Australia and Canada. He also writes for KAGE theatre company.

SuEllen Hamkins, MD, is Assistant Director of the Center for Counseling and Psychological Health at the University of Massachusetts-Amherst and Adjunct Clinical Assistant Professor at Tufts University School of Medicine. Her work focuses on helping people cultivate their values and strengths in the face of difficulties and has centred on three main areas: adolescent girls and mother–daughter relationships, college mental health, and narrative psychiatry. From 1997 to 2007, she co-created The Mother–Daughter Project, a primary prevention grassroots initiative that explored how to support the wellbeing of adolescent girls, mothers, and mother–daughter relationships. She co-authored the resulting book, *The Mother–Daughter Project: How Mothers and Daughters Can Band Together, Beat the Odds, and Thrive Through Adolescence* (Penguin, 2007). Mother–daughter groups based on the model she helped develop have formed throughout the world. Her latest book, *The Art of Narrative Psychiatry* (Oxford University Press, 2014) shows the person-centered, collaborative approach of narrative psychiatry in action through vivid case reports and offers detailed guidance in how to incorporate strengths-based narrative strategies in ones practice of psychiatry or psychotherapy. SuEllen lives in Northampton, Massachusetts, with her family, with whom she enjoys cross-country skiing, swimming, dancing, and lying around the living room reading.

David Harper is Reader in Clinical Psychology at the University of East London (UEL). He moved to UEL in 2000 after nearly a decade working as a practitioner in the North-west of the UK. He is a co-author of *Deconstructing Psychopathology* (Sage, 1995) and *Psychology, Mental Health and Distress* (Palgrave MacMillan, 2013), and co-edited *Qualitative Research Methods in Mental Health and Psychotherapy: An Introduction for Students and Practitioners* (Wiley, 2012). He also works as a consultant clinical psychologist in Newham as part of a systemic consultation service in East London Foundation Trust.

Natasha Kis-Sines is a member of the Toronto District School Board social work team. She works with young people and families from diverse communities and is deeply committed to social justice. With her colleague, Ruth Pluznick, Natasha has developed a programme for children growing up with parents with mental health difficulties; the young people share their stories with other youth and families in similar circumstances, and they "consult" to agencies and schools. Natasha and Ruth have published two articles about this project and plans are under way for a documentary film with these young people and their parents. Natasha has also produced a public education video with young men in her school about depression. The video offers a first-person account of their experience of depression, its effects on their lives and relationships, and their strategies to move forward in life, despite the challenges.

Sue McNab worked as a systemic psychotherapist in CAMHS in London before moving to adult mental health services in Oxford Health NHS Trust ten years ago. She has also been attached to the Tavistock Centre and the Institute of Family Therapy as a trainer and supervisor on the Masters courses, and currently works on the Advanced Diploma in the Supervision of Family and Systemic Psychotherapy at IFT. During a period of working in adolescent inpatient units, she became interested in mother blaming and shaming discourses and has written on this topic with her colleague and friend, Ellie Kavner. In recent years, a bevy of grandchildren has added an exciting new dimension to life.

Duncan Moss has worked for more than twenty years as a clinical psychologist, both clinically, in adult mental health contexts, and as an associate professor (senior lecturer) on the University of Plymouth Clinical Psychology Programme. In the past twelve years, he has been exploring the relevance of "mindfulness meditation" to both staff and receivers of services in the NHS and elsewhere, and is interested in the links between mindfulness and other forms of reflexivity, such as social constructionism.

Karen Partridge, PhD, is a consultant clinical psychologist and systemic psychotherapist currently working at the Tavistock and Portman NHS Trust and in private practice. Her clinical work has taken place primarily in adult mental health, but she has worked across the age range and across services. Her research was an enquiry into organisational change in hospitals, which she remains passionate about. She completed her systemic training at the KCC Foundation, where she worked as a tutor and, latterly, as Co-Director. She teaches and supervises professionals in a wide range of settings and is interested in consultation and training in staff groups and organisations and in the interface between therapy, community and organisational interventions, action research, and social justice. She lives in London with her partner, adult children, and two cats who all come and go. She enjoys music and art and enquiring into Buddhism.

Ruth Pluznick is the Director of Clinical Services at a public children's mental health centre in Toronto. She is a member of the international faculty of the Dulwich Centre and a teacher for the Narrative Therapy Centre of Toronto. Ruth has been practising and teaching narrative therapy for over twenty years, and is particularly committed to the application of these ideas in marginalised communities. With her colleague, Natasha Kis-Sines, Ruth has developed a programme for children growing up with parents with mental health difficulties; the young people share their stories with other youth and families in similar circumstances. Natasha and Ruth have published two articles about this project and plans are under way for a documentary film with these young people and their parents. Ruth is also involved with narrative projects in residential programmes and a range of community initiatives. She has just returned from working with Dulwich Centre in Ramallah, Palestine.

Jaakko Seikkula, PhD, is Professor of Psychotherapy at the University of Jyväskylä, a clinical psychologist, and a family therapist. Dr Seikkula has been mainly involved in developing family- and social network-based practices in psychiatry with psychosis and other severe crises. From the early 1980s until 1998, he was a member of a team in Western Lapland in Finland who were developing the comprehensive open dialogue approach, which he has been studying both in relation to the process of dialogues and the outcomes in treatment of acute psychosis. After moving to the University of Jyväskylä, he has become involved in the development of many research projects. Recently, ideas of open dialogues have been applied to social work with children's problems, to consultation to organisations, and to supervision and teaching. Research has focused on the outcome and process studies of family therapy with psychosis, depression, and social network interventions. A recent development focuses on a new method of research known as "dialogical methods of investigations in happenings of change". This has grown out of Jaakko's longstanding interest in Mikhail Bakhtin's work, which has been his main inspiration for understanding the power of dialogue in human life. During the past few years, the importance of being present in the moment, in the "once occurring participation in being", has become the most important aspect of therapy and writing and teaching about therapy. Jaakko is in charge of a project entitled Relational Mind, which is studying the moments of change during the "multi-actor" dialogues of family meetings.

Gail Simon, D. Prof., is interested in research into systemic practice. Her doctoral research was on writing as a relational practice. She is Principal Lecturer in Systemic Practice at the University of Bedfordshire, where she is course leader for the Professional Doctorate in Systemic Practice. She has developed and published papers on reflexive practitioner research methodologies and has presented at national and international conferences on systemic practice, the politics of psychotherapy, reflexive research methods, and research as social and political intervention. She is a member of International Advisory Board for the *International Journal for Collaborative Practice*, the Editorial Board for *The Qualitative Report*, and reviews for the *Journal of Family Therapy*, *Child Abuse Review*, *Human Systems: Journal of Therapy, Consultation and Training*, and the *International Journal for Collaborative Practice*. Gail has written on psychotherapy in the lesbian, gay, and queer communities, having co-founded and directed The Pink Practice, a systemic therapy service for the lesbian, gay, bisexual, transgender, and queer communities in London. She is a member of the Professional Affairs Committee for the Association for Systemic and Family Therapy.

Roger Stanbridge worked as Consultant Family Therapist with the Somerset Partnership NHS Foundation Trust until his recent retirement. He was Head of Family Therapy and clinical lead for the Trust's Strategy to Enhance Working Partnerships with Carers and Families and chaired the Trust's multi-agency Carers and Families Steering Group. He has published on developing family inclusive mainstream mental health services, family interventions in psychosis, and associated training programmes. Since retiring, he has continued his involvement with writing and training in these areas.

Clare Summerskill is a playwright, a singer–songwriter and a comedienne. She regularly performs her own one-woman comedy shows and tours them to theatres internationally. Clare has written and produced several plays and films in the verbatim theatre style and has also contributed to sketch shows for Radio 4. Her published works include *We're the Girls!* (Diana Publishing 2008); *Hearing Voices*, which is a play based on service users' experiences of the mental health system (Tollington Press, 2010); and, most recently, *Gateway to Heaven: Fifty Years of Lesbian and Gay Oral History* (Tollington Press, 2012).

Allan Wade, PhD, lives on Vancouver Island, where he works in private practice doing family therapy, consulting, and research. Allan and his colleagues (Linda Coates, Nick Todd, Gillian Weaver-Dunlop, and Cathy Richardson) work with individuals and families where violence (broadly defined) is at issue. The group is best known for developing response-based practice, a comprehensive framework for working with individuals who have committed, or been subjected to, violence and their families. This framework incorporates original research and analysis on social responses in cases of violence, individual and collective resistance, and the connection between violence and language, and is applied in child protection, individual and family therapy, shelter work, family law, offender and victim treatment, organisational consulting, and education. Allan works extensively for indigenous people in Canada and elsewhere, teaches locally and internationally, and has published numerous articles and book chapters read avidly by members of his immediate family.

SERIES EDITORS' FOREWORD

It is with huge pleasure that we welcome the publication of this volume, edited by two senior systemic psychotherapists, each with a wealth of experience in the field of adult mental health. The relative lack, at least in the UK, of systemic influence in adult psychiatric services as opposed to those for children and adolescents makes us particularly pleased to have this rich and inspirational volume to demonstrate and make visible both its existing impact and its potential. Sue McNab and Karen Partridge have brought a special vision to the planning of the book. As well as disseminating a range of ideas and innovative clinical approaches, they take an ethical stance that suffuses the volume and expresses itself in three main ways.

The first is that, while locating the contributions overwhelmingly within the context of public health services, the importance of maintaining a critical stance on the most widely used models of psychiatric illness remains at the core and is specifically elaborated by some of the contributors. The reader is invited to deconstruct dominant discourses of mental illness, and many contributors offer alternatives—of language and of perspective—to use for ourselves and for those with whom we work. Second, the wider questions of power, powerlessness, social marginalisation, and the effects of institutions themselves, however well meaning, are never far from the centre of contributions, so that clinical practice is always located within a wider set of questions about the impact of professional interventions. Third, the voices of users of psychiatric services are incorporated within the volume, both in the chapters themselves and in the "bookends", adding a crucial layer of richness, texture, and depth to the contributions. The presence here of multiple perspectives, individuals speaking from different positions in the adult mental health system, is, in turn, enlightening, disturbing, moving, provoking, eye-opening, and enhancing. This meticulous attention to the multiple layers of systems at work in the lives of individuals, families, and practitioners within the adult mental health context opens up to the reader the experience of double description, of reading all accounts contrapuntally, and of constantly holding in mind the question "what would this look like from another perspective?", a question which is at the heart of the systemic approach. The editors and contributors skilfully extend the dialogue between families and the wider context, between the interpersonal and intrapersonal, and between inner and outer dialogues, and, in so doing, pose important ideological and existential questions.

Systemic/family psychotherapy has, in recent years, made many contributions to adult mental health, sometimes incorporated as part of recognised treatment approaches, as in the fields of anorexia nervosa and psychosis, and at other times needing to hold a position at the margins, working "against the grain" of psychiatric orthodoxy, challenging conventional wisdom, questioning rigid boundaries such as that between adult and child services, and insisting on respecting the complexity of lives and on utilising the resources and wisdom of users and their families as well as responding to, and learning from, their feedback. In this volume, these activities achieve a new visibility as we learn from innovative projects which have led to the reconfiguration of service delivery, and from a subtle elaboration of the nuances in therapeutic communication, to provoke us to find ways to open up new meanings and ways of working while managing uncertainty, risk, and crisis. In this current climate of diminishing resources and an increasingly narrow focus on diagnosis, it is invaluable to have examples of ways in which professionals have striven to develop collaborative work with individuals and families, who so often have experiences of services which leave them feeling marginalised or stigmatised, and to share creative ways to work with individuals and families which are compassionate and effective.

We are confident that this volume, with its range of approaches and the openness and generosity of contributors in sharing many aspects of their personal and professional selves, as well as their passion and commitment, will be of interest to all those who work with, and are connected to, the adult mental health field. We are proud to include it in the series.

Charlotte Burck
Gwyn Daniel

FOREWORD

Bebe Speed

When my sister, brother, and I were children in the 1950s, our mother was depressed for a number of years and regularly saw a consultant psychiatrist at Winwick Hospital, the local asylum, one of many still dotted around the country at that time. It had opened in 1897 and eventually closed in 1998, and was one of the largest psychiatric institutions in Europe. It was a forbidding-looking place and was the nub of anxiety-laden jokes locally about being sent to the nut house if you did or said something silly or odd. Not surprisingly, it felt shameful to have a family member who was a patient there, so we kept it quiet, which cut us off even more from needed support.

Our mother was eventually prescribed ECT, the main effect of which was loss of memory, which had its good and bad sides from her perspective. To us, she seemed a bit jollier and we could sometimes even share a joke with her about whether we would get more pocket money because she could not remember whether or not she had already given it to us.

I do not know how much the ECT helped her; though she hated the memory loss, she used to say that it was worth it if it did her any good. What I do know is that she much appreciated the psychiatrist, who was kind and listened to her. She felt that she did not get very much of this from our GP, who told her to "snap out of it", or from our father, a man of his time brought up in traditional patriarchal ways. She, a gentle woman who lacked confidence, had been easily undermined.

Down the years, I have often wished that our mother's problems could have been addressed in some of the innovative ways described in this book. What a difference it might have made if, as well as being diagnosed as ill with depression and receiving physical treatments (perhaps more likely nowadays to be medication rather than ECT), she and the rest of our family could have been seen by a family therapist or someone using a "meaning framework" who would have considered her depression in the context of her relationships with her husband, children, and wider family. If someone had looked for the "soul within the symptoms" (see Introduction) and the soul within the system, what might have emerged? Maybe a story about the upheaval of our family's house move from an army camp to an austere and bitterly cold property which required a huge amount of work, our parents' strained marriage, and our mother's grief for the loss of the stability and attentive support of her family of origin and homeland in Scotland, the impact of the Second World War on my father, who had been torpedoed on his Merchant Navy ship, and on my mother, who had been without his support when my sister had been born, and the pressures both our parents were under with three young children and little money living in the Cheshire countryside miles from anywhere. As children, we could have told someone something about some of this, but, of course, nobody asked us. If we and my parents *had* been asked about the story behind the depression, I believe my mother could have been helped a great deal more, and my father along with her, and the fallout on we children would have been considerably less.

Since the 1950s, there have been many developments in the management and treatment of mental ill-health problems (see Tom Burns' excellent *Psychiatry: A Very Short Introduction*, 2006 for an overview). With the discovery of chlorpromazine and the growing awareness of the negative impact of institutionalisation, the 1960s and 1970s saw the move to community mental health teams, group homes, a few therapeutic communities, and the resultant gradual closure of the asylums. The 1970s also saw the growth of the medical disease and treatment model, with ever more detailed diagnostic manuals being produced and the development of a range of medications to treat the various diagnostic categories. But running alongside the increasing sophistication of the biogenetic medical model was the continuing influence of psychodynamic meaning approaches and the burgeoning influence of theorists and practitioners such as Laing, Bateson, Szasz, Scheff, and Goffman. Together, they presented a very different social, psychological, interpersonal, meaning view of mental illness and its appropriate treatment, quite unlike the biogenetic illness models of much of early psychiatry. And, of course, there was *One Flew Over the Cuckoo's Nest*—a required cinema outing.

My experience as a sociology student at Leicester in the heady, revolutionary late 1960s, added to my experience in my family, made a powerful mix which bred in me a deep suspicion of conventional medical psychiatry. My research dissertation was titled "Mental illness or problems in living?", in which I was at pains to show that psychiatric diagnoses covered up underlying, perfectly explicable if-only-you-spent-time-looking-for-it interpersonal problems. With more detachment now, I can see that this is a telling example of how our personal experience, training, and the contexts in which we live can powerfully influence and prejudice what we think and come to hold as "truths". It took training, time, experience, personal psychotherapy, and developments in the science of the brain for me to move to my current position of really accepting the complex mix of all the factors—intrapsychic, interactional and relational, biological, genetic, cultural, social—in any of our behaviours and feelings. Thus, a number of different stories might be told about someone's difficulties: a medical story, a meaning story, a behavioural story, all of which would have relevance and the potential for making a difference. Some difficulties would be illuminated more adequately with a medical story, others more with a meaning story, and with others an amalgam of both would be most effective.

By the time I was working in adult services in Oxford and Bucks Mental Health Trust thirty years later, it was much more likely that patients and families were being asked about meaning, not just by we family therapists and our psychological therapies colleagues, but also by psychiatrists and nursing staff. However, there were still times when it was worryingly apparent that there had been little or no enquiry about meaning; when you looked at file notes, there was no discernible "story", just symptoms, a brief history, diagnosis, and the treatment record. This might be because our psychiatric and nursing colleagues did not think a meaning discourse was particularly relevant. It might be because some people are fearful about opening themselves to the pain of others' experience and avoid enquiring too closely, but it would also have been because they had little time to construct a story with the patient, given the pressures of meeting government targets, the waiting lists, risk management strategies, cuts, and the introduction of new methods such as electronic recording, which took time to master. In addition, referral on to specialist services was not easy, given how thinly spread we were in psychological therapies.

If we, as family therapists, did become involved, it was usually not difficult to find a story, often one of loss, failure of attachment, and, surprisingly frequently, one of sexual abuse, all of which gave meaning to, and a richer description of, what had gone wrong. These understandings might then suggest different pathways to useful interventions. At the same time, we could often find and highlight considerable resilience and resourcefulness in the patient and family, sometimes against tremendous odds. Not that our meetings would lead to miraculous change and the family walking happily into the sunset, but often there would be some substantial shifts in what had been a stuck situation over many years. Or, at the very least, there would be a sense for the patient and family of their painful experiences being understood, validated, and empathised with, which meant a great deal to them and sometimes allowed a little more elasticity in their circumstances. Also, crucially in the case of children, there would be a far greater awareness of who else was in the network and who might be suffering some of the fallout from the patient's and family's problems.

In 2008, I reached sixty, and after yet another reorganisation of psychological therapies and the redeployment of staff and consequent challenge of building relationships with different teams, I decided I had run out of steam and retired. It is not always well understood by managers how the practice of working together using different approaches for the benefit of patients and their families requires a great deal of trust, empathy, and relationship building between colleagues, which takes considerable time to negotiate. In many ways, working successfully with one's colleagues can be more of a challenge than working with clients, requiring even more sensitivity, respect, curiosity, and non-judgementality, and well functioning teams should not be taken apart lightly.

In the past four years, the reorganisations have continued, with further reduction of staff numbers so that those who are left are doing more and more with increasingly disturbed patients as the gateposts of who is allowed through them are placed ever closer together. There has been an increasing emphasis and time expenditure on bureaucratic detail. I have watched mostly from the outside, but hear from insiders, too, and heard recently how a clinical manager gave the news to a member of staff that a patient she had seen for assessment had committed suicide, but that she, the clinician, had done well because all her records were up to date. This manager is well known to be normally sensitive and my shocked colleague could only think that the manager had just been overcome by current demands of the context, so that records being in order met a government imposed target and seemed more important than empathy for my colleague or, indeed, sadness about the patient's unhappiness and death. Adult services are a much more challenging context in which to think about meaning and practice systemically than are CAMHS contexts or private practice, and recent changes have not helped that. Nevertheless, despite the difficulties, there are still systemically and meaning-minded clinicians who continue to chip, and sometimes even blast, away at the clinical coalface with resolve and a high level of skill.

Also on the "up" side in adult psychiatric services, the "Increasing Access to Psychological Therapies" (IAPT) programme operating at Tier 2 has been a significant initiative both in giving a message that psychological therapies are important in general and in the actual delivery of CBT in particular to a wider group of patients. The fact that IAPT is now beginning to embrace the inclusion of systemic approaches in the programme so that more families will benefit is to be celebrated. However, in general, it seems that specialist practitioners using meaning approaches are still scarce on the ground, especially in the tertiary and inpatient services, as cuts continue. We are a long way from an ideal world where, instead of a specialist systemic approach being a very scarce resource, every patient would be seen with their family or relevant network at the point of referral by colleagues versed in medical and meaning discourses working trustingly together. In this way, problems could be understood in their context and help would be available for the family as well as the patient from the outset.

The editors of this book are to be warmly congratulated for having the inspiration and commitment to get this much-needed volume about systemic approaches in adult contexts off the ground. Their contributors show us, despite the continuing pressures, how they have made a difference in adult services, and the poignant voices of service users as well as trainees have also been given space as participants alongside us.

However useful an illness discourse might be in some situations, one of its downsides is that it can render the patient "other", the ill one, different from me, the not-ill professional. One of the powerful aspects of the meaning approach used by Sue and Karen and their contributors is that it points to the commonality of experience for all of us of what it means to be a human being coping with the sticky mix of relationships, life events, biological givens, and emotions that, at times, make up our lives, whatever position in the clinical system we occupy.

Reference

Burns, T. (2006). *Psychiatry: A Very Short Introduction*. Oxford: Oxford University Press.

Louise and Rob

Louise

I had spent two weeks as an inpatient in a psychiatric ward two years earlier and had felt so sorry for those long-term patients that I had met. I never imagined that I would one day be the one who was sectioned and then trapped in there for weeks on end. Neither did I appreciate that the most difficult part of recovering from a serious psychiatric episode would be dealing with the things that happened to me while I was in hospital.

The first and most distressing thing that I encountered after being sectioned was a sense of loss of identity. I had been missing from home for two nights before I was found and was without any of my belongings, including my own clothes. Because there were few clues as to my own identity, I felt as if I was treated as "patient X"; many of the staff failed to call me by my name, using instead the name on my hospital records, which I never use. This "patient X" was a psychiatric patient, and, therefore, non-psychiatric medical needs were seen by some of the staff as being outside of their remit. So the fact that I was dehydrated on admission (having had nothing to drink for two days) was ignored. My constantly asking for water, which should have been understandable in the circumstances, was seen as challenging behaviour.

There is also a very real sense of loss of social status as a psychiatric inpatient. Like many of us, I had previously been in a position—both socially and professionally—where my opinion was sought and valued. In short, I was used to being listened to. It was incredibly distressing to find that now there was an assumption that what I said would make no sense. Anything I said that was not obviously concrete and rational was liable to be dismissed as the ravings of manic "patient X".

The very fact of being locked in somewhere for days on end not only allows rumination, but fosters it, so that trivial issues can take on greater importance. I also realise that my mental state prevented me from expressing myself as I normally would, but, looking back on it, now that I am well, I can still see a coherent narrative in my thoughts at the time.

So, for example, I began to think a lot about being trapped in the building, and what would happen in case of a fire (a close friend nearly lost his life in a fire). When I asked members of staff to explain how we would get out, I felt patronised and ridiculed. This compounded my anxiety so I decided to take an ordinary table knife to my room to loosen the screws on the grill that was keeping me in. When this lost knife was found, just a few minutes after I had taken it, the staff *naturally* assumed that I had intended to hurt myself or someone else. Nobody seemed to listen to, or believe, my own explanation, or see my fears in context.

Overwhelmingly, at a time when I was struggling to understand what was happening to me and trying to claw back a sense of identity and self-worth, I was surrounded by people who did not seem to know or care who I was inside.

Rob

Imagine if your partner of over ten years suddenly disappears. You spend a relaxed morning shopping together, apparently enjoying each other's company. Then, with very little warning, she throws your phone into the river and drives away, leaving no clue of her intended destination. After forty-eight hours of the intimate details of your life being opened up to police scrutiny in their efforts to find her, she is finally located. You watch—bewildered, exhausted, and helpless—as the police deliver her to a secure unit where she will be detained under the Mental Health Act.

Imagine visiting nearly every day for the next fifteen weeks, sometimes for her to turn you away as unwelcome, occasionally to be shouted at. On a good day, you can sit and talk to someone who looks very much like your wife but talks like someone you have never met. At home, you feel intense grief and loneliness. During hospital visits, this is replaced with an almost visceral feeling of anger at the situation in general and towards the staff for being allowed to look after your wife when she refuses to see you.

This was my experience as Louise's husband and main carer. From my work as a GP, and before that briefly as a junior doctor working in psychiatry, I knew a little about bipolar disorder and how it can affect people's behaviour, but as a member of staff, I had no idea how easy it is to misunderstand a situation or draw the wrong conclusions. I also had little appreciation of how helpless carers and loved ones can feel.

Now in the position of a carer, feeling very much on the outside, I sensed that the staff made little effort to understand either of us as individuals, or us as a couple. Constantly being told by Louise that our relationship was over, some evidently became suspicious of me. Having been in their position and made the same assumptions myself, I knew this reaction was not malicious, but the sadness of seeing my wife in this state was certainly compounded by feeling that no one in the hospital knew who she was when she was well. It seemed that everything she said was taken at face value rather than being interpreted in the context of her acute illness. No one seemed to know what a close, loving relationship we enjoyed.

Rob and Louise

The differences between these two accounts highlight how far apart we were pushed by this episode. Two years on, and with the help of a team of family therapists, we have been able to draw our two narratives together and start to understand it as a shared experience. Through this therapy, we have been able to rebuild our relationship.

We were listened to so carefully and compassionately during our family therapy, but we cannot help wondering whether there would not have been so much damage to repair if we had been listened to more during those awful months at the hospital.

The Moving on Group

Sue McNab

Some years ago, the Moving On Group started as a multi-family group working with families where a young (and at times not so young) adult has got "stuck" living at home with their parents as a result of mental health difficulties. For some families, psychosis has taken over their lives: for others extreme anxiety, Asperger's syndrome, and obsessive–compulsive disorder means that they are, as yet, unable to take up an independent lifestyle. Sometimes, the young adults come to the meetings, but more often the parents come on their own.

The group, based on systemic principles, offers a facilitated space to share stories about their situations and worries, to offer mutual support, and to find ways of living alongside chronic struggles if they cannot be moved beyond. Its members might describe it as a "sort of family" where people can bare their souls safe in the knowledge that they will be understood and accepted. They tell each other their individual family stories, report progress or lack of it, and witness and take pride and pleasure in the "high points" of others' progress even when their own situations are highly stressful and painful. The quality of listening within this group is quite exceptional and moving to witness.

One theme which recurs is the unsurprisingly high degree of involvement between these adult children and their parents, and one beneficial intervention by the group has often been to encourage parents new to the group to look after themselves more, for example, by taking their first holiday on their own for many years. Another theme is of not being heard by professionals and of being excluded from conversations about treatment. This is particularly hard for parents to bear when their child's difficulties continue to require their close involvement emotionally, financially, and practically.

We have often thought that the people who have benefited the most have been us, the facilitators, as well as any colleagues visiting the group. A group of parents meeting in this way gives a different perspective to what it means to be a family member than when families are seen on their own. Our empathy for family members has grown exponentially as we have understood much more about what it is to bear the disappointment of having a challenging and worrying child, to feel guilty about what one has done and not done, to face the loss of a happy and contented family life and the child one had hoped for. We also came to hugely admire these families' tremendous resilience, courage, and generosity to other families, as well as the degree of humour in the face of it all. As facilitators, we have been particularly touched by this experience, as we are the parents of adult children ourselves and identify with some of the struggles that are involved in launching even relatively healthy children into the world. We feel that if all our colleagues could hear these family members speak about their experiences, this would transform the practice of partnership with carers and family members.

Over the years, a core group of parents have remained very committed to this group and, while the group has retained its original focus and embraces new families for the regular types of discussions, it has also become more political in its outlook. These parents have much wisdom and experience to offer mental health professionals and they have done this in the Trust by undertaking training of new staff members and making presentations to senior management.

In their own words below and at the end of this volume, Alan and Liz, Lynne and John, and Kevin and Jo share some of their ideas with this wider audience of readers.

Alan and Liz

Back off

"Back off," said the experts
"OK," said we—"you know that we'd love to, so who will he see?"
"Well . . . Due to the cutbacks it's quite hard to say"—the name from
last week has just gone away!
Consistency's crucial we all agree but that appointment is cancelled
there's no one to see!
The resource is closed now—the prospect is bleak so no more progress
and there goes this week!
Just what is happening? We repeatedly say, but they cannot tell US!
The "Law's" in the way.
So zilch communication the resolve now wears thin, for god's sake please
help him before he gives in!
We love and console him, encourage and cry, provide all the transport
without asking why?
So don't just say back off—you professionals beware, without us the carers
Where is MENTAL HEALTH CARE?

BOUNDARIES are the lifebelts that keep me from sinking!!
    If more mental health doctors listened to the carers' point of view,
they would have fewer patients!!!!!!

Caring for the patient, your child

The medics do not seem to listen to carers. The carers are with the
patients 24/7, they see the mood swings, how they are in the mornings, through the day, and into the evenings.
    Us carers make notes, which we then email to professionals in the
hope that they take notice! Sometimes we hope the medics might
change medication, for example, if the person concerned is becoming
too drowsy.

Engaging with the medics and professionals

This is hard, because they are busy. Nevertheless, the patient is the
most important person. If they need to talk with someone about a problem, we have to find the professional. If on holiday, we hope the locum
has read the patient notes before seeing the patient, in order to have a

meaningful discussion. If not, it could be a waste of time, which leaves the patient even more frustrated, and the carer also, because the carer deals with the backlash. It would be useful to have feedback from that sort of meeting, from the professional, to enable progress to continue.

How do parents/carers cope?

By bouncing ideas off one another to deal with a particular situation. Being patient with one another, when frustrations surface, as they always will do. One of the parents could take a couple of hours off, and relax. Sometimes, you want to find an open field and just scream, or have a damn good cry. It's amazing the energy you can find when you really need it to look after someone. Afterwards, there is a need to just relax, because if you do not keep yourself healthy, how can you hope to look after anyone else?

Diagnosis: how we wish to know what the problem is, so we know more exactly what the problem is, more importantly, how we can better can look after our child.

Lynne and John

When buying a car or some other product, you are guided through the do's and don'ts via a comprehensive manual, and when it coughs and splutters, you take it to a mechanic who will put it right. A similar exercise is followed when you are not too well. You pop along to the doctor, who will use his extensive training and do a quick diagnosis that will be followed by some form of medicine to put you on the path back to full health. How I wish it were the same when a loved one suffers with mental health problems. There is no well controlled and joined-up process. You have no idea what is going on: you wrestle to try to find a way through a system which is disparate and where sections do not effectively communicate with each other. I struggle to see how professionals and therapists can exist next door to each other and yet not know each other. As a carer, you constantly fight to be part of the process. How difficult is it for others to understand that without the carers' support, knowledge, and involvement, any treatment is always going to be put at risk? The issue becomes about the health and welfare not just of one very important person, but of the whole family.

"The soul within the symptoms"

Sue McNab

Curiously, and quite by chance, I sat down to write this introduction on the very day, 11 February, that Sylvia Plath took her life fifty years ago. Also by chance, it was snowing outside, but, unlike her, we were not in the grip of one of the coldest years on record, 1963. Various commentators, writers, and journalists are still weighing up Sylvia's life and death and, perhaps fittingly for this volume, they wonder how much of her untimely death can be ascribed to a lack of modern medicine and other medical treatments and/or attributed to the various contextual tragedies in her life.

On the day of her death, Sylvia was living in London with her two very young children, having recently separated from her husband, the poet Ted Hughes, whom she suspected had already embarked on another relationship with Assia Wevill. Sylvia, a highly intelligent woman, was trying to find her voice as a poet in the early 1960s in a land not of her birth. Her novel, *The Bell Jar*, which charts some of her earlier struggles with depression, had recently been published under a pseudonym. Her poetry told of the early death of her father and its effect on her. Her story—perhaps putting her brilliance to one side—is not so uncommon for those of us working in mental health services and its sense of complexity and tragedy seems somehow a well-timed place from which to begin a description of this book.

Another point at which to start might be to describe how this volume came to be written. On a glorious autumn day in September 2009, I was attending the Association for Family Therapy annual conference in Cambridge and found myself sitting next to Karen in a workshop. At the end, she turned to me and, quite out of the blue, asked me if I would like to join her in editing a book on adult mental health. Karen and I knew each other a little. We had worked for the same Trust in South London a few years previously, although I was in Child and Adolescent Mental Health Services and she was in Adult Mental Health Services at that time. With two other colleagues, David Amias and Jelena Manojlovic, we started a "joint clinic" which straddled child and adult services and met families where there were concerns about child and adult mental health issues. This was quite a novel idea at the time, and I remember much negotiating with managers before we got it off the ground. We learnt a huge amount from each other and discovered that, while many systemic ideas are common to any client group, there are also "things you need to know" about the particular population you work with. So David and I, from CAMHS, became more acquainted with the knowledge and power of diagnoses and their treatment, while Karen and Jelena learnt more about child development and talking with children. It was a creative space for working with mental health struggles at any age.

Back to the book: I readily agreed to such an exciting idea, being rather green about the actual process of editing and how much fun, energy, work, and heartache are involved. From the beginning, we wanted this book to speak to current ideas and practice in adult mental health settings. We wanted contributors from different countries and with different systemic orientations. We wanted less experienced as well as better-known voices to be represented and, above all, we wanted the experience of service users and their families to be central.

We are delighted by the very positive response to our invitation to contribute to this book by all the authors we approached who, like us, feel that this field has been neglected systemically. At the outset, we invited the authors to pay attention to:

- The impact on the self of working in this field, that is, personal/ professional connections.

- The contexts of social difference, that is, the "GRAACCCEEESS" (Burnham, 2012).
- Evidence-based practice/practice-based evidence.
- Foregrounding the voice of the client and their family.

We hope that together we have achieved most of these aims.

Outline of the book

In choosing the title *Creative Approaches in Adult Mental Health: Outside In–Inside Out*, there were two main influences on us. First, we were thinking about the theory of the co-ordinated management of meaning, or CMM (Cronen & Pearce, 1985), which has been an important idea in our systemic thinking and practice. In this way of thinking, the "outside" contextual forces exert a downward pressure on action while the "inside" implicative forces support or challenge these contextual forces to form an emerging co-ordination between the two. We had the idea that the first half of the book would be more theoretical, contextualising and deconstructing what is "outside", while the second half would be more practice-based, providing "inside" evidence to challenge the taken for granted in adult mental health. All the chapters are rich in exciting examples of systemic/narrative work and throughout we have attempted to privilege the perspective of people, including professionals themselves, who use these services. At times, this makes for uncomfortable reading.

The second influence in our choice of title was the book by Luise Eichenbaum and Susie Orbach, *Outside in, Inside out: Women's Psychology: A Feminist Psychoanalytic Approach* (1982). Susie Orbach continues to be a major influence in challenging the individualised notion of suffering, deconstructing gender relations, acknowledging the importance of power, and asserting that the personal is political. We wanted to echo her title in appreciation of her pioneering work and also to remind ourselves and our readers of the political edge to the personal experiences of our authors and especially of those in our "bookends", the Preface and the Afterword.

Family therapy posts in adult mental health in the UK are still relatively rare, but encouragingly there are an increasing number of systemic practitioners in the field. We hope that this book will speak to them and to all the professionals working with adult patients and their families as well as to the patients and families themselves.

The chapters

The Prefaces and the Afterwords are the pieces of writing which start and finish the volume and echo the voices of experience who movingly remind us what life is like "on the inside". Louise and Rob are a young couple who tell the story, both individually and together, about Louise's hospital admission and how couple therapy helped them regain their lives together. A group of carers from the Moving On Group share their heartfelt experiences of looking after their adult children who are in the grip of severe and enduring mental health difficulties. At times, the system lets them down. On other occasions, good practice prevails and makes a huge impact on their lives and their ability to keep going. These sections also include a description of joining an adult mental health setting as family therapy trainees, and gives a fresh look at some of the constraints and possibilities of training in this context.

The book itself is divided into two main sections, "Outside in: a stance towards theory" and "Inside out: an appreciation of practice", each of which is divided into two parts. Part I of Section One deals with deconstructing theoretical positions, and comprises Chapters One, Two and Three, while Part II is titled "Constructing alternative positions" and comprises Chapters Four, Five, and Six. Part I of the second section is titled "Space in tight corners: practice-based examples", and this subject is covered in Chapters Seven, Eight, Nine, and Ten. Chapters Eleven, Twelve, Thirteen, and Fourteen comprise Part II of the second section, which deals with the subject of "Privileging the voice of the client and therapist".

David Harper, the author of Chapter One, gives us a launch pad from which to view the history of mental health diagnoses alongside a springboard of alternative ways of understanding mental health struggles through the critique of social constructionist and post-modern ideas. He continues by presenting some suggestions for systemic practitioners about how either to live more comfortably alongside the dominant medical discourse of individual pathology or take up a challenge to it in innovative practice. We leave this chapter feeling well grounded in history, appreciative of context, and with a challenge for the future—we feel in relatively safe territory.

We lose "our perch" in Chapter Two, by Duncan Moss, on "his appointment with disappointment". His creative, experiential writing about an emotion which is little written about or spoken of, but certainly experienced by all of us, draws us into a land of uncertainty or, in the words of David Loy (2008) "lack". Duncan invites us really to experience any false sense of arriving at a resolution in our therapeutic endeavours and to reflect on all those times when "things have not quite worked out" as we or our clients would have liked. He also challenges us to resist the rush to alight on mindfulness, the "new kid on the block", as a possible saviour.

Using dance as a metaphor, as suggested by Karen Partridge, who sadly was not well enough to join me in the writing of this chapter as originally planned, I have described in Chapter Three the complex series of steps that systemic practitioners perform in their daily working lives as they bump up against other professional discourses as well as their own models of therapy in adult mental health settings. In collaboration with the Simms family, who joined me in this piece of writing, I lay out not only some of the challenges involved in this process, but also, perhaps more importantly, the richness of the movement when the steps flow together.

In Chapter Four, David Denborough presents his consistently fresh approach to pushing the boundaries of narrative practice, exploring ideas from "critical heritage practice", community memory projects "combining remembrance, politics, poetry, campaigns, history and artistry" (Rassool, 2007). David gives a compelling description of how we, as clinicians in the mental health arena, are also involved in memory projects that, in his words, "seek to link personal experience, resonance, and imagery to address broader social suffering". Through this process, he is interested in helping people and communities who have suffered trauma to find a "usable history". This chapter challenges us to pay close attention to the social, community, and political contexts of the families we meet and is an antidote to individual models of mental health theory.

Leanna's account of her experience of an armed robbery in Allan Wade's Chapter Five is hair-raising, and the negative social responses she receives after the incident are sad, unfair, and debilitating for her mental health. However, as a result of Allan's careful and nuanced response-based practice, which works to uncover " accurate descriptions that reveal the nature and extent of violence, clarify perpetrator responsibility, elucidate and honour victim responses and resistance, and contest the blaming and pathologising of victims", Leanna is able to experience herself as a person of competence and self-worth. This is inspiring work, which is readily applicable to many areas of work in adult mental health.

Expressed emotion has a long history in mental health theory and practice, which Paolo Bertrando charts with considerable skill in Chapter Six. This chapter on emotions continues with a description of the role of "attractors and repellors", a view of emotional interaction proposed by Magai and Haviland-Jones (2002), before concluding by detailing his own shift to a dialogical approach in his work with a family's emotional life. He emphasises the importance of the therapist's own emotional self-reflexivity. Paolo illustrates his theoretical ideas to very good effect through the use of a case example and throughout reflects on the impact on the family and the therapeutic team of adopting the different models of emotion.

Jaakko Seikkula and Birgitta Alakare have developed a very exciting approach to working with serious mental health difficulties in their native Finland. Drawing on the concept of "open dialogue", Chapter Seven outlines their working model that, from the earliest contact with patients in crisis, puts a priority on involving their families and social networks in a sometimes daily pattern of meetings. Through dialogue, they seek to understand the meaning of the symptoms presented without rushing to find solutions. The outcome research, which details the decline in the need for hospital admissions or antipsychotic medication, is very impressive.

SuEllen Hamkins is a passionate exponent of narrative psychiatry and in her Chapter Eight we are offered an absorbing picture of her work with a young woman over a two-year period. SuEllen describes the five key narrative elements to her work: creating a connection, who the person is without the problem and their vision for their life, the nature and experience of the problem, unique outcomes, and what other psychiatric resources are needed. SuEllen pays great respect to her psychiatric colleagues from other models. We are treated to a clear portrayal of a narrative interview that is a joy to read and to a model for using narrative practice in this field.

We have been lucky indeed in the UK to have witnessed the on-going work that Roger Stanbridge and Frank Burbach have developed in adult mental health services over the past few years. They have transformed the practice of individuals and teams working with families in Somerset and their training model, which combines systemic, narrative, and cognitive behaviour therapy, is being taken up by other Trusts in the country. Here, in Chapter Nine, we obtain a clear picture of the progress of this work at various levels and some hints about how to introduce more family-sensitive practice into our own workplaces.

Taiwo Afaupe has adopted a refreshing stance in her description of couple work in Chapter Ten by concentrating on "wellbeing" in place of "mental health". Drawing on social constructionist theories, including the "co-ordinated management of meaning", dialogical approaches, and liberation psychology, Taiwo offers us some grounded examples which demonstrate the application of theory to practice. She also invites us to consider the dominant discourses in minority Western culture and advocates a mental health system that would be enhanced by defining wellbeing dialogically.

Although this book has as its focus adult mental health, it goes without saying that the voices of children are also central in this domain. We are indebted to Ruth Pluznick and Natasha Kis-Sines for illuminating children's stories in Chapter Eleven by describing their work on the "Gathering Stories Project" initiated by Dulwich Centre. The aim of this enterprise was to hear from, and listen to, children about their experiences of living with a parent with serious mental health struggles. While in no way underplaying the difficulties that such children can experience, Ruth and Natasha highlight children's resilience by opening space for the development of multiple storylines and they privilege discovering the skills and knowledge that children develop for getting through difficult lives. It is a moving and hopeful account.

Clare Summerskill is an actor, writer, and performer who has had her own experience of mental health struggles. In Chapter Twelve, she lays bare her exposure to inpatient treatment and how she used this, together with the voices of other patients on the ward, to create Verbatim Theatre. This play has been performed across the country and its hard-hitting and unpalatable stories have had considerable impact. Professionals will not find it an easy read and it is a very timely reminder of what life can be like on our wards. However, Clare also recounts more positive examples of mental health care, which should act as a beacon for future service developments.

Silence is not a skill that systemic practitioners so easily pack into their kitbags—our training leans heavily on learning how to ask good questions. It is, therefore, with great interest that we turn the pages of Gail Simon's chapter, "Beyond the spoken word" (Chapter Thirteen), in which she deconstructs systemic ideas of working in and with silence. I particularly like her ideas of "silence as dialogue" and "silence as a relational space". Through case examples, Gail recounts the value and discomfort of silence, particularly in a "results-driven" context. She offers examples of writing and reading the written word that free the heartfelt emotions underlying the quietness.

Working in adult mental health is both an inspiring and, at times, dispiriting experience: what keeps us all going? This is the theme of Chapter Fourteen, by Iona Cook, which is based on a research project she undertook during her systemic training. Through the voices of two frontline workers, we hear of the many challenges that they increasingly face as they discuss professional growth and frustration, making a difference, and the personal/professional borderlands. Iona is a committed advocate of mental health service users and their families and her own voice in support of them comes through passionately in her writing.

And finally . . .

As editors, it has been quite a journey. To begin with, Karen joined the Tavistock Clinic in a new post in child services. With lots of new responsibilities for both of us, both personal and professional, keeping our focus on this book has at times been a challenge. We have been tried and tested by the editorial process itself and I have come to appreciate just what a personal as well as professional task this is. Late in the day, it dawned on me what a privilege it is to receive people's writings—documents very close to their hearts—and how difficult it is for both of us, authors and editors, to bear the editorial process. It is our job as editors to have an overview of the book and to help each author express themselves to the very best of their (and our) ability. But how hard it is for us and them to take the red pencil to the text and ask for changes, deletions, additions, etc.

Then, as we crept towards the last chapters pinging into our inboxes, Karen became ill, and as I write is still in the midst of treatment. She writes,

Over the last eight months of this project I was diagnosed with breast cancer and I am still in treatment at the time of writing. "Chemo brain" robbed me of my ability to think clearly and tiredness largely took over. For a person who likes to be very busy with irons in lots of fires this has been a very personal challenge. The Buddhists have the idea that life brings you all the lessons you need to learn and I have had to begin to learn, very angrily and reluctantly at times, to dwell in slowness and to pace myself, to embrace disappointment and honour endurance. As a person who puts a high value on independence, I have had to learn to rest in the love and care of family, friends and good colleagues for whom I am very fortunate and to whom I am very grateful. This unchosen and unwelcome experience has often made me think about the clients and families I know and have known and the unchosen and unwelcome life experiences they have had to endure. I have had a small experience of what it means to feel marginalised and living at the edge of one's own life. I feel privileged to have been working with Sue, my Co-Editor, who has had to step up to become sole editor for the final stages of this book, which is not a position that she would have chosen and has required huge personal sacrifices in terms of time and effort. I am grateful she has been supported by Bebe Speed and Alec McNab and by Charlotte and Gwyn the series editors. Most of all I appreciate the way that she has held me in mind during the process with great sensitivity. My hope is that I will be able to draw from this rich but painful experience in a way which may benefit those I hope to work with in the future.

It would have been easier, perhaps, to put this book on hold until Karen's recovery, but both of us felt that having come so far, we must hold faith with our authors, the families whose stories they tell, and our readers, and complete the task now. I have, therefore, taken over the process of editorship to become midwife to the book, a task I could not have completed without the generous help of others. Like Karen, I am indebted to Bebe Speed, who has shared her editing wisdom and skills with me and for me and has also written the Foreword, my husband, Alec, whose proof-reading skills with a red pen have been invaluable in pointing out linguistic and grammatical errors, and the Series Editors, Gwyn Daniel and Charlotte Burck, who have believed in this project from the very beginning and have offered Karen and me steadfast support in carrying it through.

When the author Hilary Mantel was asked, "Which book changed your life?", she was tempted to answer with a shrug, indicating that books can seldom do that by themselves. She then remembered a book titled *Migraine,* by Oliver Sacks, which, as a migraine sufferer herself, did change her life by increasing her knowledge of this strange condition. Knowledge is power. Hilary went on to write in the *Guardian* on 9 February 2013, "he (Sacks) voyages into the unknown territory inside our heads. Informed by twenty-five years of hospital experience, *he sees the soul within the symptoms*". It is my hope that this book has also been able to offer glimpses of, and great respect for, those souls.

References

Burnham, J. (2012). Developments in Social GRRRAAACCEEESSS: visible – invisible and voiced – unvoiced. In: I.-B. Krause (Ed.), *Culture and Reflexivity in Systemic Psychotherapy: Mutual Perspectives.* London: Karnac.

Cronen, V. E., & Pearce, W. B. (1985). Towards an explanation of how the Milan method works: an invitation to a systemic epistemology and the evolution of family systems. In: D. Campbell & R. Draper (Eds.), *Applications of Systemic Family Therapy: The Milan Approach* (pp. 69–84). London: Grune and Stratton.

Eichenbaum, L., & Orbach, S. (1982). *Outside In, Inside Out: Women's Psychology: A Feminist Psychoanalytic Approach.* Harmondsworth: Penguin.

Loy, D. (2008). *The Nature of Lack.* Accessed 14 January 2013 at www.zen-occidental.net/articles1/loy14-eng.html.

Magai, C., & Haviland-Jones, J. (2002). *The Hidden Genius of Emotion. Lifespan Transformations of Personality.* Cambridge: Cambridge University Press.

Rassool, C. (2007). Key debates in memorialisation, human rights and heritage practice. In: *Reflections on the Conference: Hands on District Six – Landscapes of Post-Colonial Memorialisation.* Cape Town: District Six Museum.

SECTION ONE

OUTSIDE IN:
A STANCE TOWARDS THEORY

PART I

DECONSTRUCTING THEORETICAL POSITIONS

CHAPTER ONE

Psychiatric diagnosis and its dilemmas

David Harper

I n the West, the dominant discourse for understanding mental distress is a psychiatric one and a key element in this discourse is diagnosis. Systemic practitioners encounter diagnoses every day because they are enshrined in their institutional contexts. In the USA, for example, practitioners are required by insurers to give clients a diagnosis from the American Psychiatric Association's (2013) *Diagnostic and Statistical Manual of Mental Disorders* (*DSM*). In other countries, diagnoses from the World Health Organization's (2010) *International Classification of Diseases* (*ICD*) might be required for a range of administrative reasons. In addition, in the UK, the National Institute for Health and Clinical Excellence (NICE) has published a range of clinical guidelines based on diagnostic categories. Systemic therapists have a range of responses to diagnosis. For example, in their study, Strong, Gaete, Sametband, French, and Eeson (2012) noted "counsellors shared a diverse range of views on the DSM: everything from an enthusiastic embrace to dismissal or even subversion" (p. 97).

Before I moved to my current post in clinical psychology training fourteen years ago, I practised as a clinical psychologist in the NHS for nearly a decade. Part of my clinical work involved working in a psychological therapies' service where, rather than diagnose, we formulated the problems presented by those who had been referred. However, I have also worked in a number of community mental health teams where diagnostic categories were regularly used. Although it is often claimed that use of diagnosis aids communication between professionals, in my experience such terms always needed supplementing with further information, since two people with the same diagnosis could be experiencing quite different forms of distress. For example, one person with a diagnosis of schizophrenia might have problems in getting out of bed and in motivating themselves (quite often as a result of the side-effects of neuroleptic medication), whereas another might predominantly hear voices. Thus, a diagnosis was only the beginning of a conversation: I always had to ask for a fuller description of the person's experiences and concerns.

I was influenced by systemic and narrative approaches and ideas from critical psychology, discourse analysis, and social construction-ism (e.g., Harper, 1994; Parker, Georgaca, Harper, McLaughlin, & Stowell-Smith, 1995) and developed a deconstructive reading of the diagnosis of paranoia (Harper, 1996). More recently, I have been part of collaborations seeking to move beyond diagnosis, and to view experiences of distress in their proper context (see, for example, Cromby, Harper, & Reavey, 2013). As a result, I have developed an on-going interest in both why, fifty years after critiques of diagnosis first emerged, it is still with us, and in the need to develop alternatives.

In this chapter, I attempt to address the question of how systemic practitioners might both conceptualise and engage with psychiatric diagnosis. At the end of the chapter, I discuss a number of strategies ranging from those aimed at enabling us to live alongside diagnosis to those aimed at rejecting it and moving beyond it. However, before we get to that, I think it is important to contextualise diagnosis, to understand its history and social functions. Diagnostic discourse affects both how we come to view ourselves and the interventions that we develop. Understanding its historical and social contexts helps us to realise not only that this particular way of viewing distress is merely one among many, but also that its dominance serves a number of social functions and, if we are to move away from it, we need to consider how we address those functions. I also explore critiques of both medicalisation and psychiatric diagnosis and investigate some potential alternatives.

A brief history of diagnosis

By the middle of the nineteenth century in Britain, medicine had become professionalised (e.g., in the 1858 Medical Act) and had generally won the battle to administer the new mental asylums. From then onwards, a particular form of diagnostic mentality began to take shape. One of the legacies of this mentality within contemporary psychiatry is the distinction between form and content; thus, it is regarded as more diagnostically relevant that a person hears a voice that others do not than what the voices say. However, it is easy to forget that the history of diagnosis has been a heavily contested one with a number of classificatory schemes competing with one another throughout the history of psychiatry. Only with the arrival of the *DSM* and *ICD* in the middle of the twentieth century was there a systematic attempt to impose order and these systems are really compromises between different factions within psychiatry (e.g., psycho-analytical *vs.* biological psychiatrists), hence the need for committees of experts to discuss and even vote on diagnostic categories. Despite these attempts to reach consensus, critique and debate have not been quelled.

At the time of writing, the fifth edition of the *DSM* has been published, and the process of developing *ICD-11* is under way. Blashfield and Fuller (1996) note how this has become a regular occurrence, with the number of categories of disorder gradually increasing from 128 in *DSM-I* (1952) to 357 in *DSM-IV* (1994). In the space of twenty-six years, the number of psychiatric diagnoses has doubled. This explosion of "vocabularies of deficit" (Gergen, 1990) has been accompanied by a rapid growth in the mental health professions. For example, my own discipline, clinical psychology, more than quadrupled in size in the UK between 1990 and 2011. One could argue that there has been a symbiotic relationship between the creation of new forms of knowledge (e.g., diagnostic discourse) and the proliferation of disciplines to develop this knowledge.

Alongside the growth in the number of diagnoses, their reach has also increased, and we have begun to see an increasing medicalisation of everyday life (Illich, 1976) which has since been exported to other countries (e.g., Watters, 2010). Now, increasing numbers of behaviours previously seen as part of ordinary life are seen as indications of mental pathology (Furedi, 2004; Rapley, Dillon, & Moncrieff,

2011). Allied to this increasing medicalisation has been an increasing pharmaceuticalisation of society (Healy, 1997; Moncrieff, 2008). This seems to be a result both of the desires of Western populations for a technical fix to complex human problems and the result of active marketing by multi-national pharmaceutical companies who spend more on marketing than research (Rose, 2006). Indeed, there is evidence that activity by pharmaceutical companies has led to the creation of new psychiatric categories such as "panic disorder" (Moncrieff, 2008), for which pharmaceutical companies have compounds available. Over time, this has led to more drugs being prescribed. Figure 1.1 shows the increasing amount of public money spent on antidepressant and antipsychotic medication in the community in the UK between 1991–2002. Ilyas and Moncrieff (2012) report that prescription rates have continued to climb: antidepressant prescriptions rose from 18.4 million in 1998 to 42.7 million in 2010, although costs peaked in 2004 at £400 million, dropping to £200 million in 2010. Rose, who, in the 1980s and 1990s, traced the emergence of the notion of a psychological self, has recently observed that we are increasingly starting to think of ourselves in biological and neuro-chemical terms (Rose, 2006).

Mental health is a much-contested field and criticism of psychiatric diagnosis is not new. Indeed, one of the earliest examples of a mental

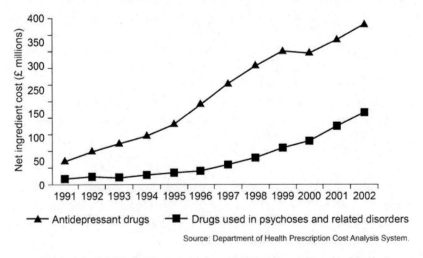

Source: Department of Health Prescription Cost Analysis System.

Figure 1.1.   Net ingredient cost of prescription items dispensed in the community (from Social Exclusion Unit, 2004).

health survivor movement is the mid-nineteenth century Alleged Lunatics Friend Society in England (Campbell, 1996), the word "alleged" introducing an element of doubt into the diagnosis of lunacy. However, probably the most sustained intellectual critiques of diagnosis and, indeed, of the project of psychiatry itself, began in the middle of the twentieth century with the publication in 1961 of books such as Szasz's *Myth of Mental Illness* and Laing's *Divided Self*. These conceptual and ethical critiques were followed by empirical demonstrations of the problems of diagnosis, such as Rosenhan's (1973) study where he sent to hospitals several "pseudo-patients" (i.e., people without diagnoses and not mentally distressed). When seen by a doctor, they were to report that they heard words such as "thud" but, once admitted to hospital, they were to act normally. What Rosenhan found was that, following diagnosis, every action performed and every statement made by the pseudo-patients was interpreted through the lens of the diagnosis. He memorably referred to the "stickiness" of diagnostic labels and, as a result, it became difficult for the pseudopatients to be discharged from hospital.

It is often claimed that problems of reliability and validity like these were resolved with the development of *DSM-IIIR*, but, in fact, despite continued revision, psychiatric diagnostic manuals still suffer from the same problems and, moreover, the past two decades have seen a new generation of critique (Bentall, 2004; Boyle, 2002; Kinderman, Read, Moncrieff, & Bentall, 2013; Kirk & Kutchins, 1992; Kutchins & Kirk, 1999). Many of these criticisms will not come as a surprise to systemic practitioners who are familiar with the way in which diagnostic frameworks individualise relational problems (Gergen, Hoffman, & Anderson, 1996; Strong, 2012a,b, in press; Strong, Gaete, Sametband, French, & Eeson, 2012; Tomm, 1991; White & Epston, 1990). From a systemic viewpoint, one of the crucial difficulties with diagnosis is that it decontextualises distress, seeing it as lying within a pathological individual rather than within the context of a problem-saturated system, as Rosenhan demonstrated. Language plays a key role here, both in effecting this decontextualisation (e.g., through an emphasis on monological rather than dialogical interaction) and in the development of alternative conceptualisations (Anderson & Goolishian, 1988; White & Epston, 1990).

Diagnosis and decontextualisation

Textbook approaches to diagnosis assume that it is simply an objective process of identifying symptoms, comparing them with the symptom checklists found in diagnostic manuals and, thus, reaching a diagnosis. However, in interviews, professionals identify factors indicating that diagnosis is a complex interactional process. In one study, my interviewees described a number of influences on the diagnostic process, for example, the personalities of colleagues (Harper, 1994). As Speed (2004) notes, there are many understandable reasons why psychiatrists diagnose: an attempt to manage complexity, a response to the pressure to "do something", a way of hiding inexperience or uncertainty, or simply because they have little time to explore fully the meaning of the person's experiences.

Of course, these processes begin at an early stage. Labelling theory (e.g., Scheff, 1999), though somewhat out of fashion now, can help us understand how a person can position themselves and be positioned by others as distressed. Drawing on the work of Coulter (1973), Rogers and Pilgrim (2005) note how often professionals are simply confirming judgements already made by the those around the person (or the person themselves), because their conduct appears to be unwarranted or hard to understand—what Sarbin and Mancuso (1980) referred to as "unwanted conduct". Such people are said to "lack insight" into their conduct if they are unable to persuade others of the intelligibility of their actions. Those around the person might mark out certain behaviour as unwarranted through the deployment of subtle rhetorical devices (Smith, 1978) and they might start to act differently around the person, sometimes unintentionally confirming a person's fears that others are conspiring against them (Lemert, 1962).

One of the dangers here is that problems of living become reified and objectified as an illness separate from the personal family and social context within which they occur. Psychiatrist Suman Fernando (1997) notes that

> in the process of making a diagnosis, judgements are hypothesized as symptoms and illnesses – as "things" that exist in some way separately from the people who make the judgements and from the people ("patients") who are said to "have" them. (p. 16)

Thus, an important aspect of systemic work is to see meaning in distress by placing it in its social context.

Despite the decontextualising effects of diagnosis, some service users are very aware of its social context and functions. Although academic interest in labelling theory has declined over the years, many service users see their diagnoses as negative labels given in a context where their power is limited. One service user with a diagnosis of personality disorder stated that this diagnosis was "a label they put on people when they can't treat you or figure out what's wrong with you" (Castillo, 2003, p. 69). Another service user with a similar diagnosis noted:

> It is no wonder that those of us with a Personality Disorder diagnosis feel like second-, or more like third-class citizens (life's rejects). You only have to look at the definitions given in ICD 10 and DSM IV and read comments such as 'limited capacity to express feelings – disregard for social obligations – callous unconcern for others – deviant social behaviour – inconsiderate of others – incompetence – threatening or untrustworthy'. The list is endless, but one thing that these comments have in common is that they are not helpful in any way. (Castillo, 2003, p. 128)

However, labelling is not the only context within which power operates: its effects can also be seen in the links between diagnosis and social inequality. Social inequality exerts its influence in a number of ways in relation to distress (Harper, 2011a). First, the very experience of distress is shaped by one's social location. Second, the way a person's distress is seen by others is also shaped by their social location. Third, access to the resources (personal, social, financial, etc.) necessary to move on from distress is influenced by inequality. These processes feed into diagnosis: thus, for example, people in certain social locations might be more likely to experience certain distressing life events (e.g., abuse, victimisation, unemployment, poverty, etc.). Black people, for instance, are more likely to experience racial abuse. Moreover, the kinds of coping strategies people use are more socially sanctioned for some social groups than others. Thus, men are much more likely to be given diagnoses of alcohol or drug abuse and are much more likely to engage in violence. This is one of the reasons why certain social groups are over-represented in certain diagnostic categories. However, at the same time, those making diagnoses might be affected by certain expectations or stereotypes about certain social groups.

The way in which distress is individualised and pathologised in the West means that the social inequalities that cause distress may be ignored and that individual, rather than family, social, or collective, therapeutic solutions (from medication to therapy) are sought (Boyle, 2011; Harper & Speed, 2012). Thus, recontextualising distress can be an important strategy. For example, the GRRAACCEESS approach (Burnham, Palma, & Whitehouse, 2008; Divac & Heaphy, 2005) can help to clarify the multiple dimensions of distress. Moreover, approaches such as Just Therapy (Waldegrave, Tamasese, Tuhaka, & Campbell, 2003) and those focused on liberation (Afuape, 2012) and collective responses (e.g., Denborough, 2008; Freedman & Combs, 2009) point to alternative ways of framing the therapeutic endeavour.

However, if we can learn anything from the fact that diagnosis and individualistic and pathologising ways of viewing distress are still with us, it is that they serve important functions and we need to understand these if we are to consider how to move beyond diagnosis (Harper, 2013).

The consequences of diagnosis

In their service user-led research study, Pitt, Kilbride, Welford, Nothard, and Morrison (2009) conducted interviews with mental health service users using service user researchers. They found that, once diagnosed, their interviewees experienced contradictory consequences. They concluded that "some people will experience diagnosis more positively or negatively than others but for all there were both elements present to a greater or lesser degree in their experience" (p. 421). So, they found that, for all participants, diagnosis provided a means of accessing services, though this was not welcomed by all. Moreover, many participants saw their diagnosis as a cause of disempowerment because of an over-reliance on medication, a lack of information, and because they felt they had been given a "prognosis of doom" (p. 421). Similarly, some found in diagnosis a way of naming their problem, helping them feel that their distress had legitimacy as it was caused by a recognised illness. This could also help them feel they were not personally to blame for the problem.

However, particularly where participants lacked information, they experienced diagnosis as primarily a negative labelling of their experience which then fed into how they saw themselves. Pitt and colleagues (2009) noted that their participants alternated between

> referring to their diagnosis as something they have, 'I've got bipolar', and something that they are, 'I'm bipolar'. This suggests that the ability of diagnosis to serve the function of externalising people's problems as an illness and protecting their concept of 'self' is never fully realised. (p. 421)

Even those seeing diagnosis as largely positive also saw it as a cause of social exclusion, with many people losing friends following their diagnosis. However, despite this, many went on to forge new relationships, drawing most strength from peer support networks.

Of course, diagnosis does not just have direct effects on the lives of those who use services and those around them. There are also wider social effects—diagnostic discourse opens up certain ways of looking at distress and closes down others (Harper, 2001):

- diagnostic categories promote pathologisation through an imperative to focus on abnormality;
- normality is defined by socially sanctioned experts;
- diagnostic categories can act as "thin descriptions" and pseudo-explanations;
- though claiming to be non-blaming, diagnostic discourse often involves implicit moral judgements;
- diagnostic discourse individualises pathology, which can serve as a form of social control (e.g., through risk discourse) and can also lead to a neglect both of structural causal factors and of collective responses to distress.

There have been attempts to counter some of these effects—for example, by normalising experiences of distress (e.g., Romme, Escher, Dillon, Corstens, & Morris, 2009) or deconstructing diagnoses (Parker, 1999). Narrative and systemic practitioners have developed innovative approaches: using language in an anti-pathologising manner (Parker, 1999; White & Epston, 1990); engaging with issues of inequality (e.g., Afuape, 2012; Waldegrave, Tamasese, Tuhaka, & Campbell, 2003); working with communities rather than individuals or families

(Denborough, 2008; Freedman & Combs, 2009). However, there are problems with trying to redress a problematic tendency simply by switching to its binary opposite (Harper, 1996). Moreover, the danger is that, by adopting different therapeutic strategies, we leave the edifice of diagnosis untouched. Recent debates triggered by the *DSM-5* revision process have led to a more explicit discussion of psychiatric diagnosis and it is possible to see a continuum in the strategies adopted by systemic practitioners towards diagnosis from being more accommodating to being more challenging and potentially transformative.

Strategies for accommodating to, and living alongside, psychiatric diagnosis

In a number of publications, drawing on a survey of therapists together with some interviews with respondents, Strong and his colleagues have identified a number of strategies to engage with diagnosis (2012a,b, in press; Strong, Gaete, Sametband, French, & Eeson, 2012). One set of responses involves therapists complying with administrative requirements to give diagnoses to clients, though some do this by simply giving all clients a *DSM* diagnosis of 309.9 — "adjustment disorder: unspecified" (Strong, Gaete, Sametband, French, & Eeson, 2012). Another set of responses involves counsellors using *DSM* diagnoses to interact with psychiatrically orientated colleagues but either challenging the diagnoses or supplementing them by introducing some of the client's preferred ways of understanding their difficulties (Strong, 2012b) or by the therapists giving a different account of the client in other contexts (Strong, Gaete, Sametband, French, & Eeson, 2012).

Some therapists have attempted to make the diagnostic process more collaborative (Strong, Gaete, Sametband, French, & Eeson, 2012). This could involve them in negotiating with the person seeking help "the potential utility and stigma associated with a DSM diagnosis" (Strong, 2012a, p. 58). One survey participant stated,

> I explain to the client the good reasons why the DSM exists (research studies etc); explain how managed care is a misuse of it; explore the potential consequences of "labelling"; then I give the client

an opportunity to read and study possible diagnoses to pick from. (Strong, 2012b)

Strong (in press) suggests that, in family work, where family members might be invested in particular diagnoses, therapists explore the "meanings and adequacy associated with the diagnosis as it relates to the member and others in the relationship or family" (p. 13).

Strong, Gaete, Sametband, French, and Eeson (2012, p. 93) also identified a position they termed as "having multiple faces". Strong (2012a) noted that some therapists ensured that clients met the diagnostic criteria for a service, for example, by categorising their clinical activity as "working with a 'depressed' client and his partner – instead of calling their work couples therapy" (p. 58). Strong (2012b) quoted an interview participant describing how they maintained "'two sets of books', practising as I consider ethically necessary, and doing the paperwork necessary to report short-term evidence-based treatment".

Other therapists have tried to move beyond the thin descriptions afforded by a diagnostic label, elaborating instead on the meaning of a person's experiences. For example, given the wide cultural availability of diagnostic discourse in the media, many clients express their concerns in diagnostic language. Strong (2012a) notes that therapists could respond to this by saying, "Well, that is how psychiatrists might talk about your concern, but what is left out of such an account of your concern?" (p. 58). Where clients express their concerns in diagnostic language and see medication as the primary active treatment, Strong (in press) suggests that the client's agency can be increased by developing Griffith and Griffith's (1994) notion of discussing with clients ways in which they *partner with their medication* so as to bring about change. By interviewing clients in this way, they could begin to reconceptualise positive changes, seeing them as a "combined effort of their initiative and the added support of their medication", p. 17) rather than being attributable to medication alone.

Strong (2012b) notes a survey participant's use of therapeutic letters to "remind clients of their voice" and their description of a "wall of wisdom" in their therapy office containing written ideas from clients emphasising "personal agency, strengths, and what they want to happen to the problem".

Of course, these strategies vary in how much they involve accommodating to diagnosis and, as a practitioner whose income does not rely on giving clients a diagnosis, I am aware that it is easy to be critical but, while at the level of the client these may be helpful, they also mean that the validity of the psychiatric diagnostic system remains unchallenged. Systemic practitioners are wary of monological accounts and prefer dialogical ones. However, although diagnosis should not necessarily close down therapeutic conversations, in practice it often does (Speed, 2004). Indeed, the biomedical psychiatric account is so powerful that approaches which claim to be multi-explanatory, like the so-called bio-psychosocial model, are, in practice, "bio-bio-bio" models (Read, 2005). Is it possible to adopt a both/and approach in this context? Gergen, Hoffman, and Anderson (1996) appeared to agree that diagnostic accounts were inherently limiting. As a result, some have considered strategies for rejecting diagnosis and moving beyond it.

Strategies for challenging and moving beyond diagnosis

The fact that, despite over fifty years of well-evidenced and conceptually sophisticated intellectual critique, diagnosis is still with us suggests that there are powerful social and even emotional influences at work and, elsewhere (Harper, 2013), I have argued for the need to adopt a political analysis of psychiatric diagnosis, identifying ways of weakening its institutional pillars of support (e.g., in the academy, health bureaucracies, the media, the pharmaceutical industry, lobby groups, etc.). To give an example from the academy, it is important to weaken the support given to diagnosis through programme curricula and textbooks. For example, undergraduate psychology programmes include courses on "abnormal psychology", "clinical psychology", or "psychopathology" and the recommended textbooks are overwhelmingly structured by the *DSM*. However, alternatives that include critiques of diagnosis and cogent alternatives are beginning to appear (Cromby, Harper, & Reavey, 2013).

Although the clinical guidelines published by the UK's National Institute for Health and Clinical Excellence appear to reinforce the use of diagnostic categories (because they are structured by "conditions" which mirror diagnostic categories), their introductory sections often raise problems with the validity and reliability of such diagnostic categories (Midlands Psychology Group, 2010) and this is something which could be publicised more and used more effectively in campaigning activities. The recent *DSM-5* revision process ignited much more debate than previously across the wider media as well as within the professional literature. The British Psychological Society's response to the revision proposals argued for the need to abandon categorical diagnostic systems such as the *DSM* (www.bps.org.uk/news/society-statement-dsm-5) and organisations representing systemic practitioners can join with such calls. Critical psychiatrist Dr Sami Timimi has founded the Campaign to Abolish Psychiatric Diagnostic Systems such as *ICD* and *DSM* (CAPSID) (www.criticalpsychiatry.net/?p=527).

If we did away with diagnosis, how else might we conceptualise distress? There seem to be at least two candidates.

One option—which refuses to cede the ground of science to diagnosis by arguing that psychiatric diagnostic categories are unscientific—is to draw on a perspective informed by a critical realist (e.g., Pilgrim, 2013) or "social materialist" (West Midlands Psychology Group, 2012) perspective. Here, the call would be to go back to basics and attempt to develop a more sophisticated, experience-based framework. Cluster analysis of symptoms indicates that they do not map on to neat diagnostic categories (Mirowsky, 1990). However, these studies use pre-defined categories from diagnostic interview schedules and what is needed is some basic qualitative research into the myriad ways in which people experience and talk about their own and others' distress, developing what Wallcraft and Michaelson (2001) refer to as a "survivor discourse". However, tricky issues to negotiate here include the need to focus on the social and relational (not simply individual) contexts of distress and to consider their meaning. Moreover, there is a danger that we assume there are ways of describing experience that are unsullied by psychiatric terminology when, in fact, Western culture is now suffused with such terminology. However, there is still a very wide range of lay terms in use.

Another path, drawing on a more relativist social constructionist approach (e.g., Anderson & Goolishian, 1988), is to abandon the naïve realism at the heart of the classificatory project and instead to be open to collaborative definition and multiple interpretations of concerns. Here, for example, one might focus on the level of fit between a person's experiences and their everyday life and relationships with others. Thus, in relation to psychotic forms of experience, we might be more interested in how someone manages to resist dominant discourses and prescriptions for living (e.g., Afuape, 2012), or how they manage to live in the everyday world while believing things others might find unusual, given the evidence that many people in the general population currently do this (e.g., Harper, 2011b).

If we reconceptualise distress, then this has implications for those offering therapeutic interventions. Formulation has been proposed as an alternative to diagnosis. Whereas a diagnosis is often little more than a label, a formulation is more like a story or narrative. Within the discipline of psychology, it has been defined as involving the development of hypotheses about experience based on psychological theory (Division of Clinical Psychology, 2011; Johnstone & Dallos, 2013). Indeed, although within mainstream British clinical psychology formulation is seen from a more critical realist perspective, when framed as a narrative it is possible to think of formulations more consistent with a social constructionist epistemology (e.g., Harper & Spellman, 2013).

Formulation is familiar to many systemic practitioners and is similar to the practice of progressive hypothesising. However, given the dominance of individual therapy approaches within adult mental health settings (especially CBT), the typical formulation is a causal formulation of a problem seen as lying within the individual. As a result, formulation practice might need to be stretched somewhat to accommodate traditions such as narrative therapy and solution-focused practice (Harper & Spellman, 2013), although there is no reason why the formulation could not be of a problem which is "externalised", as is common in narrative practice. Indeed, Carr (2006) has noted how formulations could also be about exceptions to the problems, as is common in solution-focused practice. The public appear generally to prefer formulations in psychosocial terms, where distress is located in a person's biography and social context, whereas distress explained in biomedical terms tends to be associated with stigma (Read, Haslam, Sayce, & Davies, 2006). Systemic practitioners are in an ideal position to develop rich, contextualised, and non-pathologising formulations of distress, but we need to remain vigilant of the societal pressures to individualise and pathologise distress. We also need to ensure that we do not simply replace one professionally self-serving monological account with another, as is a danger with the increasing prominence of cognitive–behavioural accounts of distress. One thing that might help with this is for systemic practitioners to engage in public debate about the societal causes of distress and their resolution.

However, although debates about diagnosis are important, equally important is the way in which we engage in therapeutic work with those who seek our help. How might we go about this work in a way that counters the pathologisation common in many mental health services? The other chapters in this volume show the exciting range of innovative forms of intervention that are now being practised in a range of contexts. No doubt these accounts will provide inspiration to those wishing to offer more helpful interventions to the people who seek their help.

Acknowledgements

Anne Cooke, Philip Messent, and Simon Platts provided useful comments on an earlier draft of this chapter.

References

Afuape, T. (2012). *Power, Resistance and Liberation in Therapy with Survivors of Trauma: To Have our Hearts Broken*. London: Routledge.

American Psychiatric Association (2013). *Diagnostic and Statistical Manual of Mental Disorders* (5th edn: *DSM-5*). Washington, VA: APA.

Anderson, H., & Goolishian, H. A. (1988). Human systems as linguistic systems: preliminary and evolving ideas about the implications for clinical theory. *Family Process, 27*(4), 371–393.

Bentall, R. P. (2004). *Madness Explained: Psychosis and Human Nature*. London: Allen Lane/Penguin.

Blashfield, R. K., & Fuller, K. (1996). Predicting the DSM-V. *Journal of Nervous and Mental Disease, 184*: 4–7.

Boyle, M. (2002). *Schizophrenia: A Scientific Delusion* (revised 2nd edn). London: Routledge.

Boyle, M. (2011). Making the world go away, and how psychology and psychiatry benefit. In: M. Rapley, J. Dillon, & J. Moncrieff (Eds.), *De-medicalising Misery* (pp. 27–43). Basingstoke: Palgrave Macmillan.

Burnham, J., Palma, D. A., & Whitehouse, L. (2008). Learning as a context for differences and differences as a context for learning. *Journal of Family Therapy*, 30: 529–542.

Campbell, P. (1996). The history of the user movement in the United Kingdom. In: T. Heller, J. Reynolds, R. Gomm, R. Muston, & S. Pattison (Eds.), *Mental Health Matters* (pp. 218–225). Basingstoke: Macmillan/Open University.

Carr, A. (2006). *Family Therapy: Concepts, Process and Practice* (2nd edn). Chichester: Wiley.

Castillo, H. (2003). *Personality Disorder: Temperament or Trauma? An Account of an Emancipatory Research Study Carried Out by Service Users Diagnosed with Personality Disorder*. London: Jessica Kingsley.

Coulter, J. (1973). *Approaches to Insanity*. London: Martin Robertson.

Cromby, J., Harper, D., & Reavey, P. (2013). *Psychology, Mental Health and Distress*. Basingstoke: Palgrave Macmillan.

Denborough, D. (2008). *Collective Narrative Practice*. Adelaide: Dulwich Centre.

Divac, A., & Heaphy, G. (2005). Spaces for GRRAACCEESS: training for cultural competence in supervision. *Journal of Family Therapy*, 27: 280–284.

Division of Clinical Psychology (2011). *Good Practice Guidelines on the Use of Psychological Formulation*. Leicester: British Psychological Society.

Fernando, S. (1997). Peeling labels. *OpenMind*, 87: 16–17.

Freedman, J., & Combs, G. (2009). Narrative ideas for consulting with communities and organizations: ripples from the gatherings. *Family Process*, 48: 347–362.

Furedi, F. (2004). *Therapy Culture: Cultivating Vulnerability in an Uncertain Age*. London: Routledge.

Gergen, K. J. (1990). Therapeutic professions and the diffusion of deficit. *Journal of Mind and Behavior*, 11: 353–368.

Gergen, K. J., Hoffman, L., & Anderson, H. (1996). Is diagnosis a disaster? A constructionist trialogue. In: F. W. Kaslow (Ed.), *Handbook of Relational Diagnosis and Functional Family Patterns* (pp. 102–118). New York: Wiley.

Griffith, J., & Griffith, M. E. (1994). *The Body Speaks: Therapeutic Dialogues for Mind–Body Problems*. New York: Basic Books.

Harper, D. (2001). Psychiatric and psychological concepts in understanding psychotic experience. *Clinical Psychology*, 7: 21–27.

Harper, D. (2011a). Social inequality and the diagnosis of paranoia. *Health Sociology Review*.

Harper, D. (2011b). The social context of 'paranoia'. In: M. Rapley, J. Dillon, & J. Moncrieff (Eds.), *De-medicalising Misery* (pp. 53–65). Basingstoke: Palgrave Macmillan.

Harper, D., & Spellman, D. (2013). Telling a different story: formulation and narrative therapy. In: L. Johnstone & R. Dallos (Eds.), *Formulation in Psychology and Psychotherapy: Making Sense of People's Problems* (2nd revised edn) (pp. 96–120). London: Brunner-Routledge.

Harper, D. J. (1994). The professional construction of 'paranoia' and the discursive use of diagnostic criteria. *British Journal of Medical Psychology, 67*: 131–143.

Harper, D. J. (1996). Deconstructing 'paranoia': towards a discursive understanding of apparently unwarranted suspicion. *Theory & Psychology, 6*: 423–448.

Harper, D. J. (2013). On the persistence of psychiatric diagnosis: moving beyond a zombie classification system, *Feminism & Psychology, 23*: 78–85.

Harper, D. J., & Speed, E. (2012). Uncovering recovery: the resistible rise of recovery and resilience. *Studies in Social Justice, 6*(1): 9–25. Available at: http://ojs.uwindsor.ca.ojs/leddy/index.php/SSJ/article/view/3499/2892.

Healy, D. (1997). *The Antidepressant Era*. Cambridge, MA: Harvard University Press.

Illich, I. (1976). *Limits to Medicine – Medical Nemesis: The Expropriation of Health*. Harmondsworth: Penguin.

Ilyas, S., & Moncrieff, J. (2012). Trends in prescriptions and costs of drugs for mental disorders in England, 1998–2010. *British Journal of Psychiatry, 200*: 393–398.

Johnstone, L., & Dallos, R. (Eds.) (2013). *Formulation in Psychology and Psychotherapy: Making Sense of People's Problems* (2nd revised edn). London: Brunner-Routledge.

Kinderman, P., Read, J., Moncrieff, J., & Bentall, R. P. (2013). Drop the language of disorder. *Evidence Based Mental Health, 16*(1): 2–3.

Kirk, S. A., & Kutchins, H. (1992). *The Selling of DSM: The Rhetoric of Science in Psychiatry*. New York: Aldine de Gruyter.

Kutchins, H., & Kirk, S. A. (1999). *Making Us Crazy: DSM – The Psychiatric Bible and the Creation of Mental Disorders*. London: Constable.

Laing, R. D. (1960). *The Divided Self*. London: Tavistock.

Lemert, E. M. (1962). Paranoia and the dynamics of exclusion. *Sociometry, 25*: 2–20.

Midlands Psychology Group (2010). Welcome to NICEworld. *Clinical Psychology Forum, 212*: 52–56.

Mirowsky, J. (1990). Subjective boundaries and combinations in psychiatric diagnoses. *Journal of Mind & Behavior*, *11*: 407–423.

Moncrieff, J. (2008). *The Myth of the Chemical Cure: A Critique of Psychiatric Drug Treatment*. London: Palgrave Macmillan.

Parker, I. (1999). Deconstructing diagnosis: psychopathological practice. In: C. Feltham (Ed.), *Controversies in Psychotherapy and Counselling* (pp. 104–112). London: Sage.

Parker, I., Georgaca, E., Harper, D. J., McLaughlin, T., & Stowell-Smith, M. (1995). *Deconstructing Psychopathology*. London: Sage.

Pilgrim, D. (2013). The failure of diagnostic psychiatry and some prospects of scientific progress offered by critical realism. *Journal of Critical Realism*, *12*(3): 336–358.

Pitt, L., Kilbride, M., Welford, M., Nothard, S., & Morrison, A. P. (2009). Impact of a diagnosis of psychosis: user-led qualitative study. *The Psychiatrist*, *33*: 419–423.

Rapley, M., Dillon, J., & Moncrieff, J. (Eds.) (2011). *De-medicalizing Misery*. Basingstoke: Palgrave Macmillan.

Read, J. (2005). The bio-bio-bio model of madness. *The Psychologist*, *18*: 596–597.

Read, J., Haslam, N., Sayce, L., & Davies, E. (2006). Prejudice and schizophrenia: a review of the 'mental illness is an illness like any other' approach. *Acta Psychiatrica Scandinavica*, *114*: 303–318.

Rogers, A., & Pilgrim, D. (2005). *A Sociology of Mental Health and Illness*. Maidenhead: Open University Press/McGraw-Hill Education.

Romme, M., Escher, S., Dillon, J., Corstens, D., & Morris, M. (Eds.) (2009). *Living with Voices: Fifty Stories of Recovery*. Ross-on-Wye: PCCS Books.

Rose, N. (2006). Disorders without borders? The expanding scope of psychiatric practice. *BioSocieties*, *1*: 465–484.

Rosenhan, D. L. (1973). On being sane in insane places. *Science*, *179*: 250–258.

Sarbin, T. R., & Mancuso, J. C. (1980). *Schizophrenia: Medical Diagnosis or Moral Verdict?* Oxford: Pergamon Press.

Scheff, T. J. (1999). *Being Mentally Ill: A Sociological Theory* (3rd edn). Piscataway, NJ: AldineTransaction.

Smith, D. E. (1978). K is mentally ill: the anatomy of a factual account. *Sociology*, *12*: 23–53.

Social Exclusion Unit (2004). *Mental Health And Social Exclusion*. London: Office of the Deputy Prime Minister

Speed, B. (2004). All aboard in the NHS: collaborating with colleagues who use different approaches. *Journal of Family Therapy*, *26*(3): 260–279.

Strong, T. (2012a). Talking about the DSM-V. *International Journal of Narrative Therapy & Community Work, 2*: 54–63.

Strong, T. (2012b). Talking about the DSM: its influence and our responses to it. Presentation to the Therapeutic Conversations X Conference, Vancouver, 12 May.

Strong, T. (in press). Brief therapy and the DSM: 13 possible conversational tensions. *Journal of Brief Therapy*.

Strong, T., Gaete, J., Sametband, I. N., French, J., & Eeson, J. (2012). Counsellors respond to the DSM-IV-TR. *Canadian Journal of Counselling and Psychotherapy, 46*, 85–106.

Szasz, T. (1984). *The Myth of Mental Illness* (revised edn). New York: HarperPerennial.

Tomm, K. (1991). Beginnings of a 'HIPs and PIPs' approach to psychiatric assessment. *The Calgary Participator, 1*(2): 21–24.

Waldegrave, C., Tamasese, K., Tuhaka, F., & Campbell, W. (2003). *Just Therapy—A Journey: A Collection of Papers from the Just Therapy Team, New Zealand*. Adelaide: Dulwich Centre.

Wallcraft, J., & Michaelson, J. (2001). Developing a survivor discourse to replace the 'psychopathology' of breakdown and crisis. In: C. Newnes, G. Holmes, & C. Dunn (Eds.), *This Is Madness Too: Critical Perspectives on Mental Health Services* (pp. 177–190). Ross-on-Wye: PCCS Books.

Watters, E. (2010). *Crazy Like Us: The Globalization of the American Psyche*. New York: Simon & Schuster.

West Midlands Psychology Group (2012). Draft manifesto for a social materialist psychology of distress. *Journal of Critical Psychology, Counselling & Psychotherapy, 12*: 93–107.

White, M., & Epston, D. (1990). *Narrative Means to Therapeutic Ends*. London: Norton.

World Health Organization (2010). *International Classification of Diseases (ICD-10)*. Geneva: WHO.

CHAPTER TWO

Missing the point: the shy story of disappointment

Duncan Moss

> And time yet for a hundred indecisions,
> And for a hundred visions and revisions,
> Before the taking of a toast and tea.
>
> (Eliot, "The Love Song of J. Alfred Prufrock" (1963, p. 14)

I t was all going to be so different. I was going to clear some space in the usual diary mess. I would sit, drink tea, and elegantly and productively enjoy this process of explorative writing, an activity rare to the point of extinction, it seems, if you are employed as a university lecturer in clinical psychology.

Yes, right. Instead, the "cleared space" has become more of a frantic, grumpy swipe at a never diminishing "things to do" list of university "blah", to stonily bleed out what follows. What a disappointment.

Fortunately, it is all rather apt.

This chapter is, in fact, about "disappointment". I have been interested in this (perhaps strange) topic for many years and want to share something of why, hoping that it might strike a chord with you. Disappointment is one of those words that is perhaps both obvious and subtle at the same time. It is, of course, in some ways, a very familiar word, but in the exploration here I want to present it as a "shy story". Partridge (2005) explored the way in which families produce narratives about "our family", often dominant narratives, or "boastful stories", to be rehearsed and retold, and held and propagated by those in the family who hold more power. At the same time, however, families are likely to have "shy stories", less visible, less comfortable perhaps, held by less powerful family members and sometimes at odds with the more dominant family narrative.

Although this chapter is more a personal "underview" rather than a conceptual overview of the shy story of disappointment, based partly on my personal experience and as an NHS clinical psychologist and lecturer, and latterly facilitator of mindfulness approaches, it is, of course, based on, and linked to, a range of other sources and inspirations. My appreciation for disappointment, at least in the way I have tried to explore it here, has been fed by Buddhist writing in particular, but I have also drawn briefly from influences from other traditions: Mason's seminal paper in the systemic tradition on "safe uncertainty" (1993), for example, and what could be called the "melancholic materialist" writing of the critical psychologist David Smail (more on that later).

None of these sources tend to speak about disappointment (the word) in great detail as such, but do talk on related themes of suffering, uncertainty, and disillusionment. In fact, part of my interest in the word is how rare it is to encounter a direct and explicit exploration of the word itself and of the lived experience of a life under its aegis. For example, if, like me, one of the first things you do with a task or project is to look it up on Google, and from there go to Amazon to see if anyone has written books on it, you might like to try Googling disappointment. You come up with seventy-three million hits. This sounds like a lot: clearly, there is a great deal of disappointment out there. But compare it with some other terms: how about trauma at 127 million, anxiety at 181 million, depression at 269 million, and crisis at 582 million!

It is, perhaps, stretching it to use such statistics to suggest that disappointment is a "shy story", but a search through psychological writing, available books and journals, and memories of training and teaching does suggest that disappointment is not a popular topic. There is one notable exception that deserves a mention: the analyst and writer Ian Craib (1994), who wrote a book specifically using disappointment as a scaffold for a broad ranging psychoanalytic critique of late modernity. Given his work is one of the few psychological explorations in this area, it might seem odd not to focus on it here. However, while his work is full of rich discussions that clearly could overlap with this present, much more modest, offering, Craib's book, in my reading of it, essentially both explores and is written within the boundaries of a strictly psychoanalytic perspective, with disappointment being more a "marker" for the exploration of a range of themes within that tradition.

In this case here, it is almost the other way round. Rather than using disappointment as a scaffold for a discussion of other topics, I want to keep coming back to the word itself, to move alongside and within it, to make an appointment with disappointment. Perhaps subtle "existential" qualities such as disappointment are not butterflies you can easily catch in your net for closer examination. Rather, it might be said, we are the butterfly and disappointment is so close and pervasive that it can feel like the net itself.

Disappointment begins at home

At this point, you might be wondering what relevance this topic has for the complexities of modern clinical practice. Surely disappointment is rather unremarkable in its everydayness, a word for the ordinary human hassles that, rightly, lie outside professionalised discourses of more uncommon human difficulties? Perhaps we could hold these questions open; my contention is that beyond the more obvious "I am disappointed in you; I am disappointed in me; in this, about that", beyond this daily marker of dissatisfaction, there may be something more subtle and more uneasy that this word touches.

This "something" to which I am alluding might be easier to connect to as a felt experience, rather than as an object of scrutiny, so how about an experiential pause? If you are reading this book at home and you are currently alone, then go to the kitchen, try to turn off your radio, your phone, the bleep of your incoming emails. Do not turn on the kettle, but do clear your kitchen table of snacks, bills, and magazines—in fact, clear it of everything. Pull up a chair and sit down—if it helps, you could drum your fingers on the tabletop as you sit there. Please, just sit there, and "hang out"; just sit there, just keep sitting there . . . now what? Well, now nothing, really . . . really; really, nothing . . .

How long can we bear it? And, more to the point, what is the point?

As I cannot ask you in person, I can only guess how you found this "exercise" (if we can even call sitting doing nothing at the kitchen table an exercise). Given the theme of this chapter, you might assume I expected this to be an aversive experience for you, but in fact maybe it felt rather nice to sit without the usual clutter and have nothing to do.

Alternatively, you might, as I have sometimes found, have had an experience of a brief sense of peace, followed by a growing sense of restlessness tinged with anxiety. Equally possibly, you might have experienced the above two lines the other way round.

So, if left to ourselves, without too many external distractions (the kitchen table is optional), we may, if we look closely, notice a range of things: moments of peace, moments of boredom and itchiness, moments of dread and nakedness, moments of wondering what is the point of these moments.

What is the "something" in this that might take us into disappointment? What I am trying to invite us to notice here is not a "state", not a static "thing", but the opposite, in fact. I am hoping we might briefly feel into the lived quality of being alive when we are not distracting ourselves—shifting, sputtering, moment-by-moment experience. Moment by moment, at the kitchen table, without our usual props, even, perhaps, the prop of being able to call this, for example, a "mindfulness exercise", what might we notice? How might this offer disappointment?

If we look a little into the belly of the word "disappointment", we can find the words "appointment", "appoint", "point". Might we begin to feel we are losing the point?

Maybe (if you are at all like me) this is what we can notice as we drum our fingers on the kitchen table—a queasy and agitated feeling as we notice our mind sliding around (as it always does, but usually we do not notice it). In other words, as Professor Dumbledore (Rowling, 2010) might say, the point is constantly "dis-apparating" (apologies—disapparating is not really a word, unless you are familiar with the world of Harry Potter, where it describes a painful, disorientating, and definitely queasy ability for a person to dissolve and reappear wherever they want to go).

It is this constant falling away from whatever state of mind we can notice when less distracted that can be unsettling, that might make us queasy. Perhaps we feel less sure of ourselves if we touch into that sputtering space, and so we shore ourselves up again with restlessness ("back to my emails—Oh, how I hate them . . . but hmm . . . wonder if so-and-so has been in contact?"). The restlessness could be both an attempt to avoid this sense of things "sliding away" and a reflection of our awareness of its lurking constancy, and our attempt at remedy.

The word from Buddhism that could be placed here is *dukkha*, usually translated as "suffering", or even, in this case perhaps, the pervasive "suffering of suffering". The word I prefer, in translation, is offered by the modern Buddhist writer, David Loy, as a pervasive sense of lack.

> The easiest way to understand lack is to think of it as the "shadow" of the sense of self. The Buddhist teaching of Anatta, or non-self, implies that our sense of self is a construct, an ever-changing process, which doesn't have any reality of its own. Because it lacks any reality of its own, any stable ground, this sense of self is haunted by what I've called a sense of lack or, for short, lack. The origin of this sense of lack is our inability to open up to the emptiness, or ungroundedness, of the self. Insofar as we're unable to cope with that emptiness, insofar as we deny it and shy away from it, we experience it as a sense of lack. (Loy, 2008)

"Why can't I get it together?" we ask ourselves . . . well, because there is a lack, an absence, in both the "it" and the "I"—neither can hold together for long. The disconcerting nature of not getting it together is expressed well by Chogyam Trungpa (the celebrated and provocative Tibetan Buddhist writer), who suggests when writing about meditation:

> Nothing happens: it is absolutely boring. Sometimes you feel silly. One often asks the question, "Who is kidding whom? Am I on to something or not?" You are not on to something. Travelling the path means you get off everything, there is no place to perch. (Trungpa, 1976, p. 53)

In this account, then, to live in the midst of disappointment is to live with our never quite achieving, never quite failing to make the appointment with something we can hold on to for sure. Never quite failing also because if we always failed utterly to get it together, that would be another static universe: one of complete failure. This, for some of us, can be a strangely desirable perch in itself.

Whether it is helpful to characterise this as disappointment is questionable. I do continue, though, to feel struck by the word, partly because it is gentler (neither "clinical" nor pathologising) than some other words that can speak to existential holes we might fall into, words such as "trauma" or "damage". It is also more personal than the generic word "suffering", able to contain both the homely and everyday ("I've had a disappointing day on eBay") and even the summation of a sense of our lives as a whole. For example, Jung, written near to his death and found in the last chapter of his memoir, *Memories, Dreams, Reflections*, writes, "I am astonished, disappointed, pleased with myself. I am distressed, depressed, rapturous. I am all these things at once, and cannot add up the sum" (Jung, 1961, p. 358).

More specifically, I am struck by disappointment because, unlike trauma and tragedy, nobody much seems to want to buy it.

From kitchen to clinic: disappointment in therapy

If disappointment could be described, as I have above, as a subtle but pervasive sense of never quite reaching a reliable point of arrival, of never quite having got it together, how does our way of living with this manifest itself, individually and collectively?

It is obviously not possible to do justice to such questions in this limited space. It also feels important to keep our feet on the ground, to keep close to the actual experience of the moment, keeping close, as it were, to the kitchen table. Perhaps when we fly with speculation, or even conceptualisation, this might be one of our strategies of avoiding touching this unsettling ground of things not quite adding up.

So, at this point, I would invite a pause: before sharing anything more with you, I wonder what you might take from this chapter so far, and if it were a lens, what do you notice about your working life, your life as a whole even, when looked at through the lens of disappointment?

> For I have known them all already, known them all:
> Have known the evenings, mornings, afternoons,
> I have measured out my life with coffee spoons.
> (Eliot, 1963, "Prufrock")

What *do* you notice when you consider disappointment in your life? Regrets, frustrations, sadnesses, boredom? Something abstract, or something concrete? Remembering perhaps some of the things, the big things and the little, that have not quite worked out as we would like? Or does disappointment take you nowhere, to nothing in particular?

Even if nothing came to mind, pausing to consider our own sense of disappointment, in any one moment, can arguably be helpful, partly as perhaps this is a refreshingly "counter-cultural" activity, and partly perhaps, writing or reading about it as a topic, as we are here, could distance ourselves too much from the "felt sense" of our own experience of "lack" right now. For myself—right now—I feel some-what "hollow chested", tired, and uninspired, but sitting pretty all the same, five floors up, in university splendour. How about you?

If, though, we turn this lens more generally on to our experience, and specifically our experience of the various therapeutic industries (which I assume many readers share), the clinics and many acronymic teams of "health and social care", what might we notice?

The clinical psychologist and writer David Smail has arguably brought an unusually honest gaze to the selling of therapeutic potency. For example, he writes,

> What seems more commonly to be the case is that therapist and patient arrive at a brilliantly illuminating formulation of how s/he got to be in his/her particular predicament, but the latter finds that, despite valiant effort and earnest desire, s/he fails miserably to put matters right. (Smail, 1999, p. 35)

Perhaps this is an overstatement? I think it does contain within it a truth, or, at least, a truth that chimes with my own experience. This is that in the midst of all the products of therapeutic potency, of outcome measures, evidence bases, and payment by results, it might be hard to acknowledge the ever-present sense of "lack" in our therapeutic endeavour.

Now, hang on a minute, writer. So much for keeping your feet on the ground and avoiding speculation—are you really making a crass generalisation that all therapy ends in failure?

No, and neither does David Smail. He argues that therapeutic spaces can be tremendously comforting and encouraging. But notice his words—comfort, encouragement. They imply no resolution, no outcome, no "working through", no point of "insight", and no place to perch. Yet, so much of the industry of therapy is predicated on resolution. As Mason explores in his paper on the close cousin of disappointment, uncertainty,

> Although the search for solutions can be seen as positive, a danger is that we can fall into the trap of seeing solutions in absolute terms. We get caught up in looking for the 'right' answer; somewhere out there is the new reality, the solution waiting to be discovered. The search for what is right, the search for solutions, the search for the correct way, I would suggest leads into a minefield. (Mason, 1993, p. 192)

Again, as well as not implying that therapy is a failure, although it might often be a disappointment (for an attempt made to acknowledge this explicitly within a therapy service, see Moss, 2002), I am not at all wanting to imply that you and I, as therapists, are not sensitive to the lack of realism in all this talk of outcomes, results, solutions, and, latterly, "payment by results".

However, it would not be surprising that if we struggle at the kitchen table to lean into the queasy "lacking" quality of moment by moment experience, this is likely to be reflected at other tables, too. One reflection of this struggle might be the increasing divergence of a public language of therapeutic potency (anyone for CBT?) and our own private experience of that potency, or otherwise. Yet, this gap between the rhetoric and the reality remains a "shy story".

How could we begin to speak up for this shy story, at work?

> It is as if I stand in the doorway of my office, waiting.
> The patient enters and makes a lunge at me, a desperate
> attempt to pull me into the fantasy of taking care of him. I step aside.
> The patient falls to the floor, disappointed and bewildered.
>
> (Kopp, 1976, p. 5)

I suspect it is getting harder to let anyone hit the floor. Yet, perhaps, if we took to heart this image, we might provide a way into acknowledging that we will, inevitably, be a disappointment to the people who "receive our service" (and to ourselves), in that we will not be able to answer that longing for "somewhere to perch", that longing for somewhere and someone to shore us up, to help us finally arrive, to really make the appointment.

For myself, I have found that curiosity about someone's expectations of what help might mean, while trying to remain neutral to that expectation, can lead us into disappointment pretty quickly. But here the issue (as I hope might be clear from this chapter as a whole) is not how/whether we might avoid disappointment, but, rather, how we make space for that quality once it is visible. We perhaps can be very helpful to others and ourselves if we can help make space to acknowledge both the disappointments within our lives and specifically of professional help (given or received, past or present).

Sometimes, there can be a sense of relief in an acknowledgement that our lives, that life itself, does not add up, that we do not arrive. It can contribute to a depathologising process, possibly, to a rejection of the cycle of hope–fear that therapy rooted in pathology can engender (hope for symptom resolution–fear of being trapped with the symptom). However, it is naïve to think it always *feels* helpful. Sometimes, disappointment can lead to anger, to the frustration, for example, of not being offered a diagnosis as a place to land, or frustration that our attempts to feel good about being helpful have not been reciprocated. And, increasingly, our health care economy arguably encourages an obscuring of the slippery outcomes of therapy. We are, after all, being paid for a successful appointment.

How we make space for disappointment in our therapeutic work, I cannot say. Perhaps we can discover it for ourselves. Extremely often I have found it more helpful to step for inspiration outside the walls of therapeutic textbooks (how often are these in the domain of modesty about therapeutic power?) and look elsewhere. If I kid myself into thinking I should be helping people (such as myself) better to overcome their difficulties, I might be well placed to watch a film such as *All or Nothing*, by Mike Leigh, which has no "closure" and no outcome . . .

> It's about connecting. I don't think it arrives at completely comfortable conclusions. You certainly don't walk away from it thinking that everything is all tied up and fine. But I do feel that the spirit of the film points towards hopeful possibilities. (Mike Leigh, quoted in Cardullo, 2008, p. 239)

Recently, I was struck by the stark, intelligent (and playful) honesty in the recent autobiographical writing of comedian and writer Stephen Fry:

It is no part of my business with you to maintain that I now fully know myself, but I think I can profess convincingly that I do at least know myself well enough to be nothing but doubtful and distrustful when it comes to any claims of solutions, cures and arrivals at final destinations. (Fry, 2010, p. 23)

The insight of Fry's alone (but also echoing Barry Mason and David Smail earlier) can be a lead into how I might inhabit disappointment in my work, and help others do so, too. For example, how might our "outcome" letters reflect Fry's comments, or our reflections in supervision, or team discussions?

Perhaps, before we begin to have an action plan on disappointment, we might just let go and connect, as Mike Leigh might suggest, connect with our felt experiences day to day, through our "evenings, mornings and afternoons".

Hmm, "let go and connect" . . . this sounds simple (or simplistic), or, maybe, just too enigmatic. How do we connect with the immediacy of our lived experience, particularly and especially in the midst of work? Perhaps we might value enlisting the services of a really good "reflecting team" that only we can see. When I think of reflecting teams, at best I think of support, attentiveness, curiosity, naïvety, friendliness, humour, and playfulness (yes, this is the systemic equivalent of fantasy football). Maybe our reflecting team can accompany us through all those moments of arrival and departure, of comings together and fallings apart, of appointments and disappointments.

But, although you are reading, and I am writing, this chapter now, for how long can you and I stay curious towards the shadowy "lack" in our professional selves; how long before we might forget our kindly attentive "team", how long before we do not really want to listen to what they might have to offer? We have appointments to keep, after all.

Maybe I should mention in passing that my only attempt to put on a workshop on disappointment for clinical psychologists was cancelled due to "lack of interest".

Mindfulness comes to the rescue?

I am no prophet—and here's no great matter;
I have seen the moment of my greatness flicker,

And I have seen the eternal Footman hold my coat, and snicker,
And in short, I was afraid.

(Eliot, 1963, "Prufrock")

Within this shy story, there is itself a shy story, about a boastful story—the story of the rise of mindfulness.

For, surely, that is what we have been talking about. I mentioned at the beginning of the chapter that I teach mindfulness, and then we have gone on to do an experiential exercise that looked suspiciously like a mindfulness practice, and from there to talk about Buddhism. Is it not time to come clean and admit that the answer to disappointment, as well as to so much else, lies in mindfulness?

Going by the advertising and marketing of mindfulness on the Internet and elsewhere, it might imply that mindfulness may well be the answer to disappointment. Promises of "greater focus and calmness", or "controlling our emotions and impulses", and other desirable forms of self-improvement can be found in some of this marketing. I suspect I have been responsible for similar promises myself. But, increasingly, I wonder if there might be more need of ambiguity, ambivalence, and uncertainty about the promises of mindfulness than the current marketing seems to suggest. In short, mindfulness as an industry may, ironically, also be reluctant to sit at its own empty kitchen table.

A vivid example at present is my role in facilitating mindfulness groups. These groups are almost always offered in the context of time-limited, eight-week courses. Our experience is that participants and facilitators alike can get caught up with the idea of a developmental journey across the eight weeks, worrying as participants that they cannot come back to week five if they missed week four, worrying as facilitators that we do not offer material in week three that comes from week seven "because they might not be ready for it". We are also increasingly aware of a narrative from a range of sources about the need for "advanced courses in mindfulness".

I am not intending to dismiss these attitudes. For example, it is quite understandable to need time to get a feel for being in a group such as a mindfulness group, either as a participant, experiencing sitting in silence with others, or as facilitators, thinking carefully about what we offer. However, at its heart, it could be said that mindfulness invites us into the unresolved present moment, where there is nowhere to develop from or to. As such, mindfulness is an extremely simple practice that, paradoxically, can feel very difficult to embody, very intangible (Moss & Barnes, 2008) and, dare I say, can feel at times rather disappointing ("I don't seem to be getting anywhere with this"). In other words, mindfulness practice is not different from our sitting at the kitchen table practice. Yet, ironically, even here as participants, facilitators, or as the new breed of "mindfulness professionals", we can get caught up in wanting somewhere to perch. This might be in the growing proliferation of manuals of mindfulness instruction, which reinforce a developmental fantasy of mindfulness, or in the ever growing range of books and CDs telling us how to practise, or in the outcome measures recording symptom reduction after attending an eight-week course. All of this could put us in danger of turning the heart of falling apart into the world of "getting it together".

None of this is intended as a critique of mindfulness *per se*, which, at its heart and its roots, is one of the few, but not the only, domains that seem able to help us move towards disappointment, to cradle our fear of lack in the arms of loving kindness. Rather, it might be more the other "m" word at fault here: marketing, the inevitable desire for a new brand of therapy to sell itself to the industry and to the consumer, and, if anything, this is the antithesis of something to buy—it is "lack".

Yet, there does seem to be something genuine here as well. We are buying into the heart of mindfulness, literally and metaphorically, if the rise in books, CDs, and courses in mindfulness, compassion, acceptance, and other related topics is anything to go by. This might suggest a greater willingness or desperation to look into our suffering and hear the message that comes through from some of the great writers in that tradition. For example, consider this quote from the dust-cover of a recent book by the writer Pema Chodron:

> Things are always in transition if we could only realize it. Nothing ever sums itself up in the way that we would like to dream about. The off-centre, in between state is an ideal situation, a situation in which we don't get caught. (1997, back cover).

Conclusion

Our appointment with disappointment need not be miserable. As we sit at our kitchen table, we might find our attention turns outwards, taking in, as if for the first time, the light of the sun falling on the home appliances that surround us, or the patina of the wood that we have eaten at a thousand times. A disquieting transience on the "inside" can sometimes become a poignant transience on the "outside", the moment-by-moment beauty of everyday objects and spaces.

David Smail coined the term "outsight" to denote a possible shift in perspective, not just for an individual, but also as a challenge to those of us in the therapeutic industry who can get caught with notions of fixed internal states. While, in his writing, "outsight" is much more than a simple possibility of "looking out", the word itself, for me, invites a turning outwards and towards the world at hand. In all that constant changing, texture, colour, and light, what is there to be disappointed in?

> And would it have been worth it, after all,
> Would it have been worthwhile,
> After the sunsets and the dooryards and the sprinkled streets,
> After the novels, after the teacups, after the skirts that trail
>   along the floor—
> And this, and so much more?
>
> (Eliot, 1963, "Prufrock")

The table I am at right now is not a kitchen table, but a library desk, high on the third floor. It is close to Christmas and the library is almost empty. Dusk has settled, but men at work are still hammering up the road outside. Through the window the imposing building opposite is now reduced to glowing squares of light, gradually going out.

Epilogue: a hundred visions and revisions

Please can you elaborate a bit more here on your influences and approaches . . . as well as explain a bit more to the uninitiated what you mean by melancholic materialism and disappointment. We wonder if you could also say something about how you are connecting disappointment and uncertainty. . .

Can you give us a bit more of a glimpse of how these ideas show in the international space between you and clients you and colleagues etc. with the odd example . . . You have more words to play with.

Hoping you can make something of these comments. Hoping you could get this back to us by end of May.

Best wishes

Karen and Sue
(Personal communication, 16 March 2012)

Perhaps one of the shadows cast by the written word is that of permanency, of having fixed your point of view, creating the final polished and finished article. Seen through the lens of disappointment, this is all rather too neat. Life is always and all the time subject to constant revision, but the finished article is not.

So where are we now? I am back in the library and, perhaps aptly, someone is sitting in "my" seat, so that I have to sit four chairs down the row. Hence, my view is slightly but significantly shifted. I can no longer see the same aspect of the building opposite; the men hammering down the road have laid down their tools and moved on; it is May and not Christmas, although the weather does not seem to have been informed, as it is foggy with wetness. My complaint that started the chapter is, if anything, worse, but right now I would love some tedious emails to attend to rather than write any more (just checked them again). Why?

A Buddhist friend once commented that a constant checking of emails is an act of reassurance that we are alive. We have a moment of openness, a moment of space without narrative, a micro moment perhaps, we touch the void, we panic, we cling to the cliff—the computer says yes.

All right, it might not be email for you; it might be text, the radio, the ironing, meetings, eating, but I wonder if most of us have these hooks to hold when "lack" opens up. Of course, emails need to be answered and the ironing needs to be done, but, if you are like me, I add an extra intent. As I sit at this library desk, my mind keeps drifting off, and it is hard work bringing it back here, right now. In fact, even writing about this makes me a bit nauseous. So, like other "creative" people (i.e., all of us), I moan about all that admin, all that blah. But without blah, we have the uncertainty of not knowing, which has to be the precursor of creativity. In this way, uncertainty and disappointment are both twins and strangers: twins because they share that uneasy sliding-away quality, sliding away from the known, and from what we are hanging on to, but also strangers—how can we be uncertain and disappointed at the same time?

As we fall off the cliff face of our expectations, disappointment looks up achingly to what we have lost, while uncertainty looks down to where we are going.

Missing the deadline

After a four week hiatus, when it rained and rained, May turned into June, the deadline for this chapter came and went, and I have attended to a lot of very important emails (do you believe me?), I have crawled back to peer anxiously at this chapter. Much to my surprise, no one has finished it for me in my absence. And, yesterday I put my knee out and am in some discomfort—or maybe I could call it a minor reminder of the melancholy in materialism:

> And what founds our common humanity is not so much the brute fact of the body's objective materiality as its subjective vulnerability. In the final analysis we all feel the same because we are all constructed in the same way. If you prick us, we bleed. It is *this* which is true whoever you are, and however strong, or weak, or beautiful, or rich or important you are. (Smail, 1993, p. 218, original italics)

The materialism at the heart of our lives that David Smail so eloquently conveys throughout his writing is the simple fact of having a body and a mind that can easily get hurt. This apparently simple fact is a revelation because it does seem as if much of the "lack avoidance" industries (including, sometimes, the therapeutic industry?) would like to move us quickly on from our "common humanity" of suffering the disappointment of our frailty. I have added the word "melancholy" to the word "materialism" simply because the opening to this reality can feel sad.

A time for toast and tea?

As for now, I am running out of steam, and would like to finish and cross the deadline. In fact, I have whimsically seated myself back in the library room I started in (now, again aptly, five chairs down from where I started) and, perhaps to mock my hope for something poetic and atmospheric to end with, the day is most unpromising in "atmosphere". It is one of those British "summer days", grey, muggy, flat, afternoon time; even heavy rain would at least give us something to talk about. The buildings through the window are equally flat and featureless today. Chodron (1997, p. 69) writes,

> As human beings, not only do we seek resolution, but we also feel that we deserve resolution. However, not only do we not deserve resolution, we suffer from resolution. We don't deserve resolution; we deserve something better than that.

That "something" is here right now, like it or not.

Dedication

This chapter is dedicated to Miller Mair (1937–2011), who saw the poetry in psychology.

References

Cardullo, B. (2008). *Soundings on Cinema*. New York: University of New York Press.

Chodron, P. (1997). *When Things Fall Apart*. Boston, MA: Shambhala.

Craib, I. (1994). *The Importance of Disappointment*. London: Routledge.

Eliot, T. S. (1963). *Collected Poems*. London: Faber and Faber.

Fry, S. (2010). *The Fry Chronicles*. London: Penguin.

Jung, C. (1961). *Memories, Dreams, Reflections*. New York: Vintage.

Kopp, S. (1976). *If You Meet the Buddha on the Road, Kill Him! The Pilgrimage of Psychotherapy Patients*. Toronto: Bantam.

Loy, D. (2008). The nature of lack. Accessed 14 January 2013 at: www.zen-occidental.net/articles1/loy14-eng.html.

Mason, B. (1993). Towards positions of safe uncertainty. *Human Systems: The Journal of Systemic Consultation and Management*, 4: 198–200.

Moss, D. (2002). Practicing from a park bench. *Mental Health Today*, *August*: 20–22.

Moss, D., & Barnes, R. K. (2008). Birdsong and footprints: tangibility and intangibility in a mindfulness research project. *Reflective Practice*, 9(1): 11–22.

Partridge, K. (2005). A systemic tale of assessment and formulation. *Clinical Psychology, 46*: 13–18.

Rowling, J. K. (2010). *Harry Potter and the Deathly Hallows*. London: Bloomsbury.

Smail, D. (1993). *The Origins of Unhappiness*. London: HarperCollins.

Smail, D. (1999). Patients' powers and the impotence of psychotherapy. *Universities Psychotherapy Association, 7*: 35–42.

Trungpa, C. (1976). *The Myth of Freedom*. Boston, MA: Shambhala.

CHAPTER THREE

Dancing between discourses

Sue McNab

L et us begin by telling a story—after all, this is what patients do when they come to an appointment with a mental health professional. How the story is told will be shaped by their view of their problem and their idea about who is listening to it, but it will also be moulded by the listener. As systemic practitioners, our listening ears attempt to hold as many positions as possible so that the story develops more depth, meaning, coherence, and purpose. This is no easy task and involves us in a number of continuing and complicated dance steps as we work to engage with the patient, their family, our professional colleagues, and the wider context.

Our story starts with Jim, a thirty-four-year-old man who has a longstanding relationship with psychosis and a diagnosis of schizophrenia. He has been attached to mental health teams since he was eighteen, when his difficulties encroached on his life to such an extent that he could not work, found living independently very stressful, and had a number of psychotic episodes. Our psychiatric colleagues have worked hard over the years to determine an appropriate and effective medication package and the clinical team has offered support in accessing assisted housing, return to work schemes, and ongoing supportive conversations. The team has been aware for some time of complex family relationships, which resulted in a referral for family therapy.

Jim came with his parents, Vicki and Alan, to a first appointment—a good-looking, gentle man entered the room, seemingly exhausted by the daily battle with his mind. He often clutched his head as if trying to "make it" do something to keep it focused or to force it to make sense of an increasingly hostile world. In contrast, his father, a small, wiry man and a keen runner, sat on the edge of his seat, seemingly unsure of his business in such a meeting, while his mother provided a quiet presence, ably aiding her son in the storytelling process. She quietly encouraged him when he stalled, adding her own ideas and memories and chivvying her husband to do the same.

So, what should a family therapist's first step be? At first glance, we have little knowledge of the "meaning" of this illness for Jim and his family—if, indeed, it has a meaning. Being strongly influenced by Seikkula's work (this volume), we might try to pay close attention to the language of the unfolding narrative to catch the glimmers of meaning in the undercurrent of the conversation. Seikkula (Seikkula, Arnkil, & Eriksson, 2003) promotes the idea that acute listening to those in a mental health crisis and beyond, who might traditionally be deemed too ill to attend meetings, actually brings forth coherent explanations of the patient's experience based on the reality of events that have happened to them—that is, apparently nonsensical ideas can make perfect sense.

However, would this route lead us to sidestep the medical diagnosis too quickly and pay insufficient respect to our medical colleagues and their long-term work? As systemic practitioners, we may rightly be taken to task for paying scant attention to the biochemical components of mental illness in our haste to privilege "meaning" over diagnosis. Such an emphasis might make us unpopular with psychiatric colleagues who might then hesitate to dance with us, leaving us as wallflowers only asked to join when all other options are exhausted and when any of our interventions may already be doomed in an entrenched and worn-out system. To avoid this, should we rather gather more information about the illness itself and its effects on the family? Or are these seemingly different ends of a continuum, diagnosis and meaning, really only the flip sides of a coin that we can keep tossing in the air in order to maintain the both/and position much loved by our field.

If this is so, our dilemmas, potential discomforts, and creative possibilities now begin as we attempt to respect a diagnosis we are not 100% sure we believe in and pursue relationship change that we are uncertain will make a substantial difference to the continuing existence of illness. We might, in addition, have to tread a careful path through the different models that exist both within other professional discourses and within our own field. There are also potential minefields of responsibility, uncertainty, blame, shame, and failure to stumble across, which do not often feel like the freedom of movement associated with our dancing metaphor. Yet, if we can co-ordinate our steps with both families and the networks of care, there are many possibilities.

Discourses in adult mental health

The dominant discourse within which we operate in Western culture is the medical/illness model of mental health. This model focuses on assessing symptoms in order to settle on the appropriate diagnosis, prescribing the correct medication or other treatment, monitoring an often exacting regimen for symptom reduction, managing symptoms and risk in a culture of blame and legal responsibility, and ensuring that family intervention programmes and daytime activities are in place. This is stressful, time-consuming work and leaves little space for "the making of meaning" attached to these difficulties. If our psychiatric colleagues want to involve families and carers, they can get caught in the ethical dilemmas around confidentiality, which can present real challenges, although such dilemmas can also be used as an excuse to minimise involvement with family work that our colleagues might have had little training to tackle. Sadly, in my experience, families are sometimes still seen as "a can of worms" best left unopened rather than the resource for recovery that they often are. Systemic practitioners must then try to find ways of working around the edges and make good working relationships with psychiatric colleagues who might have little faith in any sort of psychological interventions and in family models in particular. Questions of power and hierarchy enter the frame and we could find our voices as marginalised as those of the family. This can be a painful place to inhabit (Speed & McNab, 2006).

Another powerful discourse is cognitive behaviour therapy as the treatment of choice (National Institute for Clinical Excellence (NICE) guidelines) for a number of conditions such as depression, anxiety, OCD, etc. This model, while taking more account nowadays of the context in which patients live, remains an individual model within which family practitioners need to find a "place to perch" (Moss, this volume). Following the Layard report (2009), there has been a huge expansion of "talking therapies" through IAPT (Improving Access to Psychological Therapies) services that mostly privilege a CBT approach. Family psychotherapists are continuing to try to ensure that their ways of thinking are included within the IAPT programme and to be flexible in adopting manualised approaches that lend themselves to outcome research (Reibstein & Sherbersky, 2012).

A third discourse, closer to systemic practice, is that of family interventions. "Psychosocial interventions offered to families of persons with schizophrenia have been developed and studied over the past 20 years with increasing sophistication and methodological rigor" (Dixon & Lehman, 1995, p. 631). Family interventions approaches tend to share a belief that schizophrenia is an illness and that it will be helpful to the course of that illness to work with the family. A number of different methods have been developed over the years with different emphases, for example, working with expressed emotion (Leff & Vaughn, 1985), psychosocial education, family support, and problem solving with the aim of improving communication between family members to the benefit of patients and their families. Many National Health Service Trusts have invested in training individual members of staff in these methods but, as Burbach and Stanbridge (2006) point out, it has proved hard to continue to provide the necessary ongoing support and supervision in order to maintain a more family-inclusive stance. Their work in training whole teams in a variety of family approaches seems a much more successful way forward (Stanbridge & Burbach, this volume).

Finally, we come to our own ways of thinking, which embrace a number of substantial changes since the birth of family therapy in the 1950s. In the field of adult mental health, Bateson's theory of the double bind (1972) had a significant impact and has left a mixed legacy. Although the double bind theory has subsequently been questioned by many, including Bateson himself, I believe that we are still fighting a rear-guard action against the tendency for families and professionals to believe that systemic family therapy blames families for the illness that is afflicting their family member. In other words, that behaviour and communication within families plays a role in the development and maintenance of psychosis. Of course, the simple act of inviting a family to participate in the treatment programme can give rise to this idea.

There have been many changes in systemic theory and practice over the past sixty years. The earlier structural and strategic schools adopted a first order position in which families were seen to be functioning as systems. Therapists, taking a meta position and standing outside the family system, adopted an expert stance, devising interventions to effect the change they felt was necessary for more adaptive family functioning. The field has been transformed by the postmodern views of there being no one reality and the need to take account of multiple perspectives, as well as by the feminist discourse around power and the impact of the wider context on personal lives. Stories as an additional metaphor to systems have evolved from the influence of social constructionism and its attention to the importance of language, which shapes the ways in which we come to understand ourselves and our lives. These ideas have given birth to narrative approaches that have greatly enriched the field. These different theoretical and philosophical paradigms within an overarching frame of systems provide us with diverse, rich, but sometimes conflicting, choices for intervention.

Dancing betwixt and between discourses: finding ways to "go on"

How do I find my way through these various discourses and how might they be of service to the families that I meet? If I truly believe in, rather than just paying lip service to, the idea of "multiple perspectives" and social constructionist theories of there being no one truth (Andersen, 1997; Anderson & Goolishian, 1988; Gergen, 1985; Hoffmann, 2002), then I believe I already have the beginnings of a road map for my journey. Our systemic theories imply that we should pay due respect to the wide range of ideas and practices that we encounter and find ways of joining the dance (not stepping on our partner's toes) while maintaining the creative courage to continue our own improvisations.

Dancing with a medical discourse

This stance proved relatively straightforward when talking to John and Philippa about John's recent diagnosis of bipolar disorder. The meaning they attributed to it and its effects on their relationship brought forth very different perspectives for a couple who both work in professions allied to mine. For John, who is in his sixties, the diagnosis finally made sense of a lifetime of beliefs and actions which had caused him both concern and confusion, but which he had accommodated in a very successful career. The diagnosis had helped him to appreciate and monitor the triggers for his "high" episodes and to start to realise the need to take steps to avoid stressors or to ask for assistance. For him, as for many, the diagnosis had been very helpful. His wife, however, who tended to be more questioning of a diagnostic model, thought the "symptoms" made more sense when the wider picture of their joint retirements, her loss of professional status, and some fundamental changes in their couple relationship, together with some "break" in their relationship with their son and his family, were taken into account. At this point, we could have become caught up in a debate about which picture gave the truer account and which position we should each ally to. However, a more productive conversation about the possibility of taking a both/and position and the importance of being able to "embrace the medical discourse as well as elaborate alternatives to it" (McCarry & Partridge, 2007) helped us all out of this potential impasse.

However, the dance is not always so straightforward, particularly when our systemic dance joins that of other professional partners in adult mental health settings, where one of the major differences we will soon encounter between us is our varying beliefs about certainty and curiosity (Cecchin, 1987).

If we return to Jim and his family and hold the diagnosis respectfully in our minds while remaining curious about it without allowing it to dominate our conversations, what seems to emerge? We hear a moving account of the effects on family life of the birth of Hannah, Jim's younger sister, who has serious, complex (though, to the onlooker, not readily visible) learning disabilities. For more than twenty years, family life and relationships have been organised around her care, with each family member finding their own strategy to manage this. Through discussion with the family, we hypothesised that Vicki had become totally immersed in Hannah's daily care to prevent seizures, to keep her safe, and help her find a pathway to education, that Alan, deeply upset by his daughter's condition, had found solace in exercise, that Tom, the elder son, adopted a heroin addiction, and that Jim had retreated into schizophrenia—devastation for all. Family relationships have also been shaped by hostility and disappointment between the couple, a strong alliance between mother and younger son, and a rage from younger son to father for a lack of strong fatherly support. Such were the hypotheses that emerged as we talked with the family, which seemed to give some meaning to this illness.

On our way to trying to understand the difficulties that the family brings to us, we value ideas such as letting the dialogue develop (Seikkulla, this volume), of maintaining a stance of curiosity (Cecchin, 1987) and of not rushing to "know" too quickly (Andersen, 1987). Partridge (2010) talks movingly of the idea of "deep listening which mirrors Cecchin's curiosity, listening from a position of stillness, without prejudice and without attachment to either the past or the future" (p. 27). From such listening might emerge an apparent pathway to relationship work with Jim and his family, but will this work make a difference to the "illness" and what will our colleagues make of our hypotheses which are "just that"—evolving hypotheses, not "truths"?

Our way of taking this non-expert, exploratory position runs counter to the more expert stances of our colleagues from different professions, who both value and are valued for their ability to "know" and understand a situation swiftly and who move to finding appropriate solutions without delay. These contrasting viewpoints might trip us up in our working relationships, particularly in the current culture of evidence based practice in a high risk environment. As Speed (2004) has suggested,

> family therapists using ideas underpinned by postmodern beliefs can fear seeming wishy-washy and without much professional authority and can feel tempted into more certainty than they feel comfortable with. Or indeed they can find themselves beginning unthinkingly to conform to colleagues' more realistic discourses. (p. 262)

Neither of these positions is comfortable, and poses the question about how we can find a place of safe enough uncertainty (Mason, 1993) when we are often inviting even more complexity into the situation in order to try to make sense of it.

The issue of risk is currently all-consuming in adult mental health systems, much more so in my experience than it ever used to be, and the demands on all practitioners to talk of and log risk in the records cannot be avoided. For family therapists, this can mean trying to weave conversations around the potential for harm to self or others into each session without either becoming "dazzled" (Papadopoulos, 2002) by it or raising too much alarm for other family members. It also means that sometimes we have to "take a position" (Campbell & Groenbaek, 2006) and be prepared to stand by this if and when challenged by the family, colleagues, or the demands of the system. This might invite us to privilege an "illness" perspective and lose curiosity about underlying meanings for fear of getting our assessment of risk wrong.

Domain theory (Lang, Little, & Cronen, 1990) is a handy tool at this juncture. This theory posits that, as clinicians, we are often working within and between the different domains of "production and exploration". For example, at times we will need actively to step in to ensure that appropriate action is taken when there are potential risks to either children or adults. We will then be operating in the "production domain" through the use of safeguarding processes. The ability to take this position is part of any clinician's role and I believe it cannot be shirked, particularly in my working context where risk can be high. At other times, we will have more freedom to be in the "exploratory" domain, where our curiosity can have freer rein to understand meanings and work relationally. The third domain is one of "aesthetics", which poses the question of how "beautifully" we can move between the two domains and act to mitigate risk while remaining engaged with families. This is never an easy task in my experience, but using this theoretical idea to chart when and where we need to reposition ourselves, together with our systemic beliefs about power, transparency, and behaving ethically, can aid us in this process.

My work as a therapist on the Biomed Childhood Depression Research Project (2011) taught me that working with depression seems to invite this constant movement between "action" and "reflection", an idea further developed by Afaupe (this volume) in promoting wellbeing in her work with couples.

If we are fortunate in our working relationships with our local community mental health teams (CMHTs), we can, at times, rely on them to hold on to the major responsibility for risk which allows us more freedom to operate in the "exploratory" domain. This is a kindness on their part and we should be indebted to them. We can only hope that their work, in turn, is positively influenced by our ongoing work with family relationships.

There are also opportunities for us to work in the room together in assessment meetings, where our varying styles of production and exploration, curiosity and certainty, and diagnosis and meaning can form a coherent dance. An exciting initiative in my Trust has been the development of a systemic assessment clinic in one of the CMHTs. This pioneering project was the brainchild of two psychiatrists, Stephen Merson and Maria Turri, who are interested in including the family and wider systems in their work. A couple of years ago, they invited me to join them in their everyday outpatient clinic to broaden the assessment of individual patients. This had the dual purpose of including family perspectives on the difficulty presented and using such ideas for recovery, together with cutting down the potential number of assessments any one patient has to go through to receive an appropriate treatment package. The clinic is also used as a training model for systemic practice with the hope of spreading the word wider in the Trust about the effectiveness of this way of working.

Alma, a Spanish woman in her fifties, came to this clinic with her son and daughter, who were both in their twenties. She had been admitted to a mental health ward a few days before, following concerns about her unusual and challenging behaviour. A complicated story started to unfold of Alma having a potentially serious physical illness that she was choosing to deny. Her fervent wish to return home to the village of her birth in Spain was also clear. Her children, who had come to live in England ten years previously, were naturally very concerned about their mother and wished to make her a home with them in England. As the conversation continued, the level of tension in the room rose and Alma made accusations against her children about their lack of care. As we made space for the adult children to speak, their own story of having been in foster care as small children emerged, and it became clearer that this was a family with very fragmented relationships over many years. I very much doubt that this fuller understanding of lifelong difficulties in family relationships would have been forthcoming without the presence of these young people in the assessment appointment, together with the careful unpicking of the language they employed. Our curiosity about the term "college" to refer to schooldays could have been passed over as an error in the use of the English language, or different cultural understandings around education. Closer examination, however, revealed that they actually meant that they had been in the care of the state from a young age.

However, my systemic input alone would not be sufficient in this situation. I needed to rely on my medical colleagues, as I often do, to unpick the various strands of symptomatic behaviour exhibited by Alma in trying to understand how much these could be attributed to the onset of a serious neurological and ultimately terminal illness and/or whether they were signs of a diagnosable mental illness. These different sources of information were crucial in the pragmatic planning for Alma on her discharge from hospital and in ensuring the family's more realistic hopes and dreams for the future.

I think this example of professionals holding the tensions of diagnosis and meaning between them while working with the two discourses in a skilful dance together encouraged a fuller picture to be uncovered and addressed in a single meeting. Peter Lang talks about the importance "of holding the difference rather than trying to resolve it", while David Campbell talked about "upending the context and think of the opposite" (quoted in Partridge, 2010, p. 27). These ideas maintain the dialectic between opposite positions so that both can be fully explored in terms of possibilities and constraints. They also open up the possibility of a third, unifying context, which might unite the opposites, thus maintaining complexity rather than attempting to simplify it by coming to a compromise. Colleagues learn directly from each other and the family benefited from the understanding that we, as professionals, gained through our collective dialogue. A story emerged that would have remained untold in a psychiatric assessment alone and, while it might have come to light in a separate family meeting later down the line, this would have involved further assessments, liaison meetings, planning meetings, and so on. Managers who are anxious about the employment of a number of staff in one meeting need to be made more aware of the cost-effectiveness of this approach, particularly as the use of an interpreter was needed with this family.

I can cite many other examples of when I have depended on my psychiatric colleagues' wisdom and knowledge to work out how to go on. For example, in the case of domestic violence in a couple relationship, when the wife's belief that her partner's bipolar illness could be held responsible for his aggressive behaviour was challenged by my psychiatrist colleague, she could start to consider a different future for herself. She no longer felt that, as a Christian, she had a duty to care for a "sick man", but, rather, that she could hold to account a husband who had the capacity to take responsibility for his violent behaviour.

Dancing with CBT

The psychologists who work within my service predominantly operate within the tradition of well-researched CBT, and I greatly admire their work. They are very skilled, dedicated professionals who manage a huge throughput in a caring, thoughtful manner. We hold different positions, but there are also similarities, as "they use . . . motivational interviewing and Socratic questioning, both having some overlap with circular questioning" (Speed, 2004, p. 267). Putting together our diverse ways of working, rather than standing in competition over entrenched differences, can be very enriching.

I am indebted to one of my psychology colleagues, Khadj Rouf, who came to help me out with a young woman, Pauline, and her family, with whom I had been working for some considerable time. As good systemic thinkers, I and other members of the family therapy team had come up with a long list of hypotheses about the severe anxiety this young woman suffered from. These included her mother's chronic health problems, diagnosed when Pauline was about thirteen, the effect of which we felt kept Pauline very close to home and scared of being independent, the sudden separation from her beloved older brother, James, who married quickly at a young age and left the country, and Pauline's abusive relationship with her partner, David, and the subsequent birth of her son Tommy. We believed we had made some progress in helping Pauline decide to leave her parents to move in with her new partner and to be settled and calm in this new environment. All seemed well and we bowed out—perhaps feeling rather pleased with ourselves!

However, a few short months later, Pauline rang in crisis, having found out that she was pregnant again. Her anxieties flooded back and I realised that, while a systemic approach had been able to give plenty of meaning to why anxiety had taken over, we had not provided any strategies for tackling it in the moment. I prevailed on my psychology colleague, Khadj, to join me, and she suggested that following many anxiety provoking events in a person's life, the threat system switches on in anticipation of further catastrophes, which leads to chronic anxiety prior to any life transitions. This made perfect sense to Pauline and her family. The label of anticipatory anxiety normalised what was happening and Pauline was subsequently able to take on some very helpful techniques to keep anxiety at bay. I did not have these tools in my kitbag, and drawing on Khadj's dance enhanced our practice.

Dancing with family interventions

Bland (2007) has raised an important issue around bridging the gap between family intervention models and systemic family therapy. As she points out,

> the evidence base, usefully incorporated in the NICE guidelines for the treatment of schizophrenia is for family intervention not for family therapy. We cannot jump on their bandwagon without at least addressing the differences of emphasis of the two traditions in an open and informed way. (p. 8)

Bland also reminds us that "an impressive body of evidence has been amassed for family interventions ... and has been shown to significantly reduce relapse rates particularly in conjunction with antipsychotic medication". Once again, as systemic practitioners, we need to ask ourselves where we fit with this body of knowledge and how we can complement rather than compete with it. Perhaps a simple pyramid of family work is called for here, with a baseline where all Trust clinicians are invited to use a family sensitive approach, moving upwards to a middle tier where family interventions are called for to focus on the effect of the illness on the family and the family's responses to the illness, and last, an upper tier where the history of family relationships and current patterns of relationship call for a systemic intervention.

Dorothy is a woman in her late fifties, separated from her husband, with three young adult sons. In recent years, being single again at the same time as losing her successful career had resulted in a long period of severe psychotic depression and hospitalisation. All three of her sons were very supportive in their different ways and took advantage of the meetings on offer from a colleague of mine working in an early intervention service. This input greatly helped them to understand the nature of their mother's difficulties and to find ways of offering their support as well as gaining help themselves in stressful circumstances. This was very useful work, highly valued by the whole family. However, my colleague felt that there were undercurrents of tension between different family members that, if left unspoken, might impede his patient's progress. It was at this stage that he invited me to join him for some work on family relationships, which he did not feel equipped to tackle on his own. My engagement with the family was greatly assisted by the fact that my colleague was already a trusted professional to them, and together we were able to unpick the longer standing issues around family separation, family loyalty, and transitions—all very familiar themes for family therapists.

In all of our work with our colleagues, but perhaps most pertinently with those using a family interventions model, we must tackle headlong with them and the families that we meet any misconception that we blame families for mental health problems; it is, rather, that we see families as a resource and that working together is a positive way forward. This is not always a simple task, as I know, and demands a fleetness of foot.

Dancing within systemic discourses

The systemic tradition is rich with a variety of theoretical models and a seemingly endless assortment of ways of proceeding in our work with families. So, while stumbling across the diverse paradigms of other professionals, we also have to juggle those in our own field to try to make the best fit for families. Partridge (2007, p. 97) writes,

> We privilege some decisions over others according to the opportunities and constraints given to us in a given context. The right to make choices and the duty to choose what will be most beneficial for the client means that every action constitutes a moral choice which will enable or prohibit the way in which we can go on together with our clients.

The availability of such choices confers serious responsibilities.

Our work with Jim and his family has proved such a challenge and, as I write it, is an ongoing one. The family therapy team and I have had many conversations with the family about the impact on them of Hannah's disability, and in particular its effects on relationships over the years. In the initial stages of talking with the family, it was hard to know where best to intervene, as so many of their familial relationships had been disturbed by Hannah's birth and need for constant care. The marital relationship was full of anger and disappointment and it had been on the point of break-up for many years. However, it also felt very stuck, with neither parent wanting to grasp the nettle of an actual separation although the atmosphere between Vicki and Alan at times was painful to witness. Jim talked about his experience of "growing up quickly" and stepping into the role of supporter and confidant to his mother until his "illness" took hold. It seemed to us that Jim was still actively caught between his parents, allying strongly with his mother and joining her in her fury towards her husband for his inability to provide succour at an emotional level. I thought that some couple sessions to explore these issues might be useful, but it was hard to see how change might occur despite honest endeavours on all our parts.

We then considered the relationship between Jim and his mother, which had been a mutually close and supportive one for many long years. Before I started meeting the family, Hannah had been successfully rehoused in supported accommodation, but Vicki remained on constant call to her daughter and to the staff of the unit. Things were not easy and Jim was again called into the role of co-parent, almost unwittingly on Vicki's part—it had just been such a familiar pattern. Jim explained the almost traumatic experiences he had when the phone rang late at night and he knew that he and his mother would be called upon to respond to some crisis or other. There was one wonderfully significant moment when Vicki, monitoring her own responses, appreciated the old pattern of leaning on Jim rearing its head and stopped herself mid-flow. Jim threw up his arms, exclaiming, "I'm free!" We also talked with Vicki on her own about her hopes and dreams for her life outside of child-care, a notion that was so alien to her that she was literally lost for words.

However, it was Jim who guided us to the relationship he most wanted to sort out, and that was the one with his father. His fury, kept well contained under his gentle demeanour, about his father's inability to "be the father he wanted and needed, both as a child and as an adult" was, Jim felt, keeping him stuck in the "illness" mode. Hats off to Alan, who attended regular meetings with his son, withstood some of the criticism, acknowledged his failings, spoke emotionally about the loss of the daughter he had longed for, put his hand up to his shortcomings, and made several apologies to his son. Father and son also tried to find new ways of talking to each other, and eventually they were able to be in the same room together for longer periods before Jim felt the need to leave abruptly.

We all felt encouraged that some progress in changing relationships was being achieved; the problem was that Jim seemed as stuck in his lifestyle as ever and our colleagues in the CMHT were as involved in trying different medications, initiating individual CBT sessions, involving Jim in day-care programmes, and looking for alternative accommodation for him. We started to wonder what all our curiosity and meaning discourse had achieved, and doubt and self-doubt crept in. We began to question our systemic interventions and tried to evaluate whether we should persevere in working at the emotional level of encouraging the expression of anger repressed for many years. This would involve us in older systemic dances, using intensification and keeping family members in step until they started experimenting with a new repertoire. We might talk about the role of forgiveness and reparation. A narrative discourse might value "thickening the description" (White, 2005) of Jim's hopes and dreams and an exploration of "preferred identities" (White, 2005). It is hard to know which is the "right" path, but then, is it up to us alone to know? Reminding ourselves of the usefulness of transparency and self-reflexivity (Rober, 1999), we opened our dilemma to the family for discussion and were warmed by their wisdom. They advocated taking a both/and position: some time to be allocated for emotional talk around relationships and some time to be saved for more positive futures.

During our work with the family, we were humbled one day by directly experiencing the research findings that posit that our locus of influence is actually only about 15% and that other factors, such as life events, hold supremacy in the field of change (Lambert & Barley, 2001). Vicki had a serious biking accident and spent some time in hospital, leaving father and son to manage as best they could. Alan, in his son's words, "has really stepped up to the mark" and been the supportive and active husband that Vicki has been longing for over the years. Alan spoke movingly of realising "how close I had come to losing my wife and how much I care for her". Their relationship has subsequently improved enormously and we might have hypothesised that this would bring positive change for Jim, who could be released from his positions both as his mother's confidant and as the mediator between his parents. Of course, life is not so straightforward, and Jim found himself struggling with now feeling less important to his mother and left out of his parents' new-found happiness. I guess time will tell if and how these changes—brought about by chance—will impact on Jim and his ongoing struggle with mental health worries.

What the family have told us, however, is that the family work they are so bravely undertaking *is* making a difference to them all, and in Jim's own words, "This is a place where I am seen as a person, not as an illness."

The family themselves have, I hope, felt very much part of the writing of their story in this chapter, and they have written their comments to us in email form.

Dear Sue, Jane and Llewella

Many thanks for the email and attachment regarding the chapter about us and the invitation to comment.

We all agree that reading about ourselves is quite strange and also very humbling. We appreciate the time it has taken to support each one of us in very individual ways and how carefully you have all listened and somehow made sense of our complex lives. This is something we have all struggled with at times and so this in itself is very reassuring as we sometimes feel a very dysfunctional family and that we could/should have coped better than we did.

However, setting that aside it has been so positive to feel listened to and not judged and more importantly to have been given the tools to reflect on each other's behaviour and reactions to the dynamics of our speci-fic needs as a family. Tools we are beginning to use and to practise our ability to recognise and acknowledge each other's feelings and needs.

Family Therapy has been a painful journey and has taken commitment, complete honesty and time. Amongst our tears and pain, we have had to acknowledge our own mistakes and look at why we have made judgements and whether it was the right way to judge that person's behaviour and then to try and understand things from their perspec-tive and be able to say sorry and mean it!

Early intervention by Family Therapy could perhaps have enabled us all to have coped better. There is no manual for a marriage and the consequent pressure of having a disabled and complex daughter and sister. We all had to cope the best we could and Jim perhaps could have been spared his torment as well as Tom, who has other issues but has felt the same pain and dealt with it in a different way which we hope he will come through.

Getting help from all professionals throughout Hannah's early life was impossible – everything appeared "rationed": care managers, social workers, education, OT, speech therapy, physiotherapy and any referral for child guidance had a long waiting list even if you could get a referral.

There almost seemed to be an elite within the disabled community and we just weren't on the horizon. We did not require physical aids, hoists, etc., we had no clear label, Autism, Downs, etc., perhaps there was a hope that, after coping in the early years, her needs would disappear and Hannah's brain damage would be limited. However her problems became more complex as her world grew and she struggled to "fit in" and her epilepsy and hemaparesis grew more severe. This resulted in constant battles for Hannah to get the right support and endless meetings. She became the focus of "everything" and it was perhaps too easy to overlook what was happening to her brothers and how they were coping.

Now we all take extreme pride in the amazing young woman Hannah is and this is credit to all of us, especially her brothers who love her dearly. It must, however, be said that perhaps this was a huge price to pay when two young boys were clearly struggling to make sense of their own identity and emotions and how well (or not as the case was) their parents were coping with what had happened and how to manage it all.

Thank you all for your dedication and the very special work you do. Hopefully we will continue to repair our lives, especially Jim and his brother who deserve the very best life has to offer. We are now in a better place to move forward and use the wisdom and tools you have given us. We may stray from time to time but it is good to stop on our way up that mountain and as Llewella said "stop and look down" to reflect on how far we have come.

A very heartfelt thank you from The Simms Family.

NB I do hope I have not gone over old ground here too much.

The impact on the self of the therapist of "discourse dancing"

I often find myself having to manage my own relationship to uncertainty and how to tolerate it when things seem to be going nowhere. I work in a field of chronicity, where it is easy to lose sight of small changes and where anxiety and sadness weigh heavily on everyone. As one of a group of therapists working on the Biomed Childhood Depression Project (2011), I realised the importance of joint working when tackling the power of depression. This allowed us to support each other with the ebb and flow of curiosity and self-doubt, together with holding on to hope *vs.* despair (Flaskas, McCarthy, & Sheehan, 2007; McNab, Pentecost, Bianco, & Goldberg, 2011). The holding of hope in seemingly hopeless situations is a familiar place for those of us working in adult mental health and I often recall Karen Partridge's symbolic crystal ball, which "stands for future dreaming and the transformative power of an appreciative posture in the creation of hope" (Partridge, 2010, p. 27). However, in the current constrained context of adult mental health, the option of teamwork is becoming increasingly out of reach. We must, therefore, rely on our ability to adopt highly tuned, self-reflexive practice and, in so doing, we may again meet tensions between models.

As with psychoanalytic approaches, the systemic model holds dear the ability to reflect on our own stories and their effect on our work, and we prioritise the need for self-reflection as well as live consultations and the conversations of the supervisory process. It is not my experience that other professions necessarily share the same methods, and this could result in a difference of style in team consultations and practice. I have written elsewhere with my colleague, Ellie Kavner (2005), about the role of shame in the therapeutic relationship and I believe that emotions of shame, blame, and responsibility can operate powerfully, yet often silently, in the tensions between models. I also think this emotion is heightened in the area of adult mental health, where mental illness continues to carry stigma in the public arena and where people still carry their illness under a cloak of shame. As Iona Cook (this volume) points out, this cloak can also be worn by those of us who work alongside mental health sufferers, because the "stigma by association" principle operates (Neuberg, Smith, Hoffman, & Russell, 1994). I view with much appreciation the courage of those who suffer—both famous and lesser known—coming forward to speak openly about their troubles. This bravery is helping to shake the dominant discourse around the stereotypes of people with psychosis, depression, and anxiety, but there is still a long way to go.

In the meantime, is it possible to share more openly our own relationship to mental health, either as personal sufferers, caring for or having family members who suffer, or having lost a loved one to suicide and to use this experience to positive effect with the families with whom we work? Is it helpful to be seen as an "expert by experience" as well as having professional expertise, or should that part of the story remain untold? This is an ongoing dilemma in the systemic field and there will be many views about the usefulness and risks of sharing one's personal experience within our own profession, let alone between professions.

In our more recent work together, Bebe Speed and I decided to experiment with being more open about ourselves with our patients and their families and to ask them about the impact of this. When a particular story told in the session had a special resonance with one or other of us, we might voice something of our own experience as a way of demonstrating understanding and empathy with one or more family members, or to enrich descriptions and possibilities.

Comments from families about this way of working were overwhelmingly positive. People expressed great appreciation for what we revealed and valued highly the empathy with, and understanding of, their predicament that our comments about ourselves would often display. They also spoke about our shared "humanity", which more obviously emerged, and this sense of commonality and the witnessing of struggles, which were about being human rather than about being mad or bad, were very powerful in relieving shame. Such testimony has given me courage to continue to take risks in talking about my personal dilemmas. Being open about my experience of the impact of panic attacks and their power to make me feel as if I was going to die with a young man enduring similar experiences gave him permission to talk more about his experience and also to voice his shame and humiliation in telling his father about it. His dearest wish was to be seen as a strong person—similar to the men in his family over generations—and he had, therefore, masked the extent of his fear until this point. We were also able to agree in a more light-hearted frame that indeed panic attacks do not kill, as I am the living proof many years later!

However, this seemingly useful sharing only feels possible in working alone or with a very trusted colleague and, unfortunately, does not feel easily acceptable in wider teamwork where there is less mutual trust and confidence in colleagues' sensitivity, values, and attitudes.

Conclusion

When I started to write this chapter, my mind was centred on the complexity of this dance between discourses and how problematic the issues can be. As I have been writing, I have become much more excited about the possibilities and promise of working across models. I realise how many exceptions to the rule there have been in working with colleagues where I might have expected too much difference, only to find encouragement, interest, and a willingness to step outside of their own comfort frame to join in alternative steps. I have also come to appreciate the need for humility about any one way of doing things and how a real embracing of multiple views, even when they do not easily accord with your own, can bring small changes to seemingly intractable situations. I also keep stored in my mind the effect of the passage of time, and every now and then wonder what our successors in fifty or a hundred years' time will think when they look back at our practice in adult mental health. Will the research in neuroscience make them talk wonderingly about our belief in the power of language to make any significant difference to the brain? Who can tell—but in the here and now we "go on" to the best of our ability with the tools we have at our disposal and with the good heart to work together across disciplines, models, and professions in the service of patients and families.

Dedication

To my father, a man of fun, wit, and great wisdom, who, sadly, lost his struggle with depression.

References

Andersen, T. (1987). The reflecting team: dialogue and meta-dialogue in clinical work. *Family Process, 26*: 141–155.

Andersen, T. (1997). Researching client–therapist relationships: a collaborative study for informing therapy. *Journal of Systemic Therapies, 16*: 125–133.

Anderson, H., & Goolishian, H. A. (1988). Human Systems as linguistic systems: evolving ideas about the implications for theory and practice. *Family Process, 27*: 371–393.

Bateson, G. (1972). *Steps to an Ecology of Mind.* New York: Ballantine Books.

Bland, J. (2007). Family therapy and psychosis: struggling to integrate systemic and biological models. *Context, 93*: 7–8.

Burbach, F., & Stanbridge, R. (2006). Somerset's family interventions in psychosis service: an update. *Journal of Family Therapy, 28*: 39–57.

Campbell, D., & Groenbaek, M. (2006). *Taking Positions in the Organisation.* London: Karnac.

Cecchin, G. (1987). Hypothesising, circularity and neutrality revisited: an invitation to curiosity. *Family Process, 26*: 405–413.

Dixon, L., & Lehman, A. (1995). Family interventions for schizophrenia. *Schizophrenia Bulletin, 21*(4): 631–643.

Flaskas, C., McCarthy, I., & Sheehan, J. (Eds.) (2007). *Hope and Despair in Narrative and Family Therapy: Adversity, Forgiveness and Reconciliation.* New York: Routledge.

Gergen, K. J. (1985). The social constructionist movement in modern psychology. *American Psychologist, 40*: 255–275.

Hoffman, L. (2002). *Family Therapy: An Intimate History.* New York: Norton.

Kavner, E., & McNab, S. (2005). Shame and the therapeutic relationship. In: C. Flaskas, B. Mason, & A. Perlesz (Eds.), *The Space Between: Experience, Context and Process in the Therapeutic Relationship* (pp. 141–155). London: Karnac.

Lambert, M. J., & Barley, D. E. (2001). Research summary on the therapeutic relationship and psychology outcome. *Psychotherapy: Theory, Research, Practice, Training, 38*(4): 357–361.

Lang, W. P., Little, M., & Cronen, V. (1990). The systemic professional domains of action and the question of neutrality. *Human Systems: The Journal of Systemic Consultation and Management, 1*: 39–55.

Layard, R. (2009). *The Depression Report. A New Deal for Depression and Anxiety Disorders.* London: London School of Economics.

Leff, J. P., & Vaughn, C. E. (1985). *Expressed Emotion in Families.* London: Guilford Press.

Mason, B. (1993). Towards positions of safe uncertainty. *Human Systems: The Journal of Systemic Consultation and Management (Special Issue), 4*(3–4): 189–200.

McCarry, N., & Partridge, K. (2007). Systemic practice and psychosis; diversity and inclusion. *Context, 93*: 1–2.

McNab, S., Pentecost, D., Bianco, V., & Goldberg, H. (2011). The family therapists' experience. In: J. Trowell with G. Miles (Eds.), *Childhood Depression: A Place for Psychotherapy* (pp. 139–153). London: Karnac.

Neuberg, S. L., Smith, D. M., Hoffman, J. C., & Russell, F. J. (1994). When we observe stigmatized and "normal" individuals interacting: stigma by association. *Personality and Psychology Bulletin, 39*: 196–209.

Papadopoulos, R. (2002). Refugees, home and trauma. In: R. Papdopoulos (Ed.), *Therapeutic Care for Refugees: No Place like Home.* London: Karnac.

Partridge, K. (2007). The positioning compass: a tool to facilitate reflexive positioning. *Journal of Systemic Consultation and Management, 18*: 96–111.

Partridge, K. (2010). A bundle of treasures for a wandering therapist: an exploration of personal and professional resources to sustain a therapist on a systemic journey. *Context, 112*: 26–28.

Reibstein, J., & Sherbersky, H. (2012). Behavioural and empathic elements of systemic couple therapy: the Exeter Model and a case study of depression. *Journal of Family Therapy, 34*: 271–283.

Rober, P. (1999). The therapist's inner conversation in family therapy practice: some ideas about the self of the therapist, therapeutic impasse, and the process of reflection. *Family Process, 38*: 209–228.

Seikkula, J., Arnkil, T., & Eriksson, M. (2003). Postmodern society and social networks: open and anticipation dialogues in network meetings. *Family Process, 42*(2): 185–203.

Speed, B. (2004). All aboard in the NHS: collaborating with colleagues who use different approaches. *Journal of Family Therapy, 26*: 260–279.

Speed, B., & McNab, S. (2006). Working with couples where one partner has a psychiatric diagnosis. *Context, 86*: 21–25.

White, M. (2005). Michael White workshop notes. www.dulwichcentre.com.au

PART II
CONSTRUCTING ALTERNATIVE POSITIONS

Coming to reasonable terms with our histories: narrative ideas, memory, and mental health

David Denborough

S truggles for mental health matter to me. My extended family and friendship networks, like most, know the heartbreak and acts of bravery that accompany significant mental health struggles. My work for Dulwich Centre Foundation takes place with groups and communities who are responding to mental health concerns in the context of broader trauma and injustice. Whether it is those in my own community who are struggling for mental health, or those in communities with whom we work in partnership in Rwanda, Palestine, Iraq, or elsewhere, the suffering and courage that I regularly witness is the backdrop to this chapter. In the following pages, I wish to mention a number of hopeful recent trends, or "movements", in the field of mental health and then link these to some of our current explorations of narrative practice.

Some recent "movements" in mental health

I have recently returned to Australia after a visit to the Northern hemisphere that included the Hearing Voices World Congress[1] in Cardiff, which marked the twenty-fifth anniversary of the Hearing Voices

Movement. It was an inspiring event. One of many highlights was meeting Joseph Atukunda from Heartsounds Uganda.[2] Joseph is one of the "mental health champions" of Uganda—people who have known their own struggles and are now determined to build grass roots "consumer-led" mental health responses in Uganda and, eventually, in other African countries. I learnt from Joseph Atukunda of the ways he is using the Tree of Life (Denborough, 2008; Ncube, 2006) in his work and how they are seeking to transcend stigma in relation to mental health.

Standing in Cardiff at an event primarily led and made possible by UK and European mental health champions[3] and learning from Joseph about Ugandan forms of peer support, invited me to reflect on what is being achieved through various key trends or "movements" in relation to mental health.[4] I want to focus on just three here.

First, the efforts of the "psychiatric survivor movement",[5] the "hearing voices movement",[6] and the "recovery movement", among others, have led to a much greater appreciation of the importance of speaking about mental health concerns in ways that do not pathologise individuals, that do not locate the problem in the person, but instead externalise and contextualise problems (White 2007; White & Epston, 1990). This recognition is being accompanied by an increasing emphasis on people being the experts on their own lives, and their right to speak for and represent themselves rather than having their experience defined, interpreted, and spoken for by mental health professionals.

Second, over the past twenty years, thanks to the efforts of feminist thinkers and others, there has been an increasing recognition of a relationship between many mental health struggles in the present and past experiences of "trauma" and "abuse" (Chesler, 2005; Herman, 1997; Romme & Escher, 2000). Recognising that personal, familial, and social injustices influence the distribution of mental health struggles is posing significant challenges and providing new opportunities to our field.[7]

Third, a range of indigenous writers and majority world practitioners[8] have critiqued the cultural dominance of Western psychological approaches and have sought to ensure that responses to social suffering/mental health concerns take into account cultural meanings, honour diverse cultural knowledge, and avoid psychological colonisation (Kleinman, 1998; Tamasese, 2003a,b; Waldegrave, 1998; Watters, 2010).

The fact that Ugandan and Western approaches to recovery are now shared at conferences led by people who have their own experience of hearing voices is the combined result of at least these three "movements" and so many people's efforts to regrade and redignify responses to mental health.

Soon after the Congress in Cardiff, I flew to Kurdistan, Iraq, where I was to work alongside colleagues at the Kirkuk Center for Torture Victims.[9] While the context in Iraq is profoundly different than that in Cardiff, there are links that I wish to make. In the following section, I outline a narrative approach that aims to assist people struggling for mental health to come to reasonable terms with their own histories. I particularly relate these ideas to work occurring in Kurdistan, and also to work in Australia and the UK in relation to hearing voices.

Narrative practice and working with memory

The work of Dulwich Centre Foundation involves responding to those who are experiencing mental health difficulties as the result of trauma or "social suffering" (Kleinman, Das, & Lock, 1997), including war, military occupation, dispossession, natural disaster, racism, poverty, and so on. Our work is primarily informed by narrative therapy practices (White, 1995, 2007, 2011; White & Epston, 1990) and what we call collective narrative practice (Denborough, 2008), which comprises work with groups and entire communities in various parts of the world.

Some years ago, I spoke with Michael White about his ways of orientating to history when working with people with mental health struggles who have experienced significant trauma. In this conversation, he described the importance of enabling people to "come to reasonable terms with their own histories" (White, 2006a). Ever since hearing this phrase, I have been intrigued by exploring its possibilities. So curious, in fact, that I have explored the ways in which different fields approach problems of memory and history. During these explorations, and during community assignments in various contexts, I have come across the field of critical heritage practice and believe it has implications for our work.

Critical heritage practice

In contexts of significant historical violations in different parts of the world, various historians, writers, sociologists, social activists, and curators have established what has come to be known as Museums of Conscience.[10] In these Museums of Conscience, critical heritage practice is used to work with troubled memory, to "facilitate the recovery of the forgotten, the displaced, the marginalised, and the unspoken, and to find ways of inserting this subordinated past into the politics of the present and its futures" (Soudien, 2008, p. 24).

Critical heritage practice in these sites of conscience is characterised by a keen examination of the effects of power on memory, a commitment to the many silenced voices of history, and a determination for storytelling and performance of memory to take the form of social mobilisation (Sanger, 2007, p. 7). For example, the District Six Museum[11] in Cape Town, South Africa, acts as a site of memorial to a particular diverse cultural neighbourhood that was cleared and demolished during apartheid. At the same time, it acts as a site of social action to seek redress and to re-establish community in the site that was cleared. The "memory projects" (Rassool, 2007, p. 37) at this site take diverse forms—murals, marches, ceremonies, books, frescos, exhibits, songs, and so on. Ex-residents and visitors are invited to actively engage with re-creating history and memory through contributing reflections and participating in social actions. These "memory projects" combine remembrance, politics, poetry, campaigns, history, and artistry (Rassool, 2007, p. 37).

While these "sites of conscience" might at first seem somewhat removed from the realm of mental health, I am finding the field of critical heritage practice extremely relevant to our work. As practitioners working with individuals, groups, and communities struggling with mental health concerns, I believe we are also involved in "memory projects" that seek to link personal experience, resonance, and imagery to address broader social suffering. Let me explain.

Bridging the gap between the personal and the social

Too often, the experience of struggling for one's mental health is profoundly isolating. For many people, mental health struggles are

accompanied with the sense that no one else could possibly understand, that there is no way words can be found to adequately convey
experiences, and, therefore, a profound gap comes to exist between
the person and the rest of the world. Our Rwandan colleagues describe their first responsibility to those who are struggling for mental
health as "bridging this gap" by receiving stories of social suffering in
particular ways:

> When we meet with survivors we build trust by listening to them, by
> listening deeply and carefully. It is through our listening that we seek
> to know them and to bridge the gap between them and us. We listen
> for what they have survived, what they have endured. We listen to
> them as they speak about the suffering, the injustices, the losses, and
> the continuing difficulties they face. We listen for the effects the geno-
> cide has had on their lives. Because we are also survivors, we listen in
> ways that show we are not afraid of their stories. Sometimes we share
> our own experiences in ways that make it possible for other survivors
> to speak. We listen in ways that show we understand. (Ibuka coun-
> selors, in Denborough, 2010)

Some years ago, I interviewed the facilitators of Hearing Voices
groups in the UK, all of whom have their own experiences of hearing
voices. One of these facilitators, Sharon de Valda (2003), spoke similarly of the significance of bridging the gap through the creation of
common ground:

> From all the experiences I have had, I have learnt a lot about trust and
> making connections. I know that I can make really good connections
> with other people who hear voices . . . I know how to reach out to
> them. When I have something in common with another person,
> whether it is experiences of racism, or voices, or being in prison, we
> can find ways to trust each other differently. When I meet someone
> who is vulnerable, or who does not find it easy to trust, I try to find
> something we have in common. I am open with them, and ask about
> the content of the voices. The voices they hear might say similar things
> to what mine do and then we can talk about how we cope with this.
> (p. 10)

Once an initial bridge has been built between the individual and
the rest of the world,[12] it might then become possible to externalise
(White, 2007; White & Epston, 1990) whatever is causing the mental

distress. In situations of "psychosis", often it is the hostile voices or visions that might come to be named and externalised and their strategies and tactics articulated (Brigitte, Sue, Mem, & Veronika, 1997). When this occurs, it becomes possible to explore the broader social factors that have contributed to the emergence, the strength, and the endurance of these hostile voices and their practices. Through narrative enquiry, the hostile voices can be placed into storylines. Significantly, it is not uncommon for their emergence to be linked to experiences of personal tyranny or abuse (see Bullimore, 2003). At other times, broader social forces may be acknowledged. For instance, Sharon de Valda (2003) eloquently conveys how, as a black British woman, both racism and sexism have shaped her experiences of hearing hostile voices:[13]

> The first time I can recall hearing voices was when I was thirteen years old. The voices terrified me ... They called me 'nigger', 'coon' and 'wog'. Sometimes it was like going to a football match and being the only black person. It was like standing in the middle of the field and everyone in the crowd was white and was shouting racist names at me. That's what it was like ...

> Women shouldn't feel this guilt about abuse we have experienced, but it happens. It can manifest itself as a voice that calls us demeaning words like 'whore' or 'bitch'. It might be the voice of the abuser and it comments upon how we are as a person, how we're dressed or how we're acting. It might say things like 'you're a slag', if you'll excuse my language. The voices make these sorts of comments. And if we talk as women about these things it can be really helpful to hear that others go through similar things. You then feel like you're not the only one and this can create a sense of kinship. (pp. 9–10)

When hostile voices are externalised and placed back into history and culture, this provides new possibilities for individual, social, and cultural action. Veronika Kulwikowski was a member of Power to Our Journeys, a group that Michael White facilitated in Adelaide, South Australia, using narrative ideas, for people who heard voices. Here, Veronika explains that when the tactics of the "hostile voices" of schizophrenia are unmasked, and their links to forces of sexism, racism, and other relations of power are made visible, new options become possible for voice-hearers:

The Power to Our Journeys group sessions were amazing when we discovered that the hostile voices followed patterns. They use tactics of repression and oppression. They are terribly repressive. It made a huge difference to discover we shared similar experiences of the negative voices. You thought this was only happening to you, but then we realised that we had similar experiences. We also realised that our experience of the voices was political, that the hostile voices were often voices of culture and class. Our conversations were about changing the power relations with the voices. One of our group members would often describe her efforts at addressing the effects of sexist voices as involving 'political action in her own head'. (Kulwikowski, 2011)

I have tried to outline here two processes of "bridging the gap". The first involves building a bridge between the person experiencing mental health struggles and those who are receiving their stories. The second process involves bridging the gap between the personal and the social by placing personal experience into a wider frame. As Veronika explained above, when hostile voices are named, defined, externalised, and located back in history and culture, what initially were privatised experiences of tyranny can be responded to in solidarity with others. In this way, privatised experiences become communalised and pathology is replaced by shared concerns.

I believe there are links here between narrative practice and critical heritage practice (Table 4.1)

A memory project: vividly describing people's skills of survival

In addition to bridging the gap between the personal and the social, and creating contexts for solidarity, a second memory project involves vividly, or richly, describing people's skills of survival. As White (2006b) described, no one is a passive recipient of trauma:

People always take steps in endeavouring to prevent the trauma they are subject to, and, when preventing this trauma is clearly impossible, they take steps to try to modify it in some way or to modify its effects on their lives. These steps contribute to the preservation of, and are founded upon, what people hold precious. Even in the face of overwhelming trauma, people take steps to try to protect and to

Table 4.1.   Parallels between critical heritage practice and narrative practice in mental health.

Critical heritage practice	Narrative practice in mental health
Asking how museums can become "sites of conscience".	Asking how therapy can become a "site of conscience".
A keen examination of the effects of power on memory	A keen examination of the effects of power on the experience of hearing voices (or other mental health struggles)
A commitment to the many silenced voices of history	A commitment to the ways people have responded to and resisted these effects of power
A determination for storytelling and performance of memory to take the form of social mobilisation (Sanger, 2007, p. 7)	A determination for storytelling and performance of memory within therapy and/or collective practice to link lives, create contexts for solidarity, and enable people with shared experience to make contributions to each other's lives

> preserve what they give value to . . . in the context of trauma, and in its aftermath, these responses to trauma are often rendered invisible through diminishment and disqualification . . . Even when these responses to trauma are not disqualified in this way, they are often considered insignificant and are overlooked. This contributes to a sense of personal desolation, to the development of a sense of shame which is strongly experienced by so many people who have been subject to trauma, and to the erosion of a 'sense of myself'. (p. 28)

Similarly, no one is a passive recipient of mental health struggles, of hostile voices, or of despair. But, because the survival skills that people use to respond to mental health difficulties are rarely elicited or acknowledged, they often remain intangible, invisible even to the person themselves. Noticing these responses, these actions in a person's life, can be highly significant as Kulwikowski explains:

> While the voices were saying we were useless, we would find actions in our lives that contradicted what the voices were saying. We would talk about this. But this wasn't just words. We would find real examples in our lives that would show how we were a responsible sister or a compassionate friend. We would anchor these alternative stories about ourselves in reality. (Kulwikowski, 2011)

These responses, these "actions in our lives" and the values that inform them, which contradict the messages of the hostile voices, can be understood as openings to preferred storylines of identity (Epston & White, 1998).

Preferred storylines of identity: animating a counter-heritage

Within narrative practice, there are many different ways in which we seek to assist people to develop preferred storylines of identity. I find the following four lines of enquiry particularly helpful (Denborough, 2008); explanatory comments are given in italics:

- What is it that assists you to get through hard times? Can you name a particular value, skill, belief, or practice (something you or others do) that assists you in times of hardship?
- Can you tell me a story about this? About a time when you and/ or others have engaged with this survival skill or value? *The more vividly these stories are told, the more evocatively animated these values, skills, beliefs and practices become.*
- What is the history of these survival skills/values? Who did you learn these from or with? Who would be least surprised to hear you speaking about this? *This involves tracing the social histories or heritage of these values, skills, or practices and exploring whether these are in any way legacies from others that are being carried into the present and to the future.*
- Are these survival skills/values/practices linked to any broader collective traditions or heritage? *This could include cultural, community, familial, and political heritage.*

This rich description of survival skills contributes to developing preferred storylines of identity. It also involves eliciting what can be called "counter-heritage" (Byrne, 2009), a heritage that "counters" problematic descriptions of identity. In my experience, these four lines of enquiry often lead to links being made between a person's current methods of sustenance or survival skills and the actions or values of a treasured person in their life. Sharon de Valda (2003), for instance, speaks of the connections between her ways of seeking peace in the present and those of her mother:

One of the ways in which I try to escape is that I have put pictures up all over the walls of our lounge room. They are all pictures that tell a story of a good time, some precious memory. There are so many photographs, clippings, and pictures. The amazing thing is, when I eventually found my mum and I went into her house for the first time, I saw that she does the same thing. It was quite extraordinary. Her walls are also covered with pictures, almost every square inch of the house, many of them of old film stars. I felt like I had gone home, even though I'd never lived there. Now, when I sit in our lounge room and look at all the pictures, there is also a picture of my mother. The room and the pictures and their stories bring me glimpses of peace. (p. 11)

Sue, one of the members of the Power to Our Journeys group, had a particularly skilful method of bringing to life, or animating, a vibrant counter-heritage. She decided to give the positive voice that she heard the name of her grandmother. In this way, whenever this positive voice assisted her to participate in acts of self-care, these actions in the present were consistently linked to a rich counter-heritage.

There are a number of reasons why this process is significant. In circumstances where there is a relationship between mental health struggles in the present and past experiences of trauma and abuse, it is a matter of both healing and justice that this is recognised and acknowledged, and yet, it is also vital that this recognition is not accompanied by a pathologising or totalising of history. There is no chance of being on reasonable terms with your history if it is represented in totalising or pathologising ways. The generation of counter-heritage is an antidote to pathologising history.

In addition, I am interested in how this process can generate what Wertsch (2002) refers to as a "usable past" (p. 45). Eliciting the values, skills, and knowledge that a person is using to respond to current difficulties, and tracing the social histories of these, links these actions of the present to the actions of those in the past. This does not generate a nostalgic vision of the past, one that is separate from the dilemmas of the present. Instead, because this memory project starts in the present and then travels backwards, because this process historicises skills, values, and knowledge that are being used to respond to current hardship, it is this which can play a part in creating a "usable past"—a past that becomes more available to draw upon in order to sustain present efforts. This generation of a rich "textual heritage"

(Lowenthal, 1994, as quoted in Wertsch, 2002, p. 62) can provide the foundation for many more responses to current hardship. It seems to me that this memory project of creating a "usable past" can be particularly significant in circumstances in which people have come to consider their personal history as a burden, or as a litany of failures.

The ways that Sharon de Valda linked her skill of "escaping through pictures" to her mother, and the ways in which Sue gave her "positive voice" the name of her grandmother, are two vivid examples of ways of creating a usable past in the midst of hardship.

From personal memory to shared/social memory

We are also exploring how to move from the realms of personal memory to shared/social memory.

* * *

In our work with groups and communities, we have become very interested in the possibilities of shared or social memory. Memory can be conceived of as both interior and exterior. Exterior memory resides, or is performed, in memorial sites, in rituals, in conversations, in photographs, in documents, in relationships, and so on. It is, therefore, possible to understand memory not only as something that is experienced by an individual, but also something that people do together. We are interested in how our conversations as mental health practitioners involve certain practices of memory, certain "commemorative practices" (Jedlowski, 2001, p. 34). How might our work involve the performance of shared or social memory?

Once personal counter-heritage (or a preferred storyline of identity) is brought to life, we are interested in ways in which others can be invited to join in this memory. We seek to create collective narrative documents (Denborough, 2008), songs, and rituals through which counter-heritages can be remembered, shared, and performed. To illustrate this, I include some short extracts of a translated collective narrative document that was generated during my recent visit to Kurdistan. Using the four lines of enquiry outlined earlier (under heading "Preferred storylines of identity: animating a counter-heritage", p. 73), a collective document was developed with the workers at the Kirkuk Center for Torture Victims whose own families have experienced significant hardships and who are now working with survivors of torture.[14] The following extract offers a glimpse of the sort of stories and counter-heritage that was generated.

Survival: secret knowledge and skills of Kurdish families

As Kurdish people, we know too much about suffering. We have been through the unimaginable. But we also know so much about surviving hardship. We have included here some of the secret knowledge and skills of Kurdish families. These survival skills have long histories, as long as the history of the Kurdish people. We hope this document will be helpful to others.

Love for my country

When times are hard, some of us call upon our love of our country. I learnt to love our country from my father as he was a Peshmarga (freedom fighter). He suffered a lot because of being a Kurd and defending his country and his nation. He was tortured by the previous regime, dislocated and imprisoned. When I was one year old, I was in jail also, for seven months with my family. I remember, as a dream, my life in prison so that I always recognise who are my friends, who are my enemies, and not to depend on foreigners. I was twelve years old when I started to understand my country and my father's actions. My father was showing me pictures of his friends, fighting for freedom, and living in the mountains. His stories and his experiences have made me want to do something for my country. My mother encourages me as her daughter in this skill. It is important for her too. Love of country is tightly related to our culture. There are numerous songs, pictures, poems that we share in our family about this love of our land. And I like to have the Kurdish flag in my living room. When times are hard, some of us recall our love of our country and it helps us to continue.

Holding on to hope

Some of us have had to learn to hold onto hope. One of our group learnt this skill when he was ten years old. This was when we were forcibly removed from Kirkuk to Erbil. We left our home, our friends and family members. It was a tough experience but I could manage it and make new friends in Erbil because of a belief in optimism. I learned this from my family and from my grandma. She would always say one day we will be back and live in the same place: 'a stone is precious in its own place'. I used to tell my friends in Erbil this. I would give them my grandma's optimism. There is an Arabic phrase 'be optimistic and you will find it'. I wonder now where my grand-mother learnt her optimism, probably from her family. She would have seen a lot of hardship in her lifetime as a Kurdish woman. When I continue this optimism now, this is an honouring of my grandma. She has passed away. We owe this optimism to her.

. . . We are now planning to share these stories with the people with whom we work. We will ask them about their secret survival skills and their histories. We will ask them to share their stories of survival with us. (Kirkuk Center for Torture Victims & Dulwich Centre Foun-dation International, 2012)

As the themes in such documents combine individual and collec-tive voice, and are retold/performed in collective oral rituals, this generates a sense of shared or social memory. Another way of under-standing this is to consider that this process builds a "community of memory" (Margalit, 2002). Significantly, this community of memory includes both the living and the no longer alive: ". . . a community of memory is a community based not only on actual thick relations to the living but also on thick relations to the dead" (Margalit, 2002, p. 69).

Documenting and then performing the skills, knowledge, and counter-heritages of people struggling for mental health makes visible what otherwise goes unseen. Those engaged in critical heritage prac-tice recognise the importance of this—of making "intangible heritage" tangible (Table 4.2). For example, collective documents and songs that were created from the Power to Our Journeys group (Brigitte, Sue, Mem, & Veronika, 1997) and from others struggling for mental health (ACT Mental Health Consumers Group & Dulwich Centre, 2003) have been widely circulated. Definitional ceremonies centred on these documents have also been held, featuring resonant exchanges of messages and outsider-witness responses (White, 2007). These pro-cesses make tangible what was once unseen, enable those struggling for their mental health to experience that their hard-won knowledge is making contributions to the lives of others, and create foundations for future action. I am intrigued as to how this can be likened to a

Table 4.2. Further parallels between critical heritage practice and narrative practice in mental health

Critical heritage practice	Narrative practice in mental health
Facilitates "the recovery of the forgotten, the displaced, the marginalised, and the unspoken, and . . . find(s) ways of inserting this subordinated past into the politics of the present and its futures" (Soudien, 2008, p. 24).	Narrative practice memory projects start in the present and then travel backwards. Eliciting the values, skills, and knowledge that a person is using to respond to current difficulties, and, tracing the social histories of these, links these actions of the present to the actions of those in the past. In doing so, this creates a "usable past" and generates a rich "textual heritage", which provides the foundation for many more responses to current hardship.
"Memory projects" combine remembrance, politics, poetry, campaigns, history, and artistry and take diverse forms—murals, marches, ceremonies, books, frescos, exhibits, songs, and so on (Rassool, 2007, p. 37), and involve developing a "community of memory" (Margalit, 2002, p. 69).	Memory is not only something that is experienced by an individual, but also something that people do together. Once personal counter-heritage (or a preferred storyline of identity) is brought to life, others can be invited to join in this memory. Collective narrative documents combine individual and collective voice, and are retold/performed in collective oral rituals to generate a sense of shared or social memory.
The critical heritage practice of restoration occurs at the "moment when the intangible 'adheres' itself to the tangible and becomes the historical document of the future" (Hassard, 2009, p. 284).	Documenting and then sharing the skills, knowledge, and counter-heritages of people struggling for mental health makes visible what otherwise goes unseen and makes "intangible heritage" tangible.
	When done collectively, can this support the initiatives of the psychiatric survivor movement to create versions of history that not only name injustices but also honour resistance?
	When done collectively, can this also contribute to honouring, restoring and protecting intangible cultural heritage and culturally diverse concepts of health and healing?

critical heritage practice of restoration: ". . . the practice of restoration can . . . be understood . . . as . . . the . . . moment when the intangible 'adheres' itself to the tangible and becomes the historical document of the future" (Hassard, 2009, p. 284).

Broader considerations in relation to cultural heritage and cultural politics

"They will remember that we were sold, but they won't remember that we were strong. They will remember that we were bought, but not that we were brave" (formerly enslaved William Prescott, quoted in Hunt, 2007, p. 20).

Before I close this chapter, I wish to consider two broader themes of cultural heritage and cultural politics that relate to the trends or "movements" that I mentioned at the outset of the chapter.

One key aspect of the work of the psychiatric survivor movement and Mad Pride[15] involves projects to resurrect a collective heritage of the knowledge, perspectives, and stories of psychiatric survivors. Jackson's (2002) "In our own voice: African-American stories of oppression, survival and recovery in mental health systems", provides a particularly powerful example of "a revolutionary act of self-love and a demand for visibility for African-American psychiatric survivors" (Jackson, 2002, p. 13). Echoing the sentiment of William Prescott, Jackson is determined to create versions of history that not only name injustices but also honour resistance. Could our responses to mental health struggles include animating, documenting, and sharing counter-heritages? If so, then perhaps our work can accompany the projects of people like Jackson in contributing to regrading versions of social history.

Finally, as I mentioned earlier, indigenous writers and majority world practitioners have consistently critiqued the cultural dominance of Western psychological approaches. In fact, Tamasese (2008) has gone so far to say that psychological colonisation is now at the forefront of neo-colonialism. Alongside the necessity of self-determined mental health responses, cultural accountabilities, and partnerships, Tamasese (2003a,b) and others (Kleinman, 1998; Waldegrave, 1998; Watters, 2010) highlight the responsibilities of practitioners to ensure that responses to social suffering/mental health concerns take into account cultural meanings. Could linking responses to mental health struggles to critical heritage practice be relevant in this process? The concepts through which mental health struggles and healing knowledge are conceived within any culture are part of a people's intangible heritage (see Tamasese, 2003a,b; Watters, 2010). Perhaps finding ways to animate, honour, and link individual forms of counter-heritage could also involve restoring and protecting intangible cultural heritage. For instance, in the example offered earlier, the Kurdish trauma counsellors "restored" Kurdish concepts of "love for my country" and "holding on to hope". These are not fixed or nostalgic restorations; they are restorations of a "usable cultural past", linking contemporary actions with treasured diverse legacies from fathers and grandmothers.

These are early days in relation to exploring links between narrative practice and critical heritage studies. The conversations are just beginning. The next International Hearing Voices Congress is to be held "down under". Perhaps you will join us. It is my hope that these conversations and explorations might contribute to new options for people within my own community and within the communities in which I work to come to more reasonable terms with their own histories.

Acknowledgements

This paper has been influenced by recent conversations with Veronika Kulwikowski, Julie, Bruce Skinner, and Jussey Verco. Cheryl White and David Epston offered significant feedback on an earlier draft, as did Margaret Beels, Gaye Stockell, and Marilyn O'Neil. It is also indebted to interviews I conducted in 2003 with Sharon De Valda, Mickey de Valda, Peter Bullimore, and Jon Williams, all members of the Hearing Voices Network in Manchester. I was introduced to the concept of "intangible heritage" by Vanessa Kredler while she was working at UNESCO. Finally, I would like to acknowledge that the editorial suggestions of Sue McNab significantly improved this chapter.

Notes

1. This Congress was hosted by Karen Taylor and Ron Coleman. For more information see: www.workingtorecovery.co.uk/. The next International

Hearing Voices Congress is to take place in Australia, see: www. prahranmission.org.au/hearing_voices.htm.

2. See; http://heartsounds.ning.com/.

3. Such champions include Patsy Hague, Ron Coleman, Mickey de Valda, Sharon de Valda, Peter Bullimore, and Jon Willams, who, alongside key professionals such as Marius Romme, Sandra Escher, and Terry McLaughlin, developed the Hearing Voices movement.

4. There are many other significant trends within the field of mental health including "consumer involvement" and the development of "consumer" voice and perspectives, see: www.themhs.org/23-big-issues.

5. See European Network of (Ex) Users and Survivors of Psychiatry: www. enusp.org; the USA based Support Coalition International: www.mind-freedom.org; Psychiatric Survivors of Ottawa: http://ncf.davintech.ca/ freeport/social.services/opsa/menu.

6. See www.intervoiceonline.org.

7. There is a long and complex history in relation to the associations of "trauma" and mental health dating back to Freud. To read an account of this history, see Edkins (2003).

8. The term "majority world" is used here in place of alternatives such as "Third World" or "underdeveloped". For more discussion, see Esteva and Prakash (1998) and Mohanty (2003a,b).

9. See: www.kirkuk-center.org/welcome.html

10. See www.sitesofconscience.org.

11. See www.districtsix.co.za.

12. There are many different ways of "bridging the gap". It is not a one-off process and might require continuing efforts. Within narrative practice, if workers/group facilitators share their own life experiences, great care is taken in relation to how this is done in order to maintain a "decentred and yet influential position" (White, 2007). For further discussions about "bridging the gap", see also Stockell and O'Neill (1999) and their Friday Afternoon at Dulwich Centre video presentation: http://narrative therapyonline.com/moodle/course/view.php?id=16/#section-11

13. See M. de Valda (2003) for descriptions of the significance of class and poverty in shaping experiences of mental health challenges.

14. It is possible to view the entire document in English at: http:// issuu.com/kirkuk-center/docs/responding_to_survivors_of_torture_ and_suffering_e. In Kurdish at: http://issuu.com/kirkukcenter/docs/ responding_to_survivors_of_torture_and_suffering_k. And in Arabic at: http://issuu.com/kirkukcenter/docs/responding_to_survivors_of_ torture_and_suffering_a

15. See www.madpride.org.uk

References

ACT Mental Health Consumers Network & Dulwich Centre (2003). 'These are not ordinary lives': the report of a mental health community gathering. *International Journal of Narrative Therapy and Community Work*, 3: 29–49.

Brigitte, Sue, Mem, & Veronika (1997). Power to our journeys. Dulwich Centre Newsletter, 1, 25–34. Reprinted in: C. White & D. Denborough (Eds.), *Introducing Narrative Therapy: A Collection of Practice-based Writings* (pp. 203–215). Adelaide, Australia: Dulwich Centre, 1998.

Bullimore, P. (2003). Altering the balance of power: working with voices. *International Journal of Narrative Therapy and Community Work*, 3: 22–28.

Byrne, D. (2009). A critique of unfeeling heritage. In: L. Smith & N. Akagawa (Eds.), *Intangible Heritage* (pp. 229–252). London: Routledge.

Chesler, P. (2005). *Women and Madness*. New York: Palgrave Macmillan.

de Valda, M. (2003). From paranoid schizophrenia to hearing voices – and other class distinctions. *International Journal of Narrative Therapy and Community Work*, 3: 13–17.

de Valda, S. (2003). Glimpses of peace. *International Journal of Narrative Therapy and Community Work*, 3: 9–12.

Denborough, D. (2008). *Collective Narrative Practice: Responding to Individuals, Groups and Communities who have Experienced Trauma*. Adelaide: Dulwich Centre.

Denborough, D. (2010). *Working with Memory in the Shadow of Genocide: The Narrative Practices of Ibuka Trauma Counsellors*. Adelaide, Australia: Dulwich Centre Foundation International.

Edkins, J. (2003). *Trauma and the Memory of Politics*. Cambridge: Cambridge University Press.

Epston, D., & White, M. (1998). A proposal for a re-authoring therapy: Rose's revisioning of her life, and a commentary by Kevin Murray. In: *'Catching up' with David Epston: A Collection of Narrative Practice-based Papers published between 1991 & 1996* (pp. 9–32). Adelaide: Dulwich Centre.

Esteva, G., & Prakash, M. S. (1998). *Grassroots Post-modernism: Remaking the Soil of Cultures*. London: Zed Books.

Hassard, F. (2009). Intangible heritage in the United Kingdom: the dark side of enlightenment? In: L. Smith & N. Akagawa (Eds.), *Intangible Heritage* (pp. 270–288). London: Routledge.

Herman, J. L. (1997). *Trauma and Recovery: The Aftermath of Violence From Domestic Abuse to Political Terror*. New York: Basic Books.

Hunt, T. (2007). A bold step away from guilt and apology. *Guardian Weekly*, 31 August, p. 22.

Jackson, V. (2002). In our own voice: African-American stories of oppression, survival and recovery in mental health systems. *International Journal of Narrative Therapy and Community Work*, 2: 11–31.

Jedlowski, P. (2001). Memory and sociology: themes and issues. *Time & Society*, 10(1): 29–44.

Kirkuk Center for Torture Victims & Dulwich Centre Foundation International (2012). *Responding to Survivors of Torture and Suffering: Survival Skills and Stories of Kurdish Families*. Adelaide, Australia: Dulwich Centre Foundation International.

Kleinman, A. (1998). *Rethinking Psychiatry: From Cultural Category to Personal Experience*. New York: Free Press.

Kleinman. A., Das, V., & Lock, M. (Eds.) (1997). *Social Suffering*. Berkeley, CA: University of California Press.

Kulwikowski, V. (2011). Personal communication.

Margalit, A. (2002). *The Ethics of Memory*. Cambridge, MA: Harvard University Press.

Mohanty, C. T. (2003a). *Feminism without Borders: Decolonizing Theory, Practicing Solidarity*. Durham, NC: Duke University Press.

Mohanty, C. T. (2003b). Under western eyes: feminist scholarship and colonial discourses. In: R. Lewis & S. Mills (Eds.), *Feminist Postcolonial Theory: A Reader* (pp. 333–358). New York: Routledge.

Ncube, N. (2006). The Tree of Life Project: using narrative ideas in work with vulnerable children in Southern Africa. *International Journal of Narrative Therapy and Community Work*, 1: 3–16.

Rassool, C. (2007). Key debates in memorialisation, human right and heritage practice. In: *Reflections on the Conference: Hands on District Six – Landscapes of Post-Colonial Memorialisation*. Cape Town: District Six Museum.

Romme, M., & Escher, S. (2000). *Making Sense of Voices: A Guide for Mental Health Professionals Working with Voice-hearers*. London: Mind.

Sanger, M. (2007). Orientation to District Six and communities: engagements with Langa, Manenberg and Protea Village. In: *Reflections on the Conference: Hands on District Six – Landscapes of Post-colonial Memorialisation*. Cape Town: District Six Museum.

Soudien, C. (2008). Memory in the remaking of Cape Town. In: B. Bennett, J. Chrischené, & C. Soudien (Eds.), *City. Site. Museum: Reviewing Memory Practice at the District Six Museum* (pp. 18–31). Cape Town: District Six Museum.

Stockell, G., & O'Neill, M. (1999). Bridging the gap: conversations about mental illness experiences. In: *Narrative Therapy & Community Work: A Conference Collection* (pp. 125–136). Adelaide: Dulwich Centre.

Tamasese, K. (2003a). Honouring Samoan ways and understandings: towards culturally appropriate mental health services. In: C. Waldegrave, T. Tamasese, F. Tuhaka, & W. Campbell (Eds.), *Just Therapy – A Journey: A Collection of Papers from the Just Therapy Team, New Zealand* (pp. 183–195). Adelaide, Australia: Dulwich Centre.

Tamasese, K. (2003b). Multiple sites of healing: developing culturally appropriate responses. In: C. Waldegrave, K. Tamasese, F. Tuhaka, & W. Campbell (Eds.), *Just Therapy – A Journey: A Collection of Papers from the Just Therapy Team, New Zealand* (pp. 197–200). Adelaide: Dulwich Centre.

Tamasese, K. (2008). Personal communication, Wellington, New Zealand, 12 March.

Waldegrave, C. (1998). The challenges of culture to psychology and postmodern thinking. In: M. McGoldrick (Ed.), *Re-visioning Family Therapy: Race, Culture and Gender in Clinical Practice* (pp. 404–413). New York: Guilford Press.

Watters, E. (2010). *Crazy Like Us: The Globalisation of the American Psyche.* Carlton, Australia: Scribe.

Wertsch, J. V. (2002). *Voices of Collective Remembering.* Cambridge: Cambridge University Press.

White, M. (1995). Psychotic experience and discourse (Stewart, K. interviewer). In: M. White: *Re-Authoring Lives: Interviews & Essays* (pp. 112–154). Adelaide: Dulwich Centre.

White, M. (2006a). Personal communication.

White, M. (2006b). Working with people who are suffering the consequences of multiple trauma: a narrative perspective. In: D. Denborough (Ed.), *Trauma: Narrative Responses to Traumatic Experience* (pp. 25–85). Adelaide: Dulwich Centre.

White, M. (2007). *Maps of Narrative Practice.* New York: W. W. Norton.

White, M. (2011). *Narrative Practice: Continuing the Conversations.* New York: W. W. Norton.

White, M., & Epston, D. (1990). *Narrative Means to Therapeutic Ends.* New York: W. W. Norton.

CHAPTER FIVE

"Where the hell is everybody?" Leanna's resistance to armed robbery and negative social responses

Allan Wade

L eanna (thirty-five) and Jane (sixty-four) were robbed at gunpoint while closing a department store for the night, with "the take" for the day in hand. Two months later, Leanna phoned me to arrange counselling. We met six times over about six months while Leanna recovered and made some important life decisions. I found Leanna's descriptions of her experience especially compelling and, two years later, asked if she and I might record a conversation about the robbery. She agreed and allowed me to use the interview for training purposes. This chapter centres on a twenty-minute segment of this interview during which Leanna and I develop accounts of her responses to the robbery and to the series of negative social responses she experienced afterwards. As we explore Leanna's responses in detail, using active grammar and descriptive terms, Leanna emerges as an upright person who showed courage and composure while resisting the robbery and is justifiably indignant about the negative social responses she received.

Response-based practice

Response-based practice grew out of our work with victims and perpetrators of violence and their families, and research on the connection between violence and language. Close analysis shows that victims invariably resist violence, overtly or covertly, depending on the circumstances (Gilligan, Rogers, & Talman, 1990; Kelly, 1988; Scott, 1990; Wade, 1997, 2000). We have found that exploring victims' resistance and responses to violence and other adversities is helpful in many contexts, including child protection, victim assistance, family law, transition houses, criminal justice, and mental health settings. This has required a significant shift in practice. Resistance is a response to violence, not an effect of violence. While virtually all models of therapy contain a theory of the effects of violence on and within the victim, few acknowledge the reality of ever-present victim resistance (e.g., Kelly, 1988; Scott, 1990). The language of effects is the prevailing language used to represent victims of violence. We suggest such language is a potent political discourse that conceals victims' resistance to many types of oppression by ignoring responses that are not easily cast as effects and by recasting responses and forms of resistance as effects and symptoms to be treated. Because victim resistance is concealed, victims are widely portrayed as passive or submissive individuals who fail to discern violence or unconsciously attract offenders.

Todd (1997) extended this analysis to work with men and boys who use violence against others (Todd & Wade, 2003). Just as victims invariably resist violence and other forms of oppression, perpetrators anticipate and work to suppress that resistance (Scott, 1990). The strategies perpetrators use show that violence is more controlled than is usually presumed. However, violence is still widely seen as an effect of powerful psycho-physiological or social forces that overwhelm and compel the perpetrator to violate others. Thus, the language of effects conceals both victims' responses and resistance to violence as well as perpetrators' responsibility for violence.

Coates (1997) integrated this approach with a programme of critical analysis and research on the connection between violence and language (Coates & Wade, 2007) in professional and public settings. For example, although violence is unilateral in that it consists of actions by one person or group against the will and wellbeing of another, it is widely recast as mutual, as though the perpetrator and victim are co-agents in, and co-responsible for, the crimes. Car theft is not called automobile sharing and bank robbery is not called an unauthorised financial transaction, yet sexualised assault (even against children) is called sex or intercourse, wife assault is called a dispute or argument, invasion is called war, and workplace harassment is called a personality conflict. In contrast, in our work, we endeavour to develop complete and accurate descriptions that reveal the nature and extent of violence, clarify perpetrator responsibility, elucidate and honour victim responses and resistance, and contest the blaming and pathologising of victims.

Social responses

Before the robbery, Leanna told the store manager the security for the night deposits was too lax. The manager smugly dismissed Leanna's concerns. After the robbery, Leanna received negative social responses that were ultimately more distressing than the robbery itself. The manager imposed a back-to-work plan on Leanna without consultation, and then criticised and ultimately fired her when she refused to comply. The police were compassionate, but made no arrest. The victim assistance worker was "kinda weird", but "OK". Leanna's partner, Ken, was preoccupied because he had just lost his job. Not being close to her family of origin, Leanna did not tell them about the robbery, as she expected criticism from them. Leanna's physician said she was clinically depressed and prescribed medication and talking therapy.

In British Columbia, injured workers and crime victims are entitled to compensation for lost wages and the costs of treatment. However, the crime victim assistance manager denied Leanna's claim because, he said, her injuries were sustained at work. The workers' compensation manager denied Leanna's claim because, he said, her injuries were caused by criminal actions. Leanna appealed the latter decision and the manager, who took the odd role of reviewing an appeal of his own decision, insisted Leanna attend an "assessment" and refused to say what the assessment would entail. The assessment took three hours and Leanna was denied a break despite being hypoglycaemic. The manager pressured Leanna to talk about her family of origin, including the recent death of her brother by drug overdose. He then dismissed the appeal because, he argued, Leanna's distress was caused by family troubles, not the robbery. Collectively, the negative social responses Leanna received could be expressed as follows: "You are worthless and unimportant. We have more power than you and are not required to listen to you. You are an uneducated, isolated, and powerless woman who will present no real challenge to our authority. You are a nuisance and we will not take your concerns seriously. Go away."

Leanna's experience aligns with recent research on the correlation between social responses and victim distress (e.g., Brewin, Andrews, & Rose, 2003; Brewin, Andrews, & Valentine, 2000; Ullman & Filipas, 2005). Victims who receive negative social responses tend to experience more intense and lasting distress than do victims who receive positive social responses, are more likely to be diagnosed as having a mental disorder, and are less likely to co-operate with authorities or disclose violence again. Much of the research concerns victims of sexualised violence and domestic violence. However, our experience suggests that the same is true for victims of armed robbery, street beatings, bullying, and sexualised harassment. Many of the so-called effects of violence, including neurological effects, are better seen as responses to negative social responses, such as blame from family members and ill-conceived professional practice.

Our practice is, therefore, to ask the victim how they responded to specific negative social responses and highlight the tactics through which they worked to preserve their dignity and retain maximum control of their circumstances. Often, these are the kinds of clandestine tactics—lying (careful management of information), feigned agreement (playing cards close to the chest), unpredictability (keeping one's own schedule), ignoring advice (heeding one's own counsel), avoidance of others (self-protection or cocooning), cutting (pain release or pain management or desire to feel), substance use (self medication)—that are judged negatively and so remain unacknowledged in spite of their importance to safety and recovery. Also, once negative social responses are taken into account, so-called mental illnesses become understandable as inherently healthy and understandable, if intensely painful, responses.

So, by the time we first met, Leanna, who only weeks before was leading a normal life, was now distressed by the many negative social responses to her violent experience. She was out of work and struggling with poverty. Her relationship with Ken was in trouble. She had been told that she had a mental illness. She was becoming isolated and drinking "too much wine" to dull her feelings and get some sleep. Given the poor social responses she had encountered, Leanna was understandably reluctant to see me. She had no reason to believe I would respond fairly or effectively and immediately put me on notice, "OK, my doctor said I should come so I'm here, but I don't know what the hell you're going to do for me."

Transcript and commentary

Throughout the interview, which is divided into seven segments, I work to obtain clear physical descriptions of actions in the specific setting and interactions. The language is denotative rather than connotative, that is, aimed at revealing specifics rather than creating ambiguity and multiple meanings (Eagleton, 2007, p. 110). I focus on Leanna's responses in the physical setting and clarify details sequentially, such as who had the night deposit and where they were walking. The purpose is to elicit information that is often ignored. While developing these descriptions, I work with Leanna to identify and explore the "situational logic" of certain responses (de Certeau, 1984), that is, to contextualise those responses (i.e., actions, thoughts, emotions, physical sensations) as understandable in context, to explore how they might be understood as forms of resistance, and to highlight the pre-existing competence and awareness they evince. This process is nuanced and involves the political act of putting words to deeds (Danet, 1980). For instance, in our first meeting, I noticed that Leanna remained quite calm and thoughtful during the robbery and asked, "Where did you get such presence of mind?" I hoped this phrase would capture the quality of Leanna's responses and provide a frame we might use to explore other responses which would contest previous attributions of passivity and pathology, such as the notion that Leanna was clinically depressed, and suggest instead that she was "refusing to be content" with violence and humiliation.

Segment 1

Two minutes into the interview, Leanna describes the procedure for closing the store at 9.00 p.m. on a Friday night.

L: We worked with two younger guys as well and they left at 9.00 and then we were there to close.

A: Mhh, OK.

L: And I had only been there, I started there November 8th, so this was exactly two months later and I had mentioned to them, to management, that I didn't like the setup with the night deposits.

A: Oh?

L: This is just, really, I've been in the retail business for too long, its just not good and these girls were like taking the bag of money and just shoving it in their purse or holding it in their hands and walking to the bank at night and just, just, ahh I don't know, it just felt all wrong.

A: Mmhm.

L: So.

A: What did they say when you, you told them that you didn't like this?

L: Umm, I got the look (emphatically using hands to make scare quotes around "the look"), as far as, 'you're not going to be here long [laughs] don't stir the pot, yah umm, this is how it goes, this is what management is, you know we've been doing this for so long, you are brand new here, nothing's ever happened so far'.

A: Right, right.

L: So, so whatever umm, I let it ride and ahh . . . it was, actually it was 9.37 ahh [laughs], when we were leaving, because I remember looking at the clock.

While describing how she questioned "the setup with the night deposits", Leanna presents herself as a competent and responsible employee who is safety conscious and concerned for others. Consistent with these claims, she presents herself as precise and observant, twice noting the time to the minute and the date of the robbery. I ask, "What did they say?" to focus on interaction and social responses. The emphatic "I got the look" suggests Leanna had seen "the look" before, perhaps elsewhere. With her comment about management's view of newcomers, Leanna mimics the manager's dismissive attitude. Essentially, Leanna suggests the robbery might have been prevented if the manager had listened.

Segment 2

The first question in segment 2, "It's in the back?", keeps the focus on the physical setting. This aids recall and develops a factual basis to understand why Leanna responded one way rather than another as the robbery progressed.

A: It's in the back?

L: Yah, yah, and umm, because I was cleaning out the staff room and Jane was just finishing up cash and she . . . we grabbed our stuff and ahh, I was taking a bunch of crap that was lying around, not crap, but it was just stuff that had been there forever in lost and found, umbrellas and stuff . . .

A: Yah, yah.

L: And I was going to donate it to the food bank because I live right across from them so I was just going to say, "here", you know, for people who can't afford to buy one, "here".

A: Yah, right.

L: So I had all these bags of stuff plus my purse, and she had the night deposit in her bag.

A: Oh, OK.

L: . . . and ahh we left and . . .

A: Oh, she had the night deposit in her bag?

L: She did.

A: OK.

L: Yeah she did, she had a big bag (gesturing to show the size of the bag).

A: And you were carrying a bunch of other stuff?

L: I had my purse and then some bags . . . OK, yeah, and some plastic bags and my purse was . . . I had a strap . . .

A: Right.

L: Umm, and, you had to turn . . . Saans store was quite huge and you had to turn the lights out at the very back and then walk through the dark store.

A: Ah, OK, yeah.

L: And then on to a dark sidewalk, and, and then we closed up and then we were walking down the street.

A: You are walking down the sidewalk.

L: Yeah, yeah.

A: Beside the store?

L: Yeah, you exit (using two hands to gesture two people making a turn).

A: You turn?

L: You turn. Yeah, and you go down the sidewalk and then the parking lot's out here.

A: OK.

L: With just one little tiny feeble spotlight, I mean you can't see hardly anything.

A: Right, where is the spotlight positioned?

L: It, it was on the side of the building, near the street. It didn't illuminate the parking lot at all (shaking her head) . . .

A: OK [nodding].

L: And then ironically though because I was cleaning out the staff room and stuff, I had my car pulled out to, to the back door, which I never ever do.

A: But when you come around the corner it would be down . . . (pointing as if to the far end of the building).

L: Yeah, it was down at the far end of the building. Normally I parked near the street, just easy access.

A: Sure, yeah.

L: Umm, it's just, what I learnt from being on the road for so many years, like, just always watch right, always be aware and umm, although it was a little, there was a spotlight there, I think there was a light up above the back door . . . but umm, so we had to, we came around the corner.

Leanna presents evidence to justify her safety concerns and highlights her competence by noting the location of her car at the back door, linking this logically to cleaning the staff room. As this is something Leanna "never ever" does, she displays good knowledge of parking tactics with, "normally I parked near the street, just easy access". The statement, "it's just what I learnt from being on the road for so many years", points to a store of experience and provides a biographical context for Leanna's responses during the robbery, as we shall see.

Segment 3

I explore Leanna's experience "on the road" later, but first I return to the physical setting and pick up on "we came around the corner".

A: And she's on which side of you?

L: She's here [gesturing to right side].

A: She's on your right, OK.

L: She's here, I always make people . . . [both laughing]

A: Stand inside of you?

L: Yah, it's . . .

A: How did you acquire that habit? I mean that's ahh . . .

L: Protecting my sisters, just, it's just what you do. As the older sibling, they are safer. If I'm going to get hit by a car they're not going to be, right.

A: Yah, yah.

L: If, if there's going to be any kind of weirdness, they are protected. Its, its like right there [gesturing to her side], so . . .

A: Right. Is that something your parents coached you with or . . . or did you just . . .?

L: I don't know.

A: Yah, yah, OK.

L: A protective thing.

A: A protective thing, yah.

L: Maybe it was my, it could have been my umm, my older brothers. And sisters too . . . [long pause]

A: Oh, OK, you don't know . . .

L: I'm not sure where that ever came from . . . interesting.

Leanna ensured Jane was on her right side, away from the busy street, which she "always make[s] people" do. I finish the line, intoned as a question, "Stand inside of you?", as we smile and laugh. While this gesture is routine for Leanna, I see it as an instance of Leanna's safety awareness and regard for others, and as relevant to the robbery. The question, "How did you acquire that habit?" asks Leanna to reply from the subject position, as the agent of her own actions, not from the object position, as the recipient of others' actions. The word "how" instead of "why" asks for actions and the verb "acquire" presupposes Leanna acted over time to take up the practice. Had I asked a question that put Leanna in the object position, such as, "Who taught you that?", she would probably have presented herself as the recipient of others' actions, perhaps guidance by her parents. Instead, she recalls "protecting my sisters", which she then downplays with a matter-of-fact rationale, "it's just what you do". Leanna connects how she protected her younger sisters to how she protected Jane before and during the robbery, a theme that recurs throughout.

I refer to these as connective questions because they ask the individual to recall similar responses across times and settings. Thus, particular responses acquire a social or natural history, a flexible situational and personal logic, and a developmental dimension, like other forms of learning or acquired ability. This process provides a way to discuss previous instances of adversity while focusing on the person's competent and health-inducing responses in context.

Leanna wonders aloud if her "older brothers and sisters too" taught her to protect others, thereby opening the sensitive topic of her family, not as a source of hardship, which might have been expected given the need to protect her sisters, the expectation of criticism for being robbed, and the death of her brother by drug overdose, but as the possible source of her protective attitude to others. It was in part through her family that Leanna acquired the capacity to care for others in moments of danger, a capacity shared by her older siblings perhaps. In another context, this frame might support a useful conversation with the family.

Segment 4

I then return to the comment, "it's just, what I learnt from being on the road".

- *A:* What did you mean when you said being on the road, having been on the road . . . you learnt to watch?

- *L:* I was a long-distance truck driver for a few years, umm, forty-eight states and Canada and never in the nice parts of town . . . Always in the industrial parts of town, umm, in any city, so you learn quickly when you are walking through a truck stop in the middle of Chicago or downtown California or Denver or New York, Brooklyn, horrible, you learn not to walk in Brooklyn . . .

- *A:* Is that right . . .

- *L:* Yah, and umm, but these truck stops are huge and they can hold, you know, three hundred semis . . .

- *A:* Wow.

- *L:* Well between semis, there are a lot of dark little alleys and you don't know who these people are, and, and there's a lot of people that, umm, there's drug dealers and hookers that hang out in between and they are doing their business and there is a lot of violence that goes on so you have to be aware, and umm, I learnt, that, like if . . . you just learn to walk right down the middle right in between . . . because no one's going run at you, but if you are just kind of wandering around and not looking and walking in between trucks, that's when you get hit . . .

- *A:* Yah . . .

- *L:* Yah, yah and just be aware if there's some . . . But I've always had a strange feeling with people anyway ever since I was little I could pretty much read anybody in less than a minute and if I ever went against my gut I'd always kick myself after, but . . .

- *A:* How did you learn that, how did you learn to read people this early?

- *L:* I was a sick kid in the hospital so I, I don't know, maybe I just learnt it by just knowing who was a nice nurse and who wasn't, or just who I could trust or who I couldn't, umm . . .

- *A:* And so you learnt a little bit about, you couldn't trust everybody, you had to kind of watch. You learned how to read people pretty well.

L: Relatives as well, and just working with the public. My mum and dad opened up a store when I was five and umm they took me out of school after grade seven to work there, so I worked there full time.

A: After grade seven?

L: Yeah, to, to earn my keep (sarcastically).

Throughout, Leanna presents her concerns as a working-class woman. In Canada, retail is low paid and insecure work, regarded widely as unskilled, with no union protection. As if in response to this reality and to those who treated her poorly, Leanna presents her life experience almost as a professional would present their curriculum vitae, as proof of expertise and social worth. The phrase "its just . . . what I learnt" furthers the theme of acquired expertise begun earlier with, "I've been in the retail business for too long", and iterates the word "learnt", which is mentioned numerous times.

I felt an easy affinity with Leanna straight away, but did not give much thought to the source of this feeling. It could have been that we spoke the same dialect—she could have lived next door to me growing up and her parents might have faced the same struggles as mine. I took for granted that we got on well and found common cause addressing the injustices she had suffered.

In August 2011, I agreed to provide a book chapter, and thought the interview with Leanna would be a good choice. Then, just after I began work on the chapter, my mother, Agnes, died suddenly. I put the chapter down and looked at it indifferently once or twice. When I picked it up again in earnest, months later, I was still preoccupied with my mother and projected her life, or my view of her life, on to the transcript. I began to notice, as if for the first time, how my own outlook and sense of purpose and the easy affinity I felt for Leanna derived from the manner in which my mother lived her life. She had left school at thirteen to work as a housekeeper to earn money for her family. While raising me, she worked in retail, taking pride in her efficiency and capacity for hard work, and enjoyed treating her customers with utmost respect. In retirement, she worked in soup kitchens, blood clinics, and charity bingos. She was immensely self-conscious of her grade 6 education and alert for any social slight. She was no-nonsense, fiercely protective, and loved a laugh with friends over a cold beer.

I wondered if these memories of my mother helped me recognise Leanna's reluctance to be seen as boasting, which is almost as bad as "brown-nosing" for a working-class person. With the phrase, "it's just what you do", Leanna overtly downplays her protection of Jane. The word "just" is equivalent to the word "merely" in this instance and suggests the practice should be taken for granted. The word "you" suggests the practice is universal, or should be, as anybody would do the same. More than humility, this phrase signals Leanna's grasp of hard realities, the value she places on simple decency, and her solidarity with others who share the sentiment. In light of these comments, it was important that I acknowledge Leanna's resistance to the robbery without romanticising Leanna as exceptional or heroic.

Attending a seminar as a guest speaker, Leanna was described as "incredibly strong" by one of the participants. Leanna replied, "Thanks, yeah, I don't know." A few moments later, Leanna slipped me a note which read as follows:

> When you tell me how strong I am, I feel like you're not allowing me to be weak—to cry, to be scared, to be tired, to be angry. It's as if I have a "time limit" as to when I should be "normal" again. Because when I'm not, it's somehow wrong or bad. So I fake. I stuff. I will show you what you want to see, what you need to see. No matter what I'm feeling inside, I will make you feel comfortable by being strong.

Leanna was as alert to the restrictive potential of well-intended compliments as she was to the force of dismissive social responses.

Segment 5

The interview so far can be seen as a back and forth process, moving from discussion of social interaction in context (i.e., the robbery) to the origins of, and capacities revealed in, particular responses, and back to the social interaction. Each response is linked thematically to other responses, as yet another example of acquired competence, and located biographically in specific life events across time. My goal, in part, is to pre-empt the usual effects-based view, in which Leanna would be constructed as psychologically affected or impacted upon by the robbery and previous adversities, in favour of a response-based view, in which Leanna is seen as responding in myriad forms to a range of adversities as and after they occurred, in the process acquiring competencies (e.g., awareness, experience, skill, a sixth sense) that underpin her prudent responses during and after the robbery.

I return to the scene as the robbery begins and formulate a summary, intoned as a question, and with the distinctly Canadian "eh?".

A: As you are coming around the edge of the building with Jane, you are bringing all of this experience with you, eh?

L: I guess so, yah . . .

A: I don't know, so did that somehow influence . . . how attentive, how you paid attention to what was going on and . . .

L: We were going down a dark, ahh, sidewalk, into a dark parking lot, and I . . .

A: With money.

L: . . . never liked that. Yes, with money. I knew she had the money so I knew I'd keep her here [gesturing to right side], when we were going around the corner, and I just looked up and she was talking away about something, wasn't even paying attention.

A: Right.

L: And I looked up and it was just this, vibration I got, I don't know what it is. I don't even know how to describe it.

A: You feel it physically.

L: Physically, yeah, and I looked and I kind of nodded at this guy and he nodded because he was standing at the, at this, at the other end of the parking lot . . .

A: So he was quite a distance away then when you saw him?

L: Yeah, at the strip mall, but he was, he, he wasn't standing right. When he looked at me, it wasn't just some guy who just happened to be there smoking a cigarette or something.

A: Right, right.

L: It was deliberate and when he looked, he looked away, and then looked back at me again and I thought "Oh". And that's when all the bells went off.

A: But you nodded at him, your eyes met.

L: Yep.

A: And so you, OK . . . Why did you decide to nod at him, I mean, because right at that instance . . . or was it just sort of just automatic?

L: That's how I check people out.

A: So what did you do right then? How did you respond to that?

L: Umm, hmm, I saw him, and I knew something was a little bit, hokey. Umm, Jane kept walking towards the car. She was oblivious, she just kept walking . . .

A: Was the car in the direction of him?

L: No, opposite side. He's here, the car's over here. We're here [gesturing] and I kind of did a double take and hesitated for a minute and I thought this is, no this is Duncan, its 9.30, what the hell, right.

A: Yah, yah.

L: But yah and its two of us, one of him, but then again, you know.

A: Hm hmm

L: And then, so we kept walking and I thought I would test the water and see if we can . . . maybe I'm just being paranoid, whatever, but its just . . . and then he deliberately started walking towards us and I thought, "no, this is just too . . . for someone who was just there and now he's walking towards us very quickly." Umm, something happened inside me and I just thought, "Eww, no", and then I . . . Jane kept walking towards the car.

A: And she's still got the money?

L: She's got the, she's got the money, she's got her back to him, she doesn't even know what's going on . . . she . . . and then I actually stopped.

A: Hmm.

L: And I started backing up into the middle of the parking lot.

A: So you started backing up, you, she was walking, did she notice that you were backing up?

L: [shaking head, "no"] She was still talking to me and I had actually shut up, because when we came around the corner she said, "Oh", right out loud, "Oh get a load of this guy."

A: Right.

L: And I'm like "Shh, Jane! Don't!"

A: OK.

L: And I just, it was just this automatic reaction, "Shh, Jane don't be so loud, you don't know who this guy is", and she says, "Oh, he just looks ridiculous", and I'm trying to shut her up.

A: Yeah, yeah.

L: And I just got this really bad feeling and I thought if something's going down here its going down in the middle of the parking lot because my car is over there by the side of the building.

A: Yeah.

L: And there's an alley in behind there, you're not dragging me anywhere. You know, you want to do it, let's do it right here, there's a road, there's a highway [gesturing] right there, where . . . there were no cars that night.

A: Right, right.

L: I mean, give me a break. Police were setting up road checks there all month and then just down the sidewalk there were people at Starbucks out drinking their lattes and I'm thinking, this is insane.

The first question in this segment, phrased in a halting manner, asks Leanna to describe how she "paid attention". The question presupposes "all of this experience" is relevant and helpful in the robbery. Leanna describes her reading of the robber's actions, the limits of the situation, and her thoughts as she opted for one course of action over another. Each response is contextualised as sensible and prudent in context. This pre-empts the suggestion that Leanna did nothing, or the wrong thing, and presents an indirect complement.

Segment 6

Leanna's last comments in segment 5 concerned her thought processes, which I contextualise by asking about her overt behaviour *in situ*.

A: So you backed up?

L: Yep . . .

A: Were you near the light?

L: No, no I was right in the middle.

A: Jane's carrying on, she's got the money?

L: She's walking towards my car.

A: You know now this guy has some bad intentions.

L: 'Cause he walked in between us.

A: Oh, OK.

L: And that was what, he deliberately started toward us . . . but just the feel I got from him, that's when I started to back up, he walked in between us and he kept walking . . . and Jane was walking towards my car . . .

A: But why didn't you, sorry, but why didn't you say anything to Jane?

L: Umm, why start something I guess, like what was I supposed to say? You know.

A: Oh, well yeah.

L: Like, "Jane I don't like this guy", and then he turns around and freaks or . . . I don't know, I don't know.

A: Were you concerned about her?

L: Hmm huh.

A: Yeah, because you had already been, I noticed, protecting her, right, in the way that you were walking.

L: We used to talk all the time, she's a neat lady and, ah, she told me about her life growing up in Barbados. "I've had a perfect life. I grew up with wonderful parents, I had a beautiful education and wonderful friends." She just said, "I don't understand people that grow up in bad homes or have violence or bad husbands."

A: Right, did that go into your thinking at that moment . . . knowing who she was?

L: Naïve.

A: Naïve. How does that . . . like, you stop and you let her carry on right?

L: Maybe to take it, she, she could be safe, she's over there . . . If he wants to do something, he can do it to me.

A: Right, right.

L: Umm, I've done that before with my sisters. And it's just umm, maybe a protection thing, you know its like umm, I've watched birds do that. Birds will actually fly into the path of a cat in order to protect their babies, you know . . .

Leanna backs up to remain under the light while saying nothing to Jane, who continues towards her car. This is a complex form of resistance: Leanna works to create some safety for her and Jane while expecting an attack. I ask, "why didn't you say anything to Jane", which is unhelpful as it implies Leanna *should* have said something to Jane. I might have asked instead, "So, why did you decide to stay quiet and say nothing to Jane?", which presupposes Leanna had a good reason not to "say anything to Jane". Foot in mouth, I shift quickly to "were you concerned about her?", a closed but better question. This leads to a short story in which Leanna explains why she likes Jane. I ask awkwardly if Leanna's knowledge of Jane played any part in how she responded. Leanna guesses, "maybe a protection thing", and goes on to draw a touching analogy between her own actions and birds protecting their babies.

Segment 7

The final segment (edited for brevity) turns to the robbery itself. Leanna looked for a place to run, kept an eye on Jane, and tried to memorise the robber while the gun was pointed at her face.

L: I remember looking at the hole of the end of the gun . . .. thinking, "Jesus Christ this could be it, this isn't how I thought it was going to go down, and no one's going to know I'm here and who's going to tell my family and where the hell is everybody?" And umm . . . he kept screaming at me that I was going to fucking die, and it's when he pointed it at my heart, that I actually was pissed off because . . . he got me angry by pointing at my face because I thought, "you little piece of shit", you know, "don't think I haven't been beat up before, I got four older brothers. But you know what, because you have a gun to my face you're ten feet tall and there's not a frickin' thing I can do about it" . . . and I just looked at him . . . like "fuck you".

A: You let him know through the way you looked at him, "Fuck you".

L: Yeah, basically. But I just stood there and I thought, "I knew this was going to fucking happen. You know you didn't listen to me, you know, you don't do night deposits."

In this sequence, Leanna describes the most dangerous and terrifying point in the robbery. Notably, she uses active voice and positions herself as the subject of several dynamic verbs: "I dug in my heels", "I thought", "I don't like to be surprised", "It makes me angry", "I just stood there", "I looked at him", "I said", "I was . . . trying", "I was . . . looking at Jane", "I looked at him right in the eyes", and "I looked him up and down". The violence is clearly apparent in part because Leanna is able to detail her ongoing resistance. Moreover, Leanna's complex thoughts and emotions emerge as situated and intelligible responses that signify her pre-existing awareness of safety and danger and acute assessment of the robbery as it progressed. This reflects the shift out of the language of effects and into the language of responses, which also facilitates more complete and accurate descriptions.

Conclusion

While "looking at the hole at the end of the gun", Leanna realises she might die and thinks of her family. The desperate and ironical question, "where the hell is everybody?" can be heard in at least two ways. On one level, it captures Leanna's sense of dread and isolation in the moment: "Where the hell is everybody" who normally drives the street and drinks their latte at the coffee shop down the way? On another, it exclaims Leanna's larger sense of indignation at the negative social responses she received: "Where the hell is everybody" who should have listened to me and taken me seriously? In the same moment, Leanna expresses her outrage at both the robber ("you little piece of shit") and the store manager ("I knew this was going to fucking happen . . . you don't do night deposits").

The interview presented here is itself another social response to Leanna. It provides a platform for Leanna and I to elucidate her responses and resistance to the robbery and, equally important, her responses and resistance to negative social responses. By answering the questions raised about both the robbery and the social origins of her particular responses, Leanna is able to counter the criticisms and abuses entailed in the various negative social responses and reassert her dignity, even if only in the privacy of our conversation. In this sense, the interview becomes a means of achieving a form of social redress that could not be obtained by other means.

As the interview proceeds, Leanna counters negative assumptions about her character and, therefore, her social worth. She stresses her concern for the safety of her colleagues, because of the poor security around the night deposits. She describes how she was cleaning up the staff room and gathering items "to donate it to the food bank". She is a good neighbour and concerned about the welfare of people who cannot afford "to buy one". She explains her protection of Jane. With these situated and specific examples, Leanna presents herself as a fundamentally decent person, who is worthy of decent treatment in kind, not the negative social responses she received. Our conversation together about Leanna's situated responses and resistance to the robbery provides Leanna with a means of articulating her right to socially just and effective social responses.

References

Brewin, C. R., Andrews, B., & Rose, S. (2003). Gender, social support, and PTSD in victims of violent crime. *Journal of Traumatic Stress, 16*(4): 421–427.

Brewin, C. R., Andrews, B., & Valetine, J. (2000). Meta-analysis of risk factors for posttraumatic stress disorder in trauma-exposed adults. *Journal of Consulting and Clinical Psychology, 68*: 748–766.

Coates, L. (1997). Causal attributions in sexual assault trial judgements. *Journal of Language and Social Psychology, 16*: 278–296.

Coates, L., & Wade, A. (2007). Language and violence: analysis of four discursive operations. *Journal of Family Violence, 22*(7): 511–522.

Danet, B. (1980). 'Baby' or 'fetus'? Language and the construction of reality in a manslaughter trial. *Semiotica, 32*: 187–219.

de Certeau, M. (1984). *The Practice of Everyday Life*. Berkely, CA: University of California Press.

Eagleton, T. (2007). *Ideology*. London: Verso.

Gilligan, C., Rogers, A. G., & Talman, D. T. (Eds.) (1991). *Women, Girls, Psychotherapy: Reframing Resistance*. New York: Haworth Press.

Kelly, L. (1988). Surviving sexual violence. Minneapolis, MN: University of Minnesota Press.

Scott, J. C. (1990). Domination and the arts of resistance. New Haven, CT: Yale University Press.

Todd, N. (1997). Personal communication.

Todd, N., & Wade, A. (2003). Coming to terms with violence and resistance: from a language of effects to a language of responses. In: T. Strong & D. Pare (Eds.), *Furthering Talk: Advances in the Discursive Therapies* (pp. 145–161). New York: Kluwer Academic Plenum.

Ullman, S. E., & Filipas, H. H. (2005). Gender differences in social reactions to abuse disclosures, post-abuse coping, and PTSD of child sexual abuse survivors. *Child Abuse & Neglect, 29*: 767–782.

Wade, A. (1997). Small acts of living: everyday resistance to violence and other forms of oppression. *Journal of Contemporary Family Therapy, 19*: 23–40.

Wade, A. (2000). Resistance to interpersonal violence: implications for the practice of therapy. Unpublished doctoral dissertation, University of Victoria, Victoria, BC.

CHAPTER SIX

Psychiatry, emotion, and the family: from expressed emotion to dialogical selves

Paolo Bertrando

F amily and emotion entered the field of psychiatry together in the late 1950s as a result of working with families who had a schizophrenic member. On one side of the Atlantic, this process generated the different approaches to schizophrenic families that eventually gave rise to family therapy (Broderick & Schrader, 1991) and, on the other side, led to what has been defined as expressed emotion (Leff & Vaughn, 1985).

From that moment, the family fell, partly at least, within the domain of psychiatry. Under the psychiatric gaze, the family itself became a kind of "patient" and family problems slowly came to be considered as family pathologies. It was too easy to see a family with problems as a deviant or pathological family.

Interestingly, the American approach to family and schizophrenia, the then paradigmatic psychiatric illness, gave little emphasis to emotion, stressing instead the cognitive, as well as relational, aspects of both psychopathology and family life, as the very concept of double bind (Bateson, Jackson, Haley, & Weakland, 1956) exemplifies. The British version, however, centred on emotion, and, at the same time, subjected it to quantitative evaluation.

In a way, such an evaluative approach deepened the gap between family sanity and family pathology. It is a typical modern prejudice to believe formalised evaluation to be "truer" than clinical intuition. The distinction is sharper if the evaluation takes the form of a measurement, with a quantitative measurement invariably being seen as "truer" than a qualitative one.

Through the years, expressed emotion became the paradigmatic method for investigating families in a psychiatric setting. Such a situation contributed to creating the conviction that emotion in "psychiatric" families was a different affair from "non-psychiatric" ones. This is another interesting myth that, in my view, might usefully be dispelled.

The case of expressed emotion: from prediction to typology

Expressed emotion can be considered as a by-product of British social psychiatry, initially created by George Brown, of the London Medical Research Council (Brown, 1959), thereafter refined together with Michael Rutter (Brown & Rutter, 1966) in the investigation of relapse rates in patients discharged from mental hospitals.

The term "expressed emotion" (EE) came into being only at a relatively late time (see Brown, 1985), surfacing as an empirical predictive index which places a patient's family in one of two categories, high or low EE. Living in a high EE family environment, a typical patient will tend to show the symptoms of his or her psychiatric condition more frequently and more intensely (Brown, Birley, & Wing, 1972). This is what is usually defined as the "predictive validity" of EE.

Thus, at the very origin of EE, we have three components. First, looking for risk factors in mental illness, second, looking for them within the family, and last, making them quantifiable. If the third factor was specific to the Brown and Rutter research group, the first two strands were common to several other researchers, especially the celebrated triad of Gregory Bateson's, Lyman Wynne's, and Theodor Lidz's groups (Broderick & Schrader, 1991). There is, however, another basic difference. The triad's constructs, such as the double bind, were proposed as a causal (or, at least, a pathogenetic) hypothesis of schizophrenia, although Gregory Bateson, its spiritual father, later stated that, after all, double bind is only loosely linked to psychiatry and mental illness (see Bateson, 1969; Berger, 1978). Brown, on the other hand, was not looking for an explanation of the very origin of schizophrenia; he was simply looking for factors that could influence its course. This specificity has been extremely important for the subsequent fortunes of EE.

We need to define EE more clearly and lay bare the evaluation process. We can say that expressed emotion measures the emotional attitudes of close relatives towards a symptomatic family member (Leff & Vaughn, 1985). In the whole EE literature, interestingly, there is no mention of the exact definition of terms like "emotion" or "emotional exchanges in the family". Such an elaboration still remains to be done. However, these attitudes can strongly influence the course of the illness. As many follow-up studies have shown (Vaughn & Leff, 1976; Vaughn, Snyder, Jones, Freeman, & Falloon, 1984; see Kavanagh, 1992, for a review, Butzlaff & Hooley, 1998, for a meta-analysis), patients living in high EE homes are more likely to suffer relapse than patients in low EE families. This led to a widespread use of EE to predict the course of schizophrenia.

As to methodology, EE is evaluated through a semi-structured interview with a flexible format, the Camberwell Family Interview (Richardson, Dohrenwend, & Klein, 1965), which is administered to individual family members (Brown, Birley, & Wing, 1972). All interviews, lasting about an hour, are audio-recorded and then assessed by a trained expert. Ratings are made on five scales: "criticism", "positive remark", "hostility", "emotional over-involvement", and "warmth" (Leff & Vaughn, 1985). Space in this chapter does not allow a thorough exploration of the complicated technicalities of EE evaluation. Suffice it to say that the emotions considered should be openly and spontaneously expressed during the interview. As to its predictive value, in most studies, family EE assessment has been based mainly on criticism, over-involvement, and hostility, which are considered as predictive of relapse. It needs only one relative to be rated high EE for the whole family to be similarly rated.

We have to remember a number of implications in these ratings. First, in order to determine EE, we need the presence of an already established mental problem. Without it, no EE measurement can be performed, which emphasises again that family environment in itself has no bearing on the origin of mental problems. The underlying model is a vulnerability–stress one (Zubin & Spring, 1977): the family emotional climate acts as a chronic stress factor on a person who, for

whatever reasons, possibly biological, is vulnerable to the development of mental illness.

Second, EE is strictly unidirectional. It is measured as a sort of
emotional flux coming from non-diagnosed family members and
towards the diagnosed member. The emotional role of the diagnosed
member is not considered, although Michael Goldstein and his group
tried to explore this aspect via their measurement of "patients' coping
style" (Miklowitz et al., 1989; Strachan, Feingold, Goldstein, Miklowitz, & Nuechterlein, 1989). Neither is any consideration given to the
emotional attitude of the professional performing the evaluation. This
has therapeutic consequences: all EE-centred interventions are, in
turn, unidirectional, aiming at a "reduction" of EE through some more
or less behavioural method applied by an objective operator.

Third, there is something undefined in the very nature of what we
call EE. Sometimes, one wonders whether it is something that exists
within the family, or simply a method for investigation. In other
words, is EE something real, concrete, or something existing only
when a researcher, equipped with research tools, begins to look for it?
The answer is not simple. We think that EE surely reflects something
going on within a family; at the same time, it can be described as EE
only when a definite research method is employed. We cannot talk
about EE without immediately referring to an observation method,
with all its criteria, its procedures, its standards. This distinction is, in
our opinion, central to our subsequent discourses.

Fourth, "warmth" and "positive remark", which indicate a positive attitude towards the diagnosed family member, and may, therefore, be considered as a measurement of protective factors, are not
usually considered as relevant. This implies that EE, at least in its original formulation, is an evaluation of negative emotions: as psychiatry
centres on pathology rather than resilience, expressed emotion centres
on family risk factors rather than family support factors. Hence,
another basic question: what exactly is the relationship between EE
and psychiatry?

Expressed emotion, psychiatry, and families

Several expressed emotion characteristics dovetail brilliantly with the
tenets of contemporary psychiatry, which is a kind of psychiatry

founded on more or less overt biological assumptions and subjected to the tyranny of procedural reliability. I think that, by discussing them, we can reach some deeper understanding of contemporary psychiatry, its relationship with families, and its idea of emotion. I shall try to outline them briefly:

1. *Simplicity*. The EE factor is simple and immediately understandable. Expressed emotions deals with certain emotions that are part of the life of any family: affective warmth and appreciation, hostility and anger, involvement and over-involvement. Such simplicity and economy have been widely praised by clinicians and researchers alike.

2. *Procedures*. At the same time, EE submits those emotional elements to the rigorous filter of an assessment method: we can say that a family member is critical only if he or she satisfies a number of specific conditions. Like the *Diagnostic and Statistical Manual (DSM)* American Psychiatric Association, 2000), EE gives us some reliable criteria for investigating a muddled issue such as the emotions of family life.

3. *Induction*. EE is not grounded in any family theory. Its construction was, as we have seen, mostly inductive, observing what happened in families during carefully planned research studies. This approach is very close to the practice of psychiatry after the *DSM* revolution, where an "atheoretical" approach was stressed.

4. *Compatibility* with theories that are part of psychiatric thinking. Currently, Engel's (1977) bio-psychosocial model and Zubin and Spring's (1977) vulnerability–stress model are the most widely accepted. Both models assume the influence of endogenous factors, mostly of a biological nature, on psychiatric disorders that are, in turn, remodelled by a number of environmental factors. Any psychiatrist can, according to their ideological preference, attribute more or less weight to such factors, adjusting the theory as required. Since expressed emotion is not grounded in any aetiological theory of mental illness, it is easy to use by psychiatric practitioners, independent of their theoretical orientation.

5. As observed before, expressed emotion is a measurement of *risk factors* rather than family resources or strengths. This resonates with a long-standing psychiatric tradition, although it is alien to

the development of family and systemic theories and therapies in the past few decades (Walsh, 2008), not to mention some research in a psychiatric setting (Strauss, 1998).

6. The possibility of designing *simple empirical studies* based on EE. In such studies, it is comparatively easy to correlate patients' diagnoses, EE categories, and other simple factors (such as the presence or absence of symptomatic relapses in a given period of time). Such studies take the same format of outcome research for medication, which makes them easy to understand and appreciated by psychiatrists.[1]

7. The possibility of guiding family *treatment*, by both creating treatment procedures (e.g., aimed at reducing criticism and over-involvement) and designing treatment studies, the results of which can be investigated in terms of EE reduction (Leff, 1989).

Within this frame, expressed emotion slowly evolved "from predictive index to clinical construct", to borrow a sentence from Koenigsberg and Handley (1986, p. 1361). In time, the status of a "high" or "low" EE relative became synonymous with being a person with a number of well-defined features. According to Leff and Vaughn (1985), for example, high EE relatives tend to be intrusive, to seek contact with the ill relative independently of their wishes, and consider them responsible for all, or most, of their actions, even when they are overtly symptomatic. They have excessive expectations for the patient and often react dramatically to their symptoms, tending to show rigid responses to crises. Conversely, low EE relatives appear to be more able to adapt to the requests and needs expressed directly or indirectly by the patient. They are generally able to identify genuine symptoms, show realistic expectations, and, on the whole, appear able to control their emotions and adopt flexible responses.

Such human characteristics, which show each relative to be a person, rather than a research subject, are associated with predictions, not only about the course of psychiatric illness but also about the development of family relationships. We tend to think that any low EE relative will show exactly those traits of higher flexibility, empathy, tolerance, and realism, and will be able to help and support patients when necessary, whereas high EE relatives, rigid and unable to see and accept reality, would be unable to accept or protect their problematic relative.

The fact is that this kind of clinical use implies a treacherous shift: we take a statistical variable, which has a sense when referred to a population (e.g., criticism has a negative influence in a certain percentage of cases), and we put it in a clinical context where we try to understand why a unique family does better or worse than others. In fact, we cannot know exactly whether, in this specific case, the effect of criticism would be exactly the same as that which can be predicted for the population as a whole. We cannot even be sure that some of the typical low EE characteristics are really this advantageous: a low level of expectations might be healthy, but it can also lead to the rejection of possible courses of action or an adaptation to chronicity. (It is notable that when investigating family expressed emotion for an Italian research study (Bertrando et al., 1992), we found high and low EE parents who did not in any way resemble what we had expected.)

The Terenzi family

From what we have been saying above, it might appear obvious that expressed emotion is not enough to guide clinicians in the difficult, sometimes really hard, task of helping a family involved in the drama of mental illness. At the same time, the construct cannot be simply dismissed. It contains something precious to clinical work. My proposal is, simply, to consider expressed emotion as a part of the overall emotional system of a family. In order to support my proposal, I shall outline a family case history.

The Terenzi family was referred to me and my co-therapist by a private psychiatrist, who had been in charge of the drug treatment for Ignazio, who, at the time, was twenty-nine years old. The rest of the family comprised the father, Candido, fifty-five, a company manager, the mother, Reginella, fifty-three, who worked as an employee in a public hospital, and the first-born sister, Sara, thirty-three, who had a degree in economics. Ignazio, too, had managed to get a degree in the same subject (with more than a little help from his sister), despite a psychiatric disorder diagnosed years before, which caused him to suffer from delusions and hallucinations, following an ill-fated love affair. He had never been hospitalised, and neither had a definitive diagnosis ever been made, despite both its onset and evolution strongly hinting at schizophrenia, with a prevalence of negative symptoms. He had never worked, maintaining only a handful of distant friends, and spending most of his life in his room. He had been in and out of treatment with several psychiatrists, a psychologist, and other services, both public and private. At the time of referral, he was receiving no treatment.

On the one hand, this family could be perfectly described using the EE classifications, even without a formal interview and evaluation. Candido had all the characteristics of a typically critical father: he seemed to oscillate between recognising the severity of Ignazio's problem, and the simplistic idea that his son could be better if he only put some effort into his life, especially in the pursuit and maintenance of a job. Reginella, with all her preoccupation and over-identification with Ignazio, her constant worry coupled with a tendency to mind-read his feelings, and her inability to leave him alone, could be described as a typical over-involved mother. Sara, however, was more detached and willing to lead her own life without being too involved in her brother's problems.

In the beginning, our way of proceeding was very similar to the one indicated by Leff and his collaborators when they devised the first psycho-educational interventions for families of schizophrenics (Berkowitz, Eberlein-Vries, Kuipers, & Leff, 1984). We discovered that the family, in the previous ten years, had developed the habit of finding and dismissing professionals and institutions, both private and public, without staying with one of them for more than a few months. They came to our office imbued with a deep distrust of psychiatry in general, and public psychiatry in particular.

Ignazio came to the first session in an extremely withdrawn state, completely disinterested in establishing contact, with a wandering eye that made one suspect he was being entertained by voices in his head. All the others were talking about him, while he did not answer or intervene. He appeared oblivious to his surroundings and our attempts to make contact with him were useless. Instead, we were left to listen to the others telling the family's story.

We decided, in this instance, to be somewhat instructive with the family. We were adamant that they had to get in touch with the local psychiatric community service, in order to implement some medication treatment that had been lacking for the past few years. Also, we advised Ignazio to have some individual therapy with a psychiatrist within the service and suggested that his parents should become more tolerant towards his symptomatic behaviours. For example, he had a tendency to drive to some nearby city, get lost, and leave his father's car in the middle of nowhere, or he could spend a whole night driving around in a forbidden area, where he was detected by video surveillance, running up €5,000 fines.

In time, Candido did learn to accept this kind of behaviour, not least because such instances were immediately reduced when Ignazio accepted some medication. Reginella, for her part, complied with our gentle request to give Ignazio some space—both actual and metaphorical—in which to withdraw whenever he felt the need. Sara was able to keep a reasonable distance from her brother—neither too close nor too far removed. It seemed as though the situation was well balanced.

The fact was, however, that such a balance existed only on the surface. Underneath, the struggle in the parental couple was still very much alive. At this point, it was expressed chiefly through endless discussions about how to find Ignazio a job. Ignazio himself seemed characteristically ambivalent about his job prospects. He tended to try them once or twice, then to find all of them too demanding and, at the same time, not satisfying enough for him. After all, he had a degree from an important university. On one occasion, Candido put his own career at risk by obtaining a post for his son in his company, which entailed making various promises to colleagues. Ignazio procrastinated about taking the job for some weeks before succumbing to definite persecutory delusions. Each of Ignazio's failures reactivated the endless fight between the parents, whose recently acquired more reasonable attitudes fell by the wayside. They also returned to questioning the psychiatric treatment, thereby threatening its continuity. Clearly, useful as it had been, this EE-based intervention had been insufficient for the Terenzis. Something more was needed.

Emotional attractors and repellors

In the past few years, I have tried to develop a different approach to emotions in systemic therapy (Bertrando & Arcelloni, 2009). My basic idea is that emotions should not be considered as purely individual phenomena, but, rather, as complex events embedded in an interpersonal systemic matrix. In this way, we could look back at the Terenzi family and see its members as a network of emotional exchanges, meaningful only in the dialogical framework created by their interaction.

A useful view of such emotional interaction has been proposed by Magai and Haviland-Jones (2002). It is founded, on the one hand, on Silvan Tomkins' basic affect theory (Tomkins, 1962–1993), on the other, on dynamic systems theories (Gleick, 1987). Magai and Haviland-Jones claim that, in any human system,

> certain preferences for thoughts, feelings, and activity will develop over time; in dynamic systems terms, these are called attractors. Similarly, the system will also develop certain aversions for particular thoughts, feelings, and activities; in dynamic systems terms, these are called repellors. (Magai & Haviland-Jones, 2002, p. 44)

I think that such a conception of emotional life can be adapted to the description of interpersonal systems, such as families. In this way, we can look at the main emotional attractors within the family as a whole, as well as at individual attractors and repellors. This can enable us to gain a deeper understanding of family emotional processes.

We can easily interpret the Terenzis' emotional life in terms of emotional attractors. Individually speaking, Reginella's attractors were anger, concern/interest (strictly directed toward her offspring rather than her husband) and fear/anxiety (she also showed well-defined phobic traits), with some presence of shame. Candido's attractors were anger and sadness, and he, too, was prone to shame. It was more difficult to determine Sara and Ignazio's emotional attractors, in the former's case because of her unwillingness to be involved in family sessions and in the latter's because of his overall emotional flatness.

If we look at the family as a whole, we may see a strange attractor made up of anger, fear, and sadness, which alternated very quickly, and shifted from one interaction to the other. In dynamic system theory, a strange attractor is an attractor which shifts continually from one position to another; in human systems, a strange attractor can be seen when the emotional state of an individual or a family shifts from one emotion to another, without any discernible pattern (Magai & Haviland-Jones, 2002). Ignazio's lack of response had the paradoxical effect of centring all his parents' emotions on him. Candido's sadness, very apparent when he was reflecting on his relationship with both his son and his daughter (his relations with Sara were tense and difficult, too), triggered anger in Reginella. In turn, her constant preoccupation with Ignazio, her urgency to interpret any sign that he showed ("If only I could see within his head and know what he's up to!"), produced anger in Candido. The shift from concern to anger could be abrupt: on one occasion, a dismissive answer from Ignazio generated a furious reaction from Candido, who went to assault him, and only Reginella's desperate attempt to separate them prevented an explosion of physical violence.

At the same time, the underlying ghost of chronicity created an attractor towards sadness, depression, and grief, which in turn activated distress. The attempt to escape distress led Candido to look for jobs that each time proved unsuitable for Ignazio, and prompted Reginella to look for a miracle therapist, who each time proved unable to provide the required miracle. Usually, following any failure, anger was ignited between the two of them.

Another, more stable attractor was shame, very apparent in the refusal of both parents to accept any label of mental illness, or to find any kind of help for Ignazio apart from medication and psychotherapy. It was as if rehabilitation and group activities could precipitate him and them into the hell of schizophrenia, making them outcasts from society. Interestingly, Ignazio himself accepted drugs, meeting his psychiatrists, and even some of their suggestions, but appeared unable to accept not just any definition of his problem but even its very existence. He behaved as if he were deeply ashamed without any acknowledgement of this emotion.

Repellors, too, could be found in the Terenzi family. They seemed unable to feel joy and interest, especially when they were together. The impression was that they were able to be individually happy, but that joy was precluded from the family as a whole. Another, more subtle repellor was surprise: not one of them appeared open to novelty: everything in their lives seemed predictable, and usually unpleasant. As a family, they seemed to have reached a state close to chronicity.

Working with the Terenzis, at this point, meant first of all disentangling the strange attractor that constrained their family life. Lowering expressed emotion (i.e., reducing criticism and over-involvement) had been but a first step. Subsequent sessions centred on promoting awareness of the role of both parents in maintaining old patterns.

Ignazio preferred not to be involved in family sessions for most of this phase, and we accepted seeing him irregularly.

For Candido, the work entailed exploring the roots of his dedication to work, while for Reginella, she needed to look deeper into her anxieties in order to understand the dynamics of her involvement with her son, which was as total and unconditional as her relationship with her daughter was difficult and ambivalent. For both Candido and Reginella, it meant facing the present state of their couple relationship, long reduced to no more than discussions about Ignazio. They were able, in time, to see to what extent they needed Ignazio's involvement in order not to remain alone with each other, and to acknowledge the bitterness they had towards each other for the affairs they had both had and which were not forgotten or forgiven.

Eventually, it was possible for them to accept their own position and Ignazio's actual state of health. This, in turn, helped him to accept some rehabilitation activities, while his overall mental state, with the help of medication and regular sessions with a psychiatrist, remained free of symptoms, even if his passivity and lack of interest remained much the same. The parents, albeit remaining fairly distant from each other, were now able to think about a possible future in which Ignazio could lead a life of his own. His relationship with his psychiatrist was no longer questioned by his parents, and his outbursts of rage disappeared. The process, though, did not reach the final stage we were planning: the family dropped out of our treatment just as we were addressing the issue of an independent home for Ignazio.

Although the point we had reached could be considered very positive, if compared to the family's original situation, we needed to reflect about the reason for this sudden interruption in the treatment process. In the end, we came to the conclusion that we had probably begun to put too much pressure on the family, trying to make them conform to our own standards of family wellbeing. We wondered whether we had become too intrusive and demanding.

Probably, with the Terenzis, we were already using a different model from EE ideas, but, on the other hand, we were not exactly in the dialogical position, as described below. We were still too interested in obtaining a result (i.e., having the family accept rehabilitative activities), rather than trying to understand their needs and desires as they felt them. Anyway, the process had brought them to a better situation than the initial one, and in this respect we felt we had helped them.

Emotion: inner and outer dialogues

The changes I have outlined in my approach to emotions in families with a psychiatric problem is probably linked to a wider change in my way of doing therapy. I think that, when working on individual and family emotional attractors, a dialogical stance should prevail. I define as dialogical a therapeutic stance where the therapist is open in stating his or her position to clients, and at the same time accepts the clients' definitions, hypotheses, and feelings (Bertrando, 2007). As I try to adopt a dialogical stance myself, I attempt to accept the family members' feelings and ideas while not being afraid to hold on to, and at times express, my own emotions and use my expertise.

This implies that I must first try to understand my own emotions, both attractors and repellors. It also means that I must recognise how I may bring forth some emotions more than others. In this process, it is important to keep connected to my inner feelings while paying close attention to those of others and being aware of the relationship between the two. This is what Rober (1999) describes as being in one's inner and outer dialogue simultaneously. Emotions, here, are an essential part of the ongoing therapeutic process.

Working with attractors and repellors means I openly discuss both my emotions and the clients' in the process. My hypotheses, questions, and statements tend to refer more and more to an emotional content. I try also to be more aware of emotional interaction in the here and now, pointing my attention towards the subtle change of emotional climate and to non-verbal clues. It does not mean, though, that I use the definitions of "attractors" or "repellors" in the dialogue with clients. Rather, I refer to "emotions that I feel are very important in our talking", or "an emotion that you seem never to consider in your family", and so on.

If we look back at expressed emotion from the vantage point I have outlined, we can see it now as part of a wider picture. I think I can offer, not exactly a set of guidelines for family interventions, but at least some pointers that might be of relevance to colleagues working with the high levels of family emotion that are often present in adult psychiatric settings.

Trivial as it may seem, the first step is to get an appreciation of the overall emotional climate of the family. The emotional tone we perceive in the very first encounter could be an essential guide for creating a significant relationship with the family.

In the first stages, the expressed emotion variables are a useful index of relevant family interaction. Psycho-educational action aimed at reducing EE levels is usually essential in creating and strengthening the therapeutic alliance. If some EE reduction brings forth some easing of tension and relief of distress, family members are more likely to accept the subsequent phases of intervention.

An in-depth investigation allows us to hypothesise about emotional attractors and repellors. Family work, at this point, must become more complex and articulated. Therapists should follow their clinical skills rather than pre-determined guidelines. The actual techniques employed can be manifold, but emotions should remain the focal point.

As in any kind of therapeutic interaction, a dialogical stance is the most useful (Bertrando, 2007). This means both paying attention to outer (interpersonal) dialogues, and to our own inner dialogues. The therapist should try to accept the family members' emotional stance, without renouncing their own. This requires a fine balance, where the best guide for the therapist is a deeply respectful attitude towards all family members.

Another basic implication of such a dialogical stance is the attention to our role in the process. As we have seen, our feelings, our attitudes, our prejudices, are key factors in the success or failure of the therapeutic enterprise. The therapist should, above all, promote and be aware of his or her own inner dialogue and biases and prejudices that might get played out in the outer interpersonal dialogue with the family (see Rober, 2005).

When all is said and done, I would like to emphasise one final point. In this kind of work, no technical or professional skill is enough. Each time we meet a family or individual we are facing a drama with profound, existential implications. A good deal of compassion (from the Latin *cum-patior*, "I feel with") is required. It is this humane aspect that makes working with families involved in psychosis so challenging, and yet so rewarding.

Note

1.   I owe this reasoning to my colleague Thomas Herzog, in Heidelberg.

References

American Psychiatric Association (2000). *Diagnostic and Statistical Manual for Mental Disorders, Fourth Edition, Text Revision (DSM-IV-TR)*. Washington, DC: American Psychiatric Association.

Bateson, G. (1969). Double bind. 1969. In: *Steps to an Ecology of Mind*. San Francisco, CA: Chandler, 1972.

Bateson, G., Jackson, D. D., Haley, J., & Weakland, J. H. (1956). Toward a theory of schizophrenia. *Behavioral Science, 1*: 251–264.

Berger, M. M. (Ed.) (1978). *Beyond The Double Bind*. New York: Brunner/ Mazel.

Berkowitz, R., Eberlein-Vries, R., Kuipers L., & Leff, J. P. (1984). Educating relatives about schizophrenia. *Schizophrenia Bulletin, 10*: 418–429.

Bertrando, P. (2007). *The Dialogical Therapist*. London: Karnac.

Bertrando, P., & Arcelloni, T. (2009). Anger and boredom: unpleasant emotions in systemic therapy. In: C. Flaskas & D. Pocock (Eds.), *Systems and Psychoanalysis. Contemporary Integrations in Family Therapy* (pp. 75–92). London: Karnac.

Bertrando, P., Beltz, J., Bressi, C., Clerici, M., Farma, T., Invernizzi G., & Cazzullo, C. L. (1992). Expressed emotion and schizophrenia in Italy. A study of an urban population. *British Journal of Psychiatry, 161*: 223–229.

Broderick, C. B., & Schrader, S. S. (1991). A history of family and marital therapy. In: A. S. Gurman & D. P. Kniskern (Eds.), *Handbook of Family Therapy, Vol. II*. New York: Brunner/Mazel.

Brown, G. W. (1959). Experience of discharged chronic schizophrenic mental hospital patients in various types of living group. *Millbank Memorial Fund Quarterly, 37*: 101–131.

Brown, G. W. (1985). The discovery of expressed emotion: induction or deduction? In: J. P. Leff & C. E. Vaughn (Eds.), *Expressed Emotion in Families* (pp. 7–25). London: Guilford Press.

Brown, G. W., & Rutter, M. (1966). The measurement of family activities and relationship: a methodological study. *Human Relations, 19*: 741–763.

Brown, G. W., Birley, J. L. T., & Wing, J. K. (1972). Influence of family life on the course of schizophrenic disorders a replication. *British Journal of Psychiatry, 121*: 241–258.

Butzlaff, R. L., & Hooley, J. M. (1998). Expressed emotion and psychiatric relapse. A meta analysis. *Archives of General Psychiatry, 55*: 547–552.

Engel, G. L. (1977). The need for a new medical model: a challenge for biomedicine. *Science, 196*: 129–136.

Gleick, J. (1987). *Chaos. Making a New Science.* New York: Abacus.

Kavanagh, D. J. (1992). Recent developments in expressed emotion and schizophrenia. *British Journal of Psychiatry, 160*: 601–620.

Koenigsberg, H. W., & Handley, R. (1986). Expressed emotion: from predictive index to clinical construct. *American Journal of Psychiatry, 143*: 1361–1373.

Leff, J. P. (1989). Controversial issues and growing points in research on relatives' expressed emotion. *International Journal of social Psychiatry, 35*(2): 133–145.

Leff, J. P., & Vaughn, C. E. (1985). *Expressed Emotion in Families.* London: Guilford Press.

Magai, C., & Haviland-Jones, J. (2002). *The Hidden Genius of Emotion. Lifespan Transformations of Personality.* Cambridge: Cambridge University Press.

Miklowitz, D. J., Goldstein, M. J., Doane, J. A., Nuechterlein, K. H., Strachan, A. M., Snyder, K. S., & Magana-Amato, A. (1989). Is expressed emotion an index of a transactional process? I. Parents' affective style. *Family Process, 28*: 153–157.

Richardson, S. A., Dohrenwend, B. S., & Klein, D. (1965). *Interviewing: Its Forms and Functions.* New York: Basic Books.

Rober, P. (1999). The therapist's inner conversation in family therapy practice: some ideas about the self of the therapist, therapeutic impasse, and the process of reflection. *Family Process, 38*: 209–228.

Rober, P. (2005). The therapist's self in dialogical family therapy: some ideas about not-knowing and the therapist's inner conversation. *Family Process, 44*: 477–495.

Strachan, A. M., Feingold, D., Goldstein, M. J, Miklowitz, D. J., & Nuechterlein, K. H. (1989). Is expressed emotion an index of a transactional process? II. Patient's coping style. *Family Process, 28*:169–181.

Strauss, J. (1998). La schizofrenia può migliorare? In: C. L. Cazzullo, M. Clerici, & P. Bertrando (Eds.), *Schizofrenia e ambiente* (pp. 54–62). Milan: Franco Angeli.

Tomkins, S. (1962–1993). *Affect, Imagery, Consciousness, Vols. 1–4.* Berlin: Springer.

Vaughn, C. E., & Leff, J. P. (1976). The influence of family and social factors on the course of psychiatric illness: a comparison of schizophrenic and depressed neurotic patients. *British Journal of Psychiatry, 129*: 125–137.

Vaughn, C. E., Snyder, K. S., Jones, S., Freeman, W., & Falloon, I. R. H. (1984). Family factors in schizophrenic relapse. *Archives of General Psychiatry*, 41: 1169–1177.

Walsh, F. (2008). *Strengthening Family Resilience*. New York: Guilford Press.

Zubin, J., & Spring, B. (1977). Vulnerability: a new view of schizophrenia. *Journal of Abnormal Psychology*, 86: 103–126.

SECTION TWO

INSIDE OUT:
AN APPRECIATION OF PRACTICE

PART I

SPACE IN TIGHT CORNERS: PRACTICE-BASED EXAMPLES

CHAPTER SEVEN

Open dialogues mobilise the resources of the family and the patient

Jaakko Seikkula and Birgitta Alakare

In a severe mental health crisis, it should be normal psychiatric practice for the first meeting to take place within a day of hearing about the crisis. Furthermore, both the patient and family members should be invited to participate in the first meeting and throughout the treatment process for as long as is needed. In these meetings, all relevant professionals from primary care, psychiatry, social care, and other appropriate authorities who have contact with this family are invited to participate and openly share their thoughts and opinions about the crisis and what should be done. These professionals should stay involved for as long as required. All discussions and treatment decisions should be made openly in the presence of the patient and family members.

These are the basic guiding principles of the open dialogue approach, a treatment method that originated in the Western part of Finnish Lapland. The development of this new approach started in the early 1980s. This chapter has its background in Finnish Lapland, but describes elements that can be put into practice in other contexts. Our aim is to outline the significance of the open dialogue approach for patients and their families.

Opening the boundaries

Our current approach arose out of analysing problems in our practice and then trying to find solutions to them by reorganising the system. There were a number of phases in developing the process of open dialogue. When we began to develop the acute psychiatric inpatient system at Keropudas Hospital in Tornio, we had two primary interests. In the beginning, we were interested in individual psychotherapy with patients diagnosed with schizophrenia. At that time, Keropudas Hospital was occupied by dozens of long-term patients who had been considered "incurable" and were to be transferred to another mental hospital designated to receive patients who needed long-term inpatient treatment. In shifting to a more optimistic treatment model, the Keropudas staff had to learn how to work with the psychological resources of the patients with psychotic problems. In Finland, psychotherapeutic practice has long been part of public health care. Particularly important has been the development and research undertaken in the Turku Psychiatric Clinic by Professor Yrjö Alanen and his team since the 1960s. Starting with individual psychodynamic psychotherapy, the Turku team integrated family perspectives into their treatments in the late 1970s and called the approach "need-adapted treatment" (Alanen, 1997) in order to emphasise that every treatment process is unique and should be adapted to the varying needs of each patient.

The need-adapted treatment model was also fitted into the context of the Finnish National Schizophrenia Project in the 1980s. The revolutionary aspects of the need-adapted approach were to focus on: (1) rapid early intervention in every case; (2) treatment planning to meet the changing and case specific needs of each patient and family by integrating different therapeutic methods in a single treatment process; (3) having a therapeutic attitude as the basic orientation for each staff member in both examination and treatment; (4) seeing treatment as a continuous process; (5) constantly monitoring treatment progress and outcomes (Alanen, 2009; Alanen, Lehtinen, Räkköläinen, & Aaltonen, 1991).

In the era of evidence-based medicine, all this sounds very radical because it challenges the idea that therapists should choose the one right method of treatment after first making an accurate diagnosis of the case. By contrast, need-adaptiveness focuses on the idea that the "right" diagnosis *emerges* in joint meetings. It became clear to us that the use of dialogue to reach a full understanding by all concerned of what had happened can of itself be a very therapeutic process.

Anticipating psychotherapy research into common factors, by the early 1980s the need-adapted approach was already integrating different psychotherapies instead of choosing just one school or approach, such as systemic family therapy or individual psychodynamic psychotherapy.

Based on this long tradition of schizophrenia treatment in Finland, in Western Lapland the open dialogue approach meant that psychotherapeutic treatment was organised for all patients within their own particular support systems. The ideas of the need-adapted approach and experiences of open dialogue have been applied to some extent in most of the health districts in Finland, but Western Lapland is the exception in the sense that the entire treatment system has been organised to follow the joint guidelines.

Open dialogue refers both to the way the psychiatric system is organised and to the role of dialogue in the meetings with the patient, family members, and professionals. The term "open dialogue" was first used in 1996 to describe the entire family and social network-centred treatment. It has two aspects: first, the meetings described earlier in this chapter in which all relevant members participate from the outset to generate new understanding through dialogue, and second, the guiding principles for the entire system of psychiatric practice in one geographical catchment area.

Open dialogues in organising psychiatric practice

Several evaluations of the effectiveness and treatment process in the open dialogue approach have been completed employing an action research methodology (Aaltonen, Seikkula, & Lehtinen, 1997; Haarakangas, 1997; Keränen, 1992; Seikkula, 1991, 1994; Seikkula, Alakare, & Aaltonen, 2011; Seikkula et al., 2003; Seikkula et al., 2006). By summarising the observations in these studies, seven main principles emerged.

1.   Immediate support.
2.   A social networks perspective.
3.   Flexibility and mobility.

4.   Responsibility.
5.   Psychological continuity.
6.   Tolerance of uncertainty.
7.   Dialogism.

These principles of the open dialogue approach are enlarged upon below. It is worth noting that these principles came out of the research and were not predetermined. Later on, more general ideas about good treatment were added. Although most of the studies have focused on the treatment of psychotic problems, they are not diagnosis specific, but describe an entire network-based treatment especially suited to crisis situations.

Immediate response

In a crisis it is vital to act immediately without waiting for the patient with psychosis to become more coherent before convening a family meeting. It is preferable that the first response be initiated within twenty-four hours. The meeting is organised regardless of who first contacts the response unit. In addition, a twenty-four-hour crisis service ought to be set up. One aim of the immediate response is to prevent hospitalisation in as many cases as possible.

Everyone, including the patient, participates in the very first meet-ings during the most intense psychotic period. The patient usually seems to be experiencing something that has been unappreciated or unacknowledged by the rest of the family. Although the patient's comments might be incomprehensible in the first meetings, after a while it becomes apparent that the patient is actually speaking of real incidents in his or her life. Often these incidents include some terrify-ing issues or a threat that they have not been able to articulate before the crisis. This is also the case in other forms of difficult behaviour. In extreme anger, depression, or anxiety, the patient is describing previously unspoken themes. Thus, the main person in the crisis, the patient, reaches for something that has not been touched by others in their surroundings. The aim of the treatment becomes the open expression in a language shared by all participants of these unspoken experiences.

During the first couple of days of a crisis, it seems possible to speak of things that are difficult to discuss later. In the first days, hallucinations may be handled and reflected upon but they easily fade away and the opportunity to deal with them might not reappear until after several months of individual therapy. It is as if the window for these extreme experiences only stays open for the first few days. If the team manages to create a safe enough atmosphere by responding rapidly and listening carefully to all the themes the clients bring up, then important themes may find a space where they can be handled and the prognosis improved.

Including the social network

The patient, key members of his or her family, and their social network are always invited to the first meetings. Social networks, which might include state employment and insurance agencies, vocational rehabilitation services, fellow workers or the supervisor at the patient's workplace, neighbours, or friends can be instrumental in helping to define the problem and mobilise support for the patient and their family.

A problem is one that has been defined as such in the language of either those closest to the patient or by the patient in person. In the most severe crises, the first notion of a problem often emerges in the definition of those closest to the patient after they note that some forms of behaviour might be the result of using drugs. The young person will seldom see taking drugs as a problem, but their parents can be terrified by the first signs of possible drug misuse. From a network perspective, all these individuals should be included in the process. It is helpful to adopt a simple way of deciding who should be invited to meetings. It can be done, for instance, by asking the person who made the initial contact in the crisis the following questions:

"Who is concerned about the situation or who has been involved?"
"Who could be of help and is able to participate in the first meeting?"
"Who would be the best person to invite them, you or the treatment team?"

In this way, the participation of those closest to the patient is suggested as part of an everyday conversation, which decreases any possible suspicion about the invitation. Also, the one who has made contact with the services can decide whom they do not want to participate in the meetings. If the proposal for a joint meeting is made in an official tone, by asking, for instance, "Will you allow us to contact your family and invite them to a meeting?", problems might arise in motivating both the patient and those close to him or her. Another factor in deciding about the relevant participants is to find out whether the patient has been in touch with any other professionals, either in connection with the current situation or previously. If so, and the other professionals cannot attend the first meetings, a joint meeting can be arranged later.

The people in the patient's social network can be included in many ways. The clients are asked if they want to invite others who know of their situation and who could possibly help. They can be present or, if some of them cannot manage to attend meetings, then some other member of the network can be given the task of contacting them after the meeting and relaying the absent person's comments to the next joint meeting. Those present can be asked, for instance,

"What would Uncle Mark have said if he was present in this conversation?"
"What would your answer be?"
"And what would his response be?'"

In this way, dialogues are generated with the inner voices of some important family member or members of the social network even if they are not actually present in the meeting.

Flexibility

Flexibility is guaranteed by adapting the treatment so that it is responsive to the specific and changing needs of each patient, using the therapeutic methods best suited to each family, their specific language, and their way of living. The approach and the length of treatment should fit the actual problem instead of applying a generic programme without variation from case to case. During the first ten to twelve days of a crisis, the need is quite different compared with the need three weeks later. For instance, during the most acute phase, it is advisable, if possible, to have a meeting every day, which will no longer be necessary once the situation has stabilised. In that later period, families generally know how frequently they should be meeting. The best place for the meeting, if the family approves, might be the patient's home. However, meetings in an emergency department or a psychiatric outpatient clinic are options, if the family sees these as more suitable.

Home meetings seem to prevent unnecessary hospitalisations, since the family's own resources are more accessible in a home setting (Keränen, 1992; Seikkula, 1991). Families can easily refuse to participate in treatment (Friis, Larsen, & Melle, 2003). However, the need-adapted approach, with its emphasis on taking into account the uniqueness of each treatment process, has been more successful in engaging with families. It seems to suit the Nordic system in which every psychiatric unit has total responsibility for providing psychiatric treatment for the entire population in its catchment area. It is paid for by the State and is, therefore, free of charge to patients.

Responsibility

Organising a crisis service in a catchment area is difficult if all the professionals involved are not committed to providing an immediate response. A good rule of thumb is to follow the principle that whoever is contacted takes responsibility for organising the first meeting and inviting the team. The person contacting the professional could be, for example, the patient, a family member, a referring practitioner, or other authorities such as the family doctor or a school nurse. Organising a team or home resolution team are possibilities, with all staff members knowing whom to contact to organise an immediate first meeting. This means that it is no longer possible to respond to a request for help by saying "This has nothing to do with us, please contact the other clinic".

It is important to reassure the family member contacting the service that they have come to the right place and a meeting will be organised. One can say, for instance, "It sounds to me that alcohol misuse may be involved in your son's problem. Would you allow me to invite someone from the alcohol misuse clinic to join us in the meeting tomorrow?"

In the meetings, decisions are made as to who will best form the team that will be responsible for the treatment. In multi-problem situations, the most effective team is made up of professionals from different units, such as one from social care, one from a psychiatric outpatient clinic, and one from the hospital ward. The team mobilised for the first meeting should take all the responsibility needed for analysing the current problem and planning the treatment. Everything needed for an adequate response is available in the room, as there is no other authority elsewhere that will know better what to do. This means that all team members should take care to gather the information they need for the best possible decisions to be made. If the doctor is not able to attend the meetings, this individual should be consulted by phone, and if there is a difference of opinion about certain decisions, a joint meeting is advisable to discuss the choices in the presence of the family. This empowers family members to participate more fully in the decision-making process.

Guaranteeing psychological continuity

The team takes responsibility for the treatment for as long as necessary in both outpatient and inpatient settings. This is the best way to guarantee psychological continuity. Forming a multi-disciplinary team early on increases the possibility of crossing the boundaries of different treatment facilities and preventing people dropping out. In the first meeting, it is impossible to know how long the treatment will continue. Sometimes, one or two meetings are enough, but in other cases intensive treatment for up to two years might be needed. Problems might occur if the crisis intervention team meets three or five times and then refers the patient to other authorities. In these circumstances, even in the first meetings, there is a danger of too much focus on the actions to be taken and not enough on the process itself. Representatives of the patient's social network participate in the treatment meetings for the entire treatment sequence, including when other therapeutic methods are applied.

One part of psychological continuity is to integrate different therapeutic methods into a cohesive treatment process where different methods complement each other. For instance, if individual psychotherapy is recommended for the patient, psychological continuity is easily guaranteed by having one of the team members act as the individual psychotherapist. If this is not possible or is inadvisable, the psychotherapist could be invited to one or two joint meetings in which the ideas that are generated can serve as the basis for an individual therapy process. The therapist should be invited every now and then to meetings with the team and the family. Problems might occur if the individual psychotherapist does not want to participate in the joint meetings. This can intensify the family's suspicion towards the therapy, sometimes affecting the entire treatment process. This is particularly important to consider in the case of children and adolescents.

Tolerating uncertainty

The first task for professionals in a crisis is to increase the safety of the situation, when no one yet knows the reasons for the problem or what the solutions will be. By generating new stories about their most extreme experiences, the aim is to mobilise the psychological resources of the patient and those nearest to him or her so as to increase the agency in their own lives. This is supported by building up a sense of trust in the joint process. For example, in psychotic crises, an adequate sense of security can be generated by meeting every day at least for the first ten to twelve days. After this, meetings can be organised on a regular basis, according to the wishes of the family. Usually, no detailed therapeutic contract is made in the crisis phase but, instead, at every meeting it is decided if and when the next meeting will take place. In this way, premature conclusions and treatment decisions are avoided. Neuroleptic drugs are not given during the first few weeks. This allows for more time to understand the problem and its dimensions. There is also time for spontaneous recovery and, in some cases, the problem can dissolve by itself. A recommendation of neuroleptic drugs should be discussed in at least three meetings before implementation to clarify whether those present think the drugs are necessary.

This approach is in contrast to illness-orientated approaches, which, during the early phase of treatment, focus on trying to remove symptoms with drugs. For psychotic patients, these are typically neuroleptics. Psychiatric drugs can help, of course, but the risk is that their sedative effect, which calms psychological activity, might also be a hindrance to psychological work. The challenge is to create a process that increases safety and encourages personal work. In our study, only 33% of acutely psychotic patients used neuroleptics during the five-year follow-up period.

Besides the practical aspects of seeing that the family is not left alone with its problems, increasing safety means generating a quality in the therapeutic conversation such that everyone can be heard. Working as a team is one prerequisite in guaranteeing safety in a crisis with loaded emotions. One team member might start to listen more carefully to what the patient says when he maintains that he does not have any problems, but that it is his parents who need the treatment. Another team member could become more interested in the family's burden of guilt at not being successful in stopping the patient's drug misuse. From the very first meeting, it is important to reserve some time for a reflective discussion among the team so that different, or even contradictory, perspectives can be raised. If the team members can listen to each other, it might increase the possibility for family members to listen to each other as well.

If professionals are in a hurry to get to the next meeting and, therefore, propose a rapid decision, this is not the best use of the family members' psychological resources. It would be better to note that important issues have been discussed but no firm conclusions reached and, thus, the situation is left open. One way to put it into words might be: "We have now discussed this for about an hour, but we have not reached any firm conclusion as to what this is all about or the best way to address it. However, we have discussed very important issues. Why not leave this open and continue tomorrow?" After that, concrete steps should be agreed on before the next meeting to guarantee that family members know what they should do if they need help.

Dialogicity

In meetings, the focus is primarily on promoting dialogue and only secondarily on promoting change in the patient or in the family. Dialogue is seen as the forum through which families and patients are able to acquire more agency in their own lives by discussing the problems (Haarakangas, 1997).

A new understanding is generated in dialogue (Andersen, 1995; Bakhtin, 1984; Voloshinov, 1996). For a professional, this means eliciting new aspects of being an expert in whom clients can trust. Professionals are no longer seen as experts who, with skilful questioning or through skilful interpretations, can cause change to occur in the patient or in the family system, but instead professionals have to become skilled in promoting dialogues. Expert knowledge might be useful in cases where psychosis or eating disorders are seen as the main problems. However, professionals use their expertise not through giving advice or "psychoeducation", but, rather, by participating in dialogue.

Open dialogues in the therapy meeting

The main forum for dialogues is the treatment meetings, where the major participants in the problematic situation join with the patient to discuss all the relevant issues. All management plans and decisions are made with everyone present. According to Alanen (1997), the treatment meeting has three functions:

- to gather information about the problem;
- to build a treatment plan and make all decisions necessary on the basis of the problem that was described in the conversation;
- to generate a psychotherapeutic dialogue.

On the whole, the focus is on strengthening the adult side of the patient and on normalising the situation instead of focusing on regressive behaviour (Alanen, Lehtinen, Räkköläinen, & Aaltonen, 1991). The starting point for treatment is the language the family uses to describe the patient's problem. Problems are seen as social constructs and are reformulated in every conversation (Bakhtin, 1984; Gergen, 1994, 1999; Shotter, 1993a,b). All persons present speak in their own voices. The stance of the therapist is different to that of the traditional one in which it is the therapist who makes the interventions.

While many family therapy schools concentrate on creating specific forms of interviewing, the dialogic approach focuses more on listening and responding.

The meeting takes place in an open forum with all participants sitting in a circle. The team members who have taken the initiative for calling the meeting take charge of leading the dialogue. On some occasions, there is no prior planning regarding who initiates the questioning and, thus, all staff members can participate in interviewing. On other occasions, the team might decide in advance who will conduct the interview. The best option is when the treatment unit is accustomed to conducting family meetings in a structured way. The first questions are as open-ended as possible, so as to guarantee that family members and the rest of the social network can begin to talk about the issues that are most relevant at that time. The team does not plan the themes of the meeting in advance. From the very beginning the task of the interviewer(s) is to adapt their answers to whatever the patients say. Most often, the team's answer takes the form of a further question that is based on, and has taken into account, what the client and family members have already said. This can mean repeating word for word some part of the utterance and encouraging further dialogue on the subject. If the patient does not want to participate in the meeting, or suddenly runs out of the meeting room, a discussion takes place with the family members whether or not to continue the meeting. If the family wants to continue, a staff member informs the patient that she or he can return if she or he wants. During this discussion, no other decisions concerning the patient are made.

Everyone present has the right to comment, but is asked not to interrupt an ongoing dialogue. Every new speaker should adapt his or her utterance to what was previously said. For the professionals, this means they can comment either by enquiring further about the theme under discussion, or by commenting reflectively to the other professionals about their thoughts in response to what is being said (Andersen, 1995). Often, in these comments, specific phrases are introduced to describe the client's most difficult experiences.

When the staff members have to remind the family of their obligations and duties in this specific treatment process, it is advisable to focus on these issues towards the end of the meeting after family members have had the opportunity to speak about their most compelling issues. After deciding that the important issues for the meeting have been addressed, the team member in charge suggests that the meeting be adjourned. It is important, however, to close the meeting by referring to the client's own words and by asking, for instance, "I wonder if we could take steps to close the meeting. Before doing so, however, is there anything else we should discuss?"

At the end of the meeting, it is helpful to summarise briefly the themes of the meeting, especially whether or not decisions have been made, and, if so, what they were. The length of meetings can vary, but ninety minutes is usually adequate.

Case example: a father's voice "causes" psychosis

Anita herself contacted the psychiatric polyclinic on her mother's advice. At the beginning of the first meeting, she spoke of her fear of becoming mad. To begin with, she talked of her fear in a very coherent manner and said that over the past couple of months she had lost her memory. Although her long-term memory was not impaired, she was uncertain of more recent events in her life. She also said that she suspected she had been involved in fights and even in hitting someone, but that she could not accurately recall what had happened. She herself said that perhaps she was paranoid. The following sequences describe the very first utterances in the first meeting. Anita is represented as A, and T represents the therapists. Anita and three therapists are present in the meeting.

> T: Where should we start?
>
> A: I can't really remember anything of my whole life.
>
> T1:   Has it been like this for a long time—that you can't remember anything?
>
> A: Well, I don't know if it has been that way for two months. I do remember whether I've been in contact with someone . . . But then when I leave my place, I don't even know if I was there, and where I might suddenly pop up is here . . .
>
> T2:   Who are you living with?
>
> A: I've been living by myself, but now I've gone to my parents . . .
>
> T1:   And how long had you been living by yourself?
>
> A: Hmh . . . for three, four years. Three years.

In her answer to the first question, Anita opened up the core theme of her experience. The team constructed the subsequent questions as answers to Anita's reply. From the beginning, the conversation was very informative, so that in a short time relevant information about Anita's life situation was obtained. She herself had a suspicion that she might have severe problems, but she could describe her situation clearly. Although she spoke of odd experiences, she was not psychotic in her speech. A change started to emerge after she started to speak more about her family members.

T1:   Whose idea was it that you come here?

A: Well . . . my mother's.

T2:   And what was your mother worried about?

A: I don't know if I've been talking with her. I can't really remember anything. I have a feeling that I have even hit someone, but I can't remember.

T2:   Has someone said that to you?

A: No. But I am paranoid and have lost my memory. You think that something has happened.

T1:   What about your father? Is he worried about some specific issue?

A: I don't know but yesterday night when we were watching TV he went to bed and in the morning he left for work.

T1:   And what was the situation when he returned home?

A: Well . . . I was afraid of others, I was quarrelling with these kind of guys umm . . . afraid of them and you see . . . they had keys made to my place and them . . . They came in and raped me and did all these things.

T1:   In May?

A: I was living in my apartment. You see, someone who came into my flat, had they been blackmailing or something . . .? And forced to steal a key. And they made a copy of it and could come in whenever they wanted. I don't know if that happened when I was asleep . . . and they gave some pills and I got mixed up and started to . . . I don't know. Or if you take some drug without knowing it and then when you get into her flat, they wait until you are asleep and after that come in with their own keys . . ."

In the beginning, Anita described her odd experiences in a way that she could see them as her thoughts. The team could understand the difficult situation. Although the experiences she described may have included psychotic experiences, she herself was not psychotic until the coherence of her story started to disappear after the team member's questions about her parents' concerns. Her anxiety increased, especially in speaking about her father. She described how a gang from the street came into her apartment and sexually assaulted her. Her story changed into a more sinister one, so that she no longer talked of her fear of having lost her memory but, rather, of her terror at describing what she saw as a true situation. Later on in the treatment process, it became evident that Anita really had been involved with a group of adolescents who were mixed up in criminal activities for the procurement of money for drugs, although Anita herself was probably not actively using drugs. Things that in the first session were uttered as a part of her psychosis were later seen as a part of her real life incidents.

All this seemed to happen after the team asked about her father's concern for her. In this first meeting, all this seemed incomprehensible, but later in the treatment process severe marital problems between the father and mother became evident. Her father had a drinking problem and her mother was depressed. The patient also had a belief that people who disappear are dead, which might also have affected her description of her father's concerns, since he had disappeared off to work in the morning. In a way, the psychotic behaviour was "caused" by the team's question about her parents and especially about her father. The team cannot, of course, avoid this type of question, because they cannot know in advance what the unspoken experiences are that might be connected to the psychotic behaviour. But what the team should do is to respond by encouraging the patient to say more about what has happened to them. The psychotic story becomes simply one voice among others in the dialogue and the task of the therapist is to understand this.

In a dialogical therapy, little information is needed in advance. All that is relevant is present in the therapy room. There is neither a need to define the rules of behaviour nor the function of the psychotic symptoms, as in systemic family therapy, but to be present by responding in the dialogue. Dialogue becomes an aim in itself.

The effectiveness of the open dialogue approach

In Western Lapland, the effectiveness of open dialogue has been assessed in follow-up studies for first-episode psychotic patients. The results, compared with traditional treatment (comparison group), are promising (Seikkula & Arnkil, 2006). Patients diagnosed with schizophrenia were hospitalised for significantly less time than is usual: an average of fourteen days per person, compared with 117 days for the comparison group over a two-year period. Only 33% used neuro-leptics during some phase of treatment, compared with 100% in the comparison group. Families were actively involved in all of the cases, averaging twenty-six meetings over two years.

When comparing outcomes, open dialogue patients diagnosed with schizophrenia seem to recover better from their crises. Seventy-one per cent of the comparison group of patients had at least one relapse, whereas only 24% of the open dialogue group suffered a relapse. Only 17% of the open dialogue patients had at least occasional mild symptoms, compared with 50% in the comparison group. As many as 81% had returned to full employment, compared with only 43% in the comparison group.

The results with open dialogue patients remained positive at the five-year follow-up (Seikkula et al., 2006). Only 29% of open dialogue patients experienced one or more relapses during the five-year follow-up. At the five-year follow-up interview, 82% of open dialogue patients had no residual psychotic symptoms. Employment status was better than in any other outcome study, with 86% of the open dialogue patients returning to their studies, work, or active job seeking.

Because of the extraordinary outcomes in first-episode psychosis, some critics believed that the results could not have been that good (Friis, Larsen, & Melle, 2003). In order to see if the results had remained consistent, further research was conducted to include the first-episode psychotic patients who were treated between 2003 and 2005 (Seikkula, Alakare, & Aaltonen, 2011). In this study the very same outcomes were verified: 84% of the patients returned to full employment or studies. There was a change in the population of psychotic patients in that the mean age had fallen to around twenty years compared to twenty-six in the 1990s. This might be related to the notion that the duration of untreated psychosis (DUP) was now approximately only three weeks compared to three and a half months in the 1990s. The incidence of schizophrenia patients had declined to three new schizophrenia patients per 100,000 inhabitants. The decline is dramatic since in the mid 1980s the incidence was thirty-three new schizophrenia patients per 100,000 inhabitants (Aaltonen, Seikkula, & Lehtinen, 2011). When the group of psychotic patients is younger, it could mean that there are no longer so many psychotic patients.

Conclusions and reflections

The results show a remarkable change in the prognosis for severe mental illness. As one well-known professor of psychiatry noted in a personal communication, "we have not previously seen any of these kinds of results with psychosis". This suggests that our approach to psychiatric crises should change. We are used to thinking of psychosis as a sign of schizophrenia and schizophrenia as a relatively stable state that affects the patient throughout his or her entire life. For instance, a third of the patients with schizophrenia are said to need ongoing treatment, a third will need intermittent treatment, and a third will fully recover and actively work. In the few long-term follow-up studies of first-time psychotic patients treated by traditional methods, after five years more than a half, often nearer 60%, are said to be living on a disability pension (Lenior, Dingemans, Linszen, de Haan, & Schene, 2001; Svedberg, Mesterton, & Cullberg, 2001). The positive outcomes using the open dialogue approach could indicate that psychosis no longer needs to be seen as a sign of a long-term illness but can be viewed as one way of dealing with a crisis, and when this crisis is resolved, most people are capable of returning to an active life. In addition, given that so few patients actually need neuroleptic drugs, we could ask whether our understanding of the underlying problem needs to change. Instead of seeing psychotic crises or schizophrenia as a lifelong illness, the open dialogue approach in Western Lapland has taught us that psychotic behaviour is one way to live through a crisis. Thereafter, the large majority of patients return to an active social life, are no longer dependent on the treatment system or on medication, as they might have been previously, or which they could continue to be where this approach is not adopted.

New ways of thinking about psychoses have emerged through the introduction of open dialogues. Does this mean that we should rethink the way psychiatric services are organised? Instead of focusing primarily on controlling the symptoms and removing them as rapidly as possible, attention should be directed at organising meetings for all those involved, including family members and other relevant individuals from the personal, social, and professional networks. In these meetings, we should then be more interested in generating dialogues by paying close attention to what family members are saying rather than planning interventions aimed at effecting change in the patient or the family. This would mean that the training of professionals should be restructured to promote not only an understanding of medical interventions, but also an active reflection on the philosophy of human experience. This would lead to an emphasis on the art of generating dialogue and listening to people instead of dominating the therapeutic process.

References

Aaltonen, J., Seikkula, J., & Lehtinen, K. (2011). The comprehensive open dialogue approach in Western Lapland. I: The incidence of non-affective psychosis and prodromal states. *Psychosis, 3*: 179–191.

Alanen, Y. (1997). *Schizophrenia. Its Origins and Need-Adapted-Treatment.* London: Karnac.

Alanen, Y. (2009). Toward a more humanistic psychiatry. Development of need adapted approach of treatment of schizophrenia group psychosis. *Psychosis, 1*: 156–166. DOI: 10.1080/17522430902795667.

Alanen, Y., Lehtinen, K., Räkköläinen, V., & Aaltonen, J. (1991). Need-adapted treatment of new schizophrenic patients: experiences and results of the Turku Project. *Acta Psychiatrica Scandinavica, 83*: 363–372.

Andersen, T. (1995). Reflecting processes. Acts of informing and forming. In: S. Friedman (Ed.), *The Reflective Team in Action* (pp. 11–37). New York: Guilford Press.

Bakhtin, M. (1984). *Problems of Dostojevskij's Poetics: Theory and History of Literature (Vol. 8).* Manchester: Manchester University Press.

Friis, S., Larsen, T. K., & Melle, I. (2003). Terapi ved psykoses. *Tidsskr Nor Laegeforen, 123*: 1393.

Gergen, K. (1994). *Realities and Relationships. Soundings in Social Construction.* Cambridge, MA: Harvard University Press.

Gergen, K. (1999). *An Invitation to Social Construction.* London: Sage.

Haarakangas, K. (1997). Hoitokokouksen äänet [The voices in treatment meeting. A dialogical analysis of the treatment meeting conversations in family-centred psychiatric treatment process in regard to the team activity]. *Jyväskylä Studies in Education, Psychology and Social Research, 130*: 119–126.

Keränen, J. (1992). The choice between outpatient and inpatient treatment in a family centred psychiatric treatment system. *Jyväskylä Studies in Education, Psychology and Social Research, 93*: 124–129.

Lenior, M., Dingemans, P., Linszen, D., de Haan, L., & Schene, A. (2001). Social functioning and the course of early-onset schizophrenia: five-year follow-up of a psychosocial intervention. *British Journal of Psychiatry*, *179*: 53–58.

Seikkula, J. (1991). Family-hospital boundary system in the social network. *Jyväskylä Studies in Education, Psychology and Social Research*, *80*: 227–232.

Seikkula, J. (1994). When the boundary opens: family and hospital in co-evolution. *Journal of Family Therapy*, *16*: 401–414.

Seikkula, J., & Arnkil, T. E. (2006). *Dialogical Meetings in Social Networks*. London: Karnac.

Seikkula, J., Alakare, B., & Aaltonen, J. (2011). The comprehensive open-dialogue approach in Western Lapland. II: Long-term stability of acute psychosis outcomes in advanced community care. *Psychosis*, *3*: 192–204.

Seikkula, J., Aaltonen, J., Alakare, B., Haarakangas, K., Keränen, J., & Lehtinen, K. (2006). Five-year experience of first-episode non-affective psychosis in open dialogue approach: treatment principles, follow-up outcomes, and two case studies. *Psychotherapy Research*, *16*: 214–228.

Seikkula, J., Alakare, B., Aaltonen, J., Holma, J., Rasinkangas, A., & Lehtinen, V. (2003). Open dialogue approach: treatment principles and preliminary results of a two-year follow-up on first episode schizophrenia. *Ethical Human Sciences and Services*, *5*: 163–182.

Shotter, J. (1993a). *Conversational Realities. Constructing Life Through Language*. London: Sage.

Shotter, J. (1993b). *Cultural Politics of Everyday Life*. Buckingham: Open University Press.

Svedberg, B., Mesterton, A., & Cullberg, J. (2001). First-episode non-affective psychosis in a total urban population: a 5-year follow-up. *Social Psychiatry*, *36*: 332–337.

Voloshinov, V. (1996). *Marxism and the Philosophy of Language*. Cambridge, MA: Harvard University Press.

CHAPTER EIGHT

Narrative psychiatry

SuEllen Hamkins

N arrative psychiatry brings together narrative and biological understandings of human suffering and wellbeing. It relishes discovering untold but inspiring stories of a person's resilience and skill in resisting mental health challenges while exposing and deconstructing discourses that fuel problems. It examines what the doctor's kit of psychiatry has to offer in light of the values and preferences of the person seeking consultation, authorising the patient as the arbiter of what is helpful and what is not.

Narrative psychiatry, as I theorise and practise it, arises from the confluence of several streams of inspiration in my life. Postmodern philosophy (Foucault, 1979) and feminist theory (Gilligan, 1982; Morgan, 1970) inspired me early on to discern and unpack operations of power in society. I studied medicine with the intention of becoming a doctor who could selectively draw from bio-medical discourses while resisting their hegemony, with hopes of attending more empathically to my patients (Lewis, 2011). Narrative psychotherapy (Freedman & Combs, 1996; Freeman, Epston, & Lobovits, 1997; Maisel, Epston, & Borden, 2004; White, 1989, 1995, 1997, 2000, 2004, 2007; White & Epston, 1990) gave me a playground of ideas, a workshop full of therapeutic tools, and a community of colleagues. These influences led me to practise what I call narrative psychiatry (Hamkins, 2004, 2010), which brings together the understanding that we experience our lives and identities through stories, that meaning is socially created, that we can interrogate the discourses that influence us, that we are embodied creatures beholden to the resplendence and vulnerabilities of biology, and, finally, that when these ideas are gracefully combined in com-passionate practice, tremendous healing is possible.

In this chapter, I present the key ideas and practices of narrative psychiatry through telling the story of my work with Addie Mackie-wicz, focusing on the first two years that we worked together. While the practices of narrative psychiatry often lead to a rapid resolution of problems, in sharing Addie's story I am illustrating how a narrative approach can be particularly helpful when problems are complex and tenacious.

"I want my mind to stop obsessing about scary things," Addie said to me at our first meeting when I asked her what her hopes were for our consultation. Addie was then sixteen years old, with dark brown hair, blue eyes, an athletic build, and a demeanour that was both polite and guarded. She was in eleventh grade at a small, local, public high school.

When the three of them arrived at my sunny office that November, the love and care that Addie's parents, Tim and Connie, felt for her was palpable, as well as worry and confusion about what could possi-bly be so troubling to their attractive, smart, successful daughter. Addie was a star athlete in basketball, an honours student, and had a lot of friends. "We see Addie acting well but saying she isn't feeling well," they said. They told a story of how Addie was developing debil-itating anxiety, leading her to miss many days of school.

What might narrative psychiatry offer Addie?

Narrative psychiatry has five key elements. My core priority as a narrative psychiatrist was to form a connection with Addie that respected who she was and where she was emotionally. In this, I hoped to create a collaborative therapeutic alliance in which she felt seen and heard and felt. Second, I wanted to hear and strengthen the story of who Addie was without the problem, and what her vision was for her life. Third, I wanted to hear her experience of the problem and come to a common understanding of the nature of the prob-lem, with attention to the cultural discourses that were affecting her experience of the problem. Fourth, I wished to determine the ways, however small, that she was succeeding in mitigating the problem's effect on her life. My hope was to actively develop and extend this story of success with further detail, additional examples over time, connection with important people in her life, and opportunities to share and retell it. Finally, in collaboration with Addie and her parents, I wanted to consider what next steps they might take and what psychiatric resources, such as medicine and psychotherapy, might be helpful.

In the light of these considerations, one of my first questions to Tim and Connie was, "What do you love about Addie?" My intentions were three-fold: to further cultivate the story of Addie's identity separate from the problem, to nurture Addie's experience of her parents' love, and to foster Addie's trust that I could see these things.

"She's a great kid," they said promptly. "She has a good sense of humour. She's good with her older brother. She works hard and seems to enjoy things."

Addie readily told me she was a good student who loved psychology, sociology, and English. I was struck by the love and care within which she was held by her family, and within which she held them. Neither she nor her parents identified any troubling life stressors and she had never experienced trauma or abuse.

Working narratively, I am always seeking to understand and deconstruct the influence of wider cultural discourses of privilege and oppression on a person's life and identity. For Addie, these discourses were predominantly, but not wholly, beneficial. She was a cherished member of her local community, many of whom shared her Polish-American ethnicity, including me. The local community embraced a range of discourses on race, gender, gay rights, and other aspects of identity that might prove relevant to Addie. The wider national culture largely celebrated the equal worth of girls and boys, but it put particular pressure on girls to achieve faultless standards of appearance and performance, discourses that were affecting Addie.

When I met with Addie alone, she told me that throughout every day, she felt and thought that her life was not real and she felt separated from herself. This experience of feeling unreal and feeling that there was something terribly wrong with her terrified her. The effect of this problem of "unreality" was that she felt consumed by obsessive worries that she might be insane. It took great effort to sit through a class at school due to the terror she felt, and Addie said she often would need to leave class to go to see Mrs Sanderson, the school nurse who had been her main emotional support in school since seventh grade. It helped her momentarily when people told her, "This is real," but it was disruptive to repeatedly ask for reassurance. She also felt that she had to do her homework "perfectly". Rarely, she thought she heard a voice call her name when no one was there. She had an uncle, her mother's brother, who was living with schizophrenia, and she was afraid she, too, had serious mental health problems. She noted that many friends and teachers did not understand how tormented she felt, and this led her to feel isolated. She wanted to feel better, but did not know what might help her.

Sitting with Addie, I was struck by her anguish and her terror. From that first appointment and throughout our treatment, in creating a connection with Addie I sought to be attuned to both her experiences of suffering as well as her experiences of wellbeing. She needed to know that I "got it" about how bad she felt, especially since a key aspect of her suffering was how alone she felt in it. At the same time, to feel connected with me, she needed to know that I saw her as more than her symptoms, that I could see that she was a gifted, feisty young woman with a droll sense of humour and a commitment to helping others.

In coming to understand the nature of a problem, in narrative psychiatry I am guided by the idea that the problem is separate from the person's identity. Externalising the problem in this way helps to circumscribe and characterise it, and permits us to compare the effects of the problem with the person's own hopes and intentions. Together, Addie and I reflected on what the problem was like for her and how we could describe it, seeking names for the components of the problem that were near to Addie's experience and that she felt comfortable using. In our initial meetings, we came to understand the problem as unwanted obsessive negative thoughts, perfectionism manifest as compulsions of redoing her homework until it was perfect, severe anxiety, illusions of hearing her name, but not frank hallucinations, and a feeling of unreality, but not an actual loss of touch with reality. We also discussed diagnostic considerations. Despite the hegemony of *DSM's* (*Diagnostic and Statistical Manual*, American Psychiatric Association, 1994) diagnostic discourses in psychiatry, any diagnosis can be deconstructed (White, 1995). We can ask: "What is helpful about using this diagnosis to describe your experience? What don't you like about using this diagnosis?" Addie felt that understanding her problems as a form of obsessive–compulsive disorder honoured their severity and also gave her hope that she was not insane. We held these understandings lightly, with awareness that the full picture of what Addie was facing might still be emerging.

Another key practice in narrative psychiatry is developing stories of success in mitigating a problem. With Addie, from the first appointment, we developed the narrative of how she was succeeding in constraining the effects of the problem by reaching out for support from her teachers, the principal, and Mrs Sanderson, touching base with them between classes to help her maintain a positive focus. She wrote down quotes from them, such as "Things will get better", and used these to help herself get through difficult days. She said at our first meeting, "If I wasn't at Anderson High, I'd be in the hospital." She saw her friends, was connected with her parents, and met with her psychotherapist twice a week. Despite the pervasiveness of the problem, she was still prioritising what was most important to her: her education, her family, and her friends. Honouring this story of her success supported Addie's awareness of who she was separate from the problem and offered hope and direction for reducing the influence of the problem in her life.

In addition to attending to developing healing narratives, in practising narrative psychiatry I collaborate with my patients in considering whether additional psychiatric resources, such as medication or particular psychotherapy approaches, might be useful for them. One resource that Addie and her parents thought could be helpful was cognitive–behavioural therapy. I supported her efforts to use the CBT skills she was learning with her psychotherapist, such as bringing forward positive thoughts such as *I am not insane* and *I know this is my life*, and resisting acting on compulsive urges to ask for reassurance. She said that these efforts brought her a "nanosecond of feeling sane."

None the less, terror and anguish still dominated her days. What other psychiatric resources might be helpful for her? Perhaps medicine would be useful.

In addition to attending to the power of narrative in shaping people's lives, narrative psychiatry also attends to the influence of biological factors. When I speak of biology, I am speaking about the physical aspects of living in a body—things like doing yoga, drinking a glass of wine, suffering a concussion, taking a pill, or synthesising neurotransmitters. Biology has direct effects that are not mediated by language. At the same time, the stories we tell about biology also influence us. For example, what we experience when we take medicine is influenced by the direct biological effect of the medicine and by what it means to us, the story we tell about it. We are both biological and narrative creatures. As a narrative psychiatrist, I seek to help those consulting with me to evaluate the helpfulness of a variety of resources that have both biological and narrative effects, such as exercise, vitamins, medicine, mindfulness practices, and getting enough sleep.

In discussing medicine with Addie and her parents, I held in awareness many different psychopharmacologic discourses that were influencing us. Since pharmaceutical companies are interested in expanding the indications for prescribing their drugs, they promote a neurobiological understanding of emotional challenges, and currently this perspective enjoys a wide following in the medical profession and among the public (Carlat, 2010). Another discourse criticises this tendency to see complex human problems as a "chemical imbalance" and focuses on the lack of long-term efficacy of most psychiatric drugs (Whittaker, 2010). I am not in favour of understanding complex human problems as a "chemical imbalance" best solved by drugs, but when I listen carefully to those who consult with me, many of them find that psychotropic medicines are an invaluable resource that help relieve their suffering—similar to how many of us feel about novo-caine when we have a cavity filled. In addition, I have seen the relief that many people feel when I offer the possibility that, rather than being inexplicable or evidence of a failure of character, their troubles could be understood as due to neurochemical causes, for which they feel less personally culpable. Furthermore, I find some psychological explanations of why someone feels terrible and cannot function to be more pejorative and damaging to identity than biological ones.

Addie was seeking relief from terror and anguish. She wanted to try a new medicine that might help with her anxiety and obsessive negative thoughts and I wished to honour her preferences. Her parents were willing but unenthusiastic. They left with a prescription for a very small dose of citalopram.

Every medicine has the potential for both beneficial and harmful effects and the choice of whether to use a medicine rests on whether the benefits, according to the patient, outweigh the "side effects".

Sometimes, negative effects are negligible, but frequently they are problematic. The positive and negative effects of medicines include not only helpful or discomforting physical and psychological experiences, but also the impact of taking a medicine on the story of the patient's identity.

Addie tried the citalopram, but did not like it because it seemed to make the problem of the unreality worse. She elected to try a different medicine and, while it seemed to help reduce the negative thoughts, it caused dizziness. After three meetings, Addie wanted a "break from all psychological treatment" and "did not want to use medicine to solve an emotional problem." We said good-bye.

Six months later, in July, Addie returned. She said she was feeling "a hundred times worse" than she had before. She had initially felt better after stopping treatment, but then her experiences of anxiety and unreality had worsened, and were now accompanied by severe feelings of what she named depression and continual thoughts of suicide. She pointed to the small chest in my office. "My mind tells me that that is full of dead babies. I feel as if my parents are not really my parents, my room is not really my room." When I asked her what the effect was on her of this, she said, "I am feeling miserable." She noted she would not kill herself because she did not want to hurt her parents. No, she was not hearing voices or experiencing paranoia, but she did feel as if she was losing her mind. She had found a new psychotherapist she liked and she also wanted to consult with me. Years later, in reflecting on this time, Addie conveyed that key considerations in her desire to consult with me again was that she felt that I really listened to her, that I was respectful, compassionate, and collaborative, and that I helped her to feel a sense of hope that recovery would be possible for her.

Addie was newly committed to working with me to ameliorate her suffering, but she was doubtful that we could be effective. Addie's anxiety bombarded her with thoughts that she would never have a family or a job and that everything was unreal, while the depression brought her constant thoughts that she would be "better off dead". One challenge we faced was that the negative conclusions of the thoughts seemed to Addie to be accurate. These are complicated moments in narrative psychiatry, when a person insists that the problem's perspective on things is her own, especially when the person's life is in danger. Since narrative psychiatry prioritises what the patient values over what the psychiatrist values and seeks to create collaborative therapeutic relationships in which power disparities are minimised, there is an inherent tension in suggesting that there might be a preferable narrative to the one a person espouses. However, I draw guidance from those who have recovered from problems such as depression or anorexia, who are clear that such problems can separate a person from what would be valued in the absence of the problem. Therefore, I do not accept the problem's version of a person's prospects as the sole version, even if an alternative story is nowhere to be seen. Rather, gentle, persistent, creative means are used to discover untold stories that are free from the influence of the problem. The imposition of the psychiatrist's perspective is in suggesting that there *is* another story; *what* that story is flows from the person's values.

In addition, I am clear with my patients that my personal value is to stand on the side of life, and I let them know that if I have grounds to believe that they are at imminent risk of life-threatening actions, I will take steps to protect them. This transparency helps preserve the patient's authority as much as possible. In the first years of her treatment with me, Addie's urges to take her life were a constant worry for me and I checked in with her about them at every appointment, but her desire not to hurt her family always prevailed.

In co-creating an alternative narrative not dominated by hopelessness, Addie and I began by identifying neutral thoughts and times she felt connected to reality. Early on, she was able to identify two or three minutes several times a day when she felt a sense of wellbeing and reality, such as when she was working with children at the pre-school where she volunteered. We also discussed her successes in living her life according to what she cared most about, despite the problem, notably completing her high school courses and applying to college.

We also sought to externalise and name negative thoughts as such, with the intention of circumscribing them and making them feel less pervasive and more open to question. Addie tried countering the negative thoughts with positive ones, but felt stymied by how "true" the negative thoughts felt, thoughts such as "you're just going to die anyway, so you might as well kill yourself."

To help weaken the influence of problems and to inspire patients in their efforts to resist them, in narrative psychiatry we seek not only to counter, but also to "unpack" problems to reveal how they operate and the values on which they are based. This allows us to compare the kind of life the problem promotes with the life that the patient wants to be living. One way of doing this is to use the therapeutic strategy of personifying the problem, that is, to query the problem as if it were a person. So, we had conversations that went along the following lines.

I asked Addie, "What would you say the goals of the negative thoughts are for your life?"

"To be as pathetic as possible," she blurted out. She was sitting in a blue armchair in my office on a bright January day.

"And what are your own goals for your life?"

"To live my life."

"You want to live your life. And what are the important parts of living your life?"

"Doing activities that I enjoy. Having friends—anything fun with friends."

"OK," I said, taking notes. "Having fun with friends."

"And going to St Michaels for college, and doing well so that I can transfer to a better college."

"And your hope of going to St Michaels and transferring to a better college," I asked, "is that linked with a vision you have for your life?"

"I want to be a kindergarten teacher, and get married," Addie said.

We spent some time fleshing out this vision of her life, and then I said, "So those are your goals. And you said that the thoughts' goal for you is, 'To be as pathetic as possible.' What does that say about the intentions of the thoughts for your life?"

"The thoughts say, 'We know best. We don't want you to be happy because you are going to die anyway.'"

"The thoughts don't want you to be happy. And would your own goal be to be happy?"

"Yes, but the thoughts want me to face reality. Everything is pointless because you're going to die in the end."

"The thoughts claim that they want you to face reality, but the main aspect of reality they want you to focus on is dying, is that right?" Addie nodded. "With the goal of making you feel pathetic and unhappy?" Addie nodded again. "And let's see how that compares with your own goals," I said, and read the list we had created, as Addie listened intently. I made a copy of her list of goals to take with her.

The next week, Addie came in and said, "I'm not thinking about death so much. I'm just living my life." She had made plans with friends. "It's fun to do things with people my own age." Since our conversation the week before, it had been easier for her to counter the negative thoughts. "I shrank its power," she said. She was living a more active and socially engaged life, and the depression was reduced.

Meaning is socially created and stories are strengthened by being told and retold by important figures in a person's life. If they are told only in the doctor's office, new stories are vulnerable to being over-shadowed by the old, problem-dominated story back home. I frequently invited in Addie's parents, and, later, her brother and her friends, helping her share the new narratives she was developing and soliciting from her loved ones narratives of what they valued about Addie as a person and appreciated about her efforts to alleviate the problems she was facing. I was, likewise, in regular contact with other helping professionals in her life. We continued to deconstruct the operations of the negative thoughts and identify and celebrate Addie's successes in pursuing the life she wanted to be living. In addition, we continued to use CBT and we tried a variety of psychotropic medications.

Over the ensuing months, from mere "nanoseconds", she noticed times free of the problem "1/2 of 1%" of the time, then 2% of the time, then 5%, and one day she came in saying, "The thoughts about death aren't really there". Her family, teachers, and therapist noted that her mood was better and she seemed noticeably more energised.

Then Mrs Sanderson, her beloved school nurse, died from an aggressive cancer. The negative thoughts returned with intensity, and when I asked Addie how often they were present she said, "195.734% of the time". The thoughts were telling her "Just kill yourself, people will get over it. There's no difference between dying at seventeen or when you are older. You can't do college, it's pointless. It's a false hope to think you might get better." She missed many days of school and spent her evenings on her computer reading about suicide.

In my work with Addie at that time, I focused first on her safety.

"What is helping you not take your life?" I asked.

"The one thing that stops me is the pain it would bring my parents."

"Not wanting them to be in pain, would that be a sign of your love for them?"

"Yes, they are my best friends."

I strengthened this story by asking Addie more about the love she felt for her parents and they for her, with questions such as: "What kinds of loving things do you and your parents do for one another? What do you think it means to your parents that you love them so much? What helps you feel connected with your parents when you are apart?"

It was clear to me that while a medication adjustment might be helpful, medicine alone would not eliminate the problem. Over the following months, I focused on strengthening the narratives that brought Addie comfort and hope and taking apart those that fuelled the problem.

I invited Addie to remember what Mrs Sanderson meant to her and what she meant to Mrs Sanderson, hoping to keep the story of their mutual appreciation alive for Addie as an emotional resource.

"What did it mean to you, to have Mrs Sanderson there at school?"

"I went to her office every day. She would let me stay as long as I wanted."

"How was that for you?"

"It meant everything to me. It made it possible to get through the day."

"What do you think that meant to her?"

"I don't know."

"What might it have meant to Mrs Sanderson, as a nurse, that going to her office made it possible for you to stay in school?"

"She would have liked that, to know she was helping me."

Although the depression was more powerful than ever, "an army of one thousand with steel plate armour and loaded guns" while she was "an army of one with paper plate armour and plastic knives," as she put it in a poem she wrote at that time, I persisted in my efforts to help Addie deconstruct the story the depressive thoughts were telling and to develop a compelling narrative of strength, hope and meaning.

"What is it that you hope for, for yourself?"

"Ordinary happiness."

We lingered here to speak about what ordinary happiness would look like, and then I asked, "And what are the negative thoughts' intentions for your life?"

"To make me miserable."

Naming the intentions of the depression for her life energised Addie in her determination to free herself from it, putting her in touch with what she called an "inner fierceness".

"And if that fierceness took a form, what might it look like?" I asked.

Addie thought for a moment, tilting her head to one side. "Simba," she said finally, the lion cub in the film *The Lion King*, who grew up to vanquish treachery and restore wellbeing to the kingdom.

"Tell me more about this Simba," I said. She described him as "a lion who can vanquish misery". He was a metaphor for her "bravery and spunkiness", while suicidal thoughts were the evil lion Scar and negative thoughts were vicious hyenas.

Over the ensuing months, when Addie felt as if she was being "trampled" by a stampede of negative thoughts, we developed the story of Addie's fierceness further, identifying her parents as the benevolent lion Mufasa and her knowledge about how to get out of danger as Zazu, the red-billed hornbill who gives the morning report on the state of the kingdom. In addition to staying connected to family and friends, this knowledge included drawing on the resources of family meetings, weekly sessions with me, intensive day treatment, CBT, and trials of new medications. In fits and starts, over the next months, her hopefulness returned and the depression and suicidal thoughts became less constant, but did not fully remit. Feelings of unreality persisted, and we focused on how to make them more bearable. She graduated from high school and started college.

The psychiatrist at her college was convinced that she was developing schizophrenia and told her so. While I seriously considered that possibility and sought consultation with experts who concluded that she had prodromal symptoms, I also held a wider lens that resisted narrow categorisation of the nature of the problems she faced, seeking instead to closely follow her experiences of what was challenging and what was helpful.

Addie is now twenty-one, about to start her senior year at college. Incrementally, over the five years we worked together, her symptoms steadily decreased to the point that depression and anxiety are now negligible. She has had no psychotic symptoms and is not taking antipsychotic medication. Feelings of unreality come and go, and Addie has refined her skills in managing them. She has found the "ordinary happiness" that she had sought, has begun student-teaching, and remains connected with her parents, other relatives, close friends, a wide circle of acquaintances, and professors. We see one another weekly for meetings in which we continue to deconstruct and dismantle problems, cultivate stories of her vision for her life, collaboratively consider the use of psychiatric resources, including medications, and enjoy humour and connection (Hamkins, 2014).

Addie offers the following reflection about our work together:

> There are three components of the type of therapy Dr Hamkins and I engage in that I believe helped the most. First, a teamwork mentality exists, so I have felt like I can be more honest with my opinions and I do not feel like demands are being directed at me with an agreement that I will follow the demands exactly. Second, confidentiality here is treated exactly as the definition states, which is seemingly basic, but never achieved with my previous mental health professionals. Lastly, issues faced and ideas discussed are both described so exactly that the lack of confusion eases the strain of dealing with such complex issues. Dr. Hamkins also does not over-simplify possible solutions, which gives me reassurance that the issues I am dealing with are not simple. Being hopeful while maintaining realistic expectations has been found to be a reliable sentiment for our work together. I do still experience symptoms now, and while negligible, they are proof that transformation does not occur overnight. Symptoms are now a part of my life, instead of my complete life. Family and friends are happier because I am happier.

In conclusion, narrative psychiatry combines narrative values and practices with psychiatric resources. In practising narrative psychiatry,

I value the incredible capacity of the human spirit to heal. I seek empathic attunement with those who consult with me. I assume that every person has skills they are using and effort they are putting forth to try to overcome their problems, even if those skills and efforts are not apparent to them or others. In my work, I seek to help people connect more fully with those who support them and with resources, such as medicines, that they find helpful. I strive to honour what each person gives value to, rather than imposing my own values. I seek to create collaborative therapeutic relationships in which power disparities are minimised. My core intention is to alleviate suffering and foster joy.

In my work, I have been sustained by local and international communities of narrative therapists and psychiatrists. I have found my work with Addie to be among the most meaningful of my career. It showed me that loving perseverance in applying narrative psychiatry can help pave the way for someone to experience long stretches of joy and peacefulness after years of unremitting torment.

References

American Psychiatric Association (1994). *Diagnostic and Statistical Manual-IV*. Washington, DC: American Psychiatric Press.

Carlat, D. (2010). *Unhinged: The Trouble with Psychiatry: A Doctor's Revelations about a Profession in Crisis*. New York: Free Press.

Foucault, M. (1979). *Discipline and Punish: The Birth of the Prison*. Prescott, AZ: Peregrine Books.

Freedman, J., & Combs, G. (1996). *Narrative Therapy: The Social Construction of Preferred Realities*. New York: W. W. Norton.

Freeman, J., Epston, D., & Lobovits, D. (1997). *Playful Approaches to Serious Problems*. New York: W. W. Norton.

Gilligan, C. (1982). *In a Different Voice*. Cambridge, MA: Harvard University Press.

Hamkins, S. (2004). Introducing narrative psychiatry: narrative approaches to initial psychiatric consultations. *International Journal of Narrative Therapy and Community Work, 1*: 5–17.

Hamkins, S. (2010). Bringing narrative practices to psychopharmacology. *International Journal of Narrative Therapy and Community Work, 1*: 56–71.

Hamkins, S. (2014). *The Art of Narrative Psychiatry: Stories of Strength and Meaning*. London: Oxford University Press.

Lewis, B. (2011). *Narrative Psychiatry*. Baltimore, MD: Johns Hopkins University Press.

Maisel, R., Epston, D., & Borden, A. (2004.) *Biting the Hand That Starves You*. New York: W. W. Norton.

Morgan, R. (Ed.) (1970). *Sisterhood is Powerful*. New York: Random House.

White, M. (1989). *Selected Papers*. Adelaide, Australia: Dulwich Centre.

White, M. (1995). *Re-Authoring Lives: Interviews and Essays*. Adelaide, Australia: Dulwich Centre.

White, M. (1997). Workshop. Family Institute of Cambridge, 15 March 1997.

White, M. (2000). Workshop. Family Institute of Cambridge, 14 September 2000.

White, M. (2004). Workshop. Family Institute of Cambridge, 13 March 2004.

White, M. (2007). *Maps of Narrative Practice*. New York: W. W. Norton.

White, M., & Epston, D. (1990). *Narrative Means to Therapeutic Ends*. New York: W. W. Norton.

Whittaker, R. (2010). *Anatomy of an Epidemic: Magic Bullets, Psychiatric Drugs, and the Astonishing Rise of Mental Illness in America*. New York: Crown.

CHAPTER NINE

Family needs, family solutions: developing family therapy in adult mental health services

Roger Stanbridge and Frank Burbach

Introduction

In this chapter, we consider the needs of families where a member is involved with mental health services and the roles that family therapists might play in shaping and delivering both routine and specialist services. In considering this we begin by focusing on families' experience of mental health services, the evidence base for family work, and the policy guidance. Although working in partnership with families is part of all national guidelines, feedback from families suggests that many mental health services have not, as yet, managed to achieve this routinely. We shall describe ways in which we have approached this in the county of Somerset and consider the implications for family therapists. We hope that our experiences will encourage the further development of systemic ideas and practice in other adult mental health services.

Family needs

When asked about their experiences, family members eloquently express the impact of mental health difficulties and their own practical and emotional needs. For example,

> At the time when my relative joined the service I felt completely lost. Here was a set of new experiences I could not have imagined. I needed to know the ropes, who was there to help and what was going on. I especially needed to believe in the professionals—that they understood my connection to this precious person now in their care. I needed to have confidence they knew how to help him recover and that they saw me as part of that recovery. (Family carer, quoted in Worthington & Rooney, 2010, p. 6)

Another family member writes,

> . . . We take the bulk of caring and the worry, we are the ones who cope in the night or who drive miles in the hope that he will attend his programme . . . How can you professionals think you care for someone who cannot articulate his needs? We are, or feel, totally excluded from your updates on his condition. It makes me angry that when we say something is wrong it takes a major incident for someone to listen to us. (Family carer, quoted in Shepherd, Murray, & Muijen, 1994, p. 50)

Research studies (Pinfold et al., 2004; Shepherd, Murray, & Muijen, 1994) and carers' organisations (Age Concern, 2007; Barnardo's, 2008; Rethink, 2003; The Schizophrenia Commission, 2012) have recommended ways in which mental health services can more effectively meet the needs of informal carers, including young carers, and families. Families have identified specific features that they would like from services: to be listened to, to be involved in planning their relative's care, and emotional and practical support, including respite care. In addition, they require information about diagnosis, treatment, services, benefits, and whom to contact in an emergency. They also request advice on ways to respond to their relative and express a wish to develop additional coping skills.

Evidence base for family work

There is now considerable evidence that family interventions are effective for a wide range of mental health difficulties (Stratton, 2011).

Reviews (e.g., Carr, 2009) report that family therapy is at least as effective as other psychological therapies for a range of conditions experienced by adults, including mood disorders, substance misuse, eating disorders, and anxiety disorders. The evidence is particularly strong in relation to family interventions in psychosis (Pharoah, Mari, Rathbone, & Wong, 2010).

This emerging evidence has led to the development of clinical guidelines recommending the use of family interventions for a range of conditions, including schizophrenia (National Institute for Clinical Excellence (NICE), 2002), anorexia nervosa (NICE, 2004a), and depression (NICE, 2004b). In addition to the recommendations for specific family interventions, NICE guidelines recommend the routine involvement of families in the package of care for a range of disorders. An Association of Family Therapy document (AFT, 2011) provides a summary of the NICE guidelines that recommend family/couple therapy as well as collaborative working with families, family members, partners, or carers. These recommendations are based on our increasing knowledge of the stress involved in caring for family members who experience serious and/or enduring mental health problems (Cuipers, 2005; Kuipers & Bebbington, 2005; Singleton et al., 2002).

Policy context

The evidence has also shaped a range of mental health and social care policies. Perhaps the most significant policy development was the establishment, in the National Service Framework (Department of Health (DoH), 1999), of a carer's right to an assessment of their own needs and their own care plan as part of the interventions provided to their relative using secondary mental health services. This meant that there was an expectation that mental health services would meet the needs of family members. The way in which these services should be developed was outlined in *Developing Services for Carers and Families of People with Mental Illness* (DoH, 2002).

Building on this, a cross-government initiative led by the Cabinet Office Social Exclusion Task Force argued that health and social care services should *Think Family* (2008). They proposed that adult and child services should combine around the needs of the whole family, build on family strengths, and provide support tailored to need. This systemically orientated policy proposed that there should be "No wrong door", so that, whichever service a family member approached, that service would consider the needs of all family members and help them access other services as appropriate.

Most recently, a guide to best practice in acute mental health care has identified six key elements (Table 9.1) required to achieve better collaboration and partnership with families and carers. "'The Triangle of Care' is a therapeutic alliance between service user, staff member, and carer that promotes safety, supports recovery, and sustains well-being" (Worthington & Rooney, 2010, p. 3). This initiative is being taken forward by the Carers Trust and other mental health charities, in conjunction with National Health Service (NHS) mental health trusts throughout England.

The challenge of implementing family-orientated services

Despite the evidence base for family interventions and the clear policy and guidelines regarding working in partnership with families, many mental health services have found it difficult to meet the needs of carers. In adult mental health services, the focus tends to be on the individual, both in terms of how presenting problems are formulated and the policies and procedures themselves. This can be understood in terms of both the wider culture and the health service context. In the health service setting, the relationship between professionals, especially doctors, and people using services ("patients") is predicated on the individual's right to confidentiality. The default position,

Table 9.1. The triangle of care: six key elements.

1. Carers and the essential role they play are identified at first contact or as soon as possible thereafter.

2. Staff are "carer aware" and trained in carer engagement strategies.

3. Policy and practice protocols relating to confidentiality and information sharing are in place

4. Defined post(s) responsible for carers are in place.

5. A carer induction to the service and staff is available, with a relevant range of information across the acute care pathway.

6. A range of carer support services is available.

therefore, is to provide assessment and treatment for the "autono-mous" adult and to have a strong boundary around this professional relationship. It is not surprising, thus, that in this context many people would find it challenging to acknowledge the rights of family members as well and to involve relatives as equally important members of this professional relationship.

Furthermore, it is still the case that, in spite of evidence and policy supporting family work, most mental health professionals do not develop skills in working with families as part of their basic training (Fadden, 2006; Stacey & Rayner, 2008). It is also noteworthy that many of the mental health professionals who subsequently undertake train-ing in working with families find it difficult to do this in practice. The main reasons given for this are related to the unsupportive service context, including lack of management support, lack of supervision, and difficulty in prioritising family work due to other workload demands (Brooker, 2001; Fadden, 1997). Further evidence of the lack of a "family" culture in adult mental health services is the small number of designated family therapy posts and the relatively small proportion of adult mental health staff who pursue training in systemic therapy. The emphasis on meeting carers' needs accompany-ing the introduction of the National Service Framework has been a challenge to implement in this individually based culture, and mental health trusts have found it difficult to meet their targets in this area.

Given this dominant discourse, the challenge for systemic thinkers is to take every opportunity to develop an alternative narrative to enable a more family-inclusive practice to take hold. Different contexts will present different opportunities for taking this forward. In the next section, we explore some of the ways this might be progressed, with examples from work we have carried out in Somerset.

Enabling more family-inclusive services

Linking with others

Family therapists are skilled in creating therapeutic alliances with all parts of the family system and recognising that the family system is also a part of wider systems. Our skills at connecting and enabling people to link empathically with each other are also the core skills which can be drawn on to change the focus of services. Linking with family and carer representatives and like-minded colleagues, both family-orientated clinicians and managers concerned about quality and targets, is one of the most effective ways of bringing about organisational change. Individuals who leave their "tight corners" can together create a bulwark from which to develop family work further.

An example of this on a national level is the "Triangle of Care" initiative in which a partnership between a carer's organisation and the Department of Health has resulted in the publication of best practice guidelines. The subsequent development of a national and regional structure has created a forum for mutual support, problem solving, and sharing of ideas and resources to create more family-inclusive mental health services. The wide and representative membership means that it has more chance of success than previous "top-down" Department of Health initiatives.

In Somerset, an inquiry into a tragic death recommended that, in line with many previous national inquiries, mental health services should work more closely with relatives, particularly regarding the sharing of information about risk. As a result, we were asked by the Trust's Director of Operations to develop a strategy to enhance our working partnerships with families and carers. This provided an opportunity to consult widely and bring together interested parties from across the Trust. Following the endorsement of this by the Trust board in 2002, a steering group was established to encourage all staff to respond to the needs of families and carers (Stanbridge & Burbach, 2004; 2007a).

We had been concerned that the employment of a small team of Carers Assessment Workers might lead to other staff seeing working with families as a separate role, which they could leave to the new team. Bringing together carers' workers and carer representatives, clinicians, and managers enabled the development of best practice guidelines, for example, on confidentiality and information sharing, and team operational policies. This ensured that all staff saw working with families, including identifying the needs of children involved, as a core part of their role. The strategy was revised and updated in 2010 following a consultation process with families and carers using our services. The involvement of representatives from non-statutory organisations, such as Rethink and The Alzheimer's Association, provided both support and encouragement for the Trust in developing services in this direction.

Training and service development

In Somerset, as in other areas, staff had received little prior training in family work and reported a lack of confidence and skills to hold meetings with families (Stanbridge & Burbach, 2007a). We have developed a range of training initiatives to address this.

In order to meet the needs of all families to work in partnership with the person using services and mental health staff, we have developed a three-day training package that we are systematically providing to all teams within the Trust (Stanbridge, Burbach, & Leftwich, 2009, Stanbridge, Burbach, Rapsey, Leftwich, & McIver, 2013). This course in family-inclusive ways of working is designed to increase staff understanding of families' needs and to develop a positive attitude towards partnership working. The main aim, however, is to develop family-inclusive team processes and practices and to develop confidence and the basic skills to hold an initial meeting with families as part of the assessment/admission process.

In order to provide a specialist, Trust-wide, family intervention in psychosis service, we have also developed a one-year accredited course in which we have trained four teams (Burbach & Stanbridge, 1998, 2006). In this course we focus on skills training and the development of the family intervention in psychosis service. Although this course also has a considerable academic component, the three course assignments are closely linked with clinical practice (Burbach, Donnelly, & Stanbridge, 2002). These courses are complementary service and workforce development initiatives (Burbach & Stanbridge, 2008) that are part of Trust-wide strategies. We have found that a team training approach is the most effective way of achieving and sustaining change, as it ensures that a critical mass of staff can support each other in taking forward new ideas and practices (Bailey, Burbach, & Lea, 2003).

In addition, we provide a two-day introduction to systemic therapy aimed at staff who might be considering joining a family therapy clinic, or are regular referrers to family therapy services. This short course introduces systemic theory and practice and, although it includes clinical examples and experiential work, it is not designed to equip people with clinical skills.

We are aware of other initiatives designed to provide training to broad groups of staff with the aim of developing family-based approaches. In Germany, Schweitzer and colleagues (Haun, Kordy, Ochs, Zwack, & Schweitzer, 2013) have developed an eighteen-day multi-disciplinary training course to establish systemic interventions as routine practice on six psychiatric wards. In Australia, the Bouverie Centre, a systemic therapy training institute, delivered a state-wide three-day training programme to encourage family-sensitive practice (Farhall, 2000). In our West Midlands, the Meriden Project has devised a five-day training programme in behavioural family interventions for psychosis for mental health staff across the region (Fadden, 2006). Subsequently, this training has become more widespread and has been supplemented by short training packages on working with carers.

It is interesting to note that none of these initiatives has found that training alone automatically leads to increased meetings with families. Although there are a number of reasons for this, the solutions have often focused around providing ongoing supervision and creating supportive service structures. Similarly, our experience has highlighted the importance of focusing on implementation of training in practice and the maintenance of cultural change in services. There is an emerging consensus about the key factors which are required to develop sustainable family interventions services and which facilitate practice following training (Burbach, Fadden, & Smith, 2010; Froggatt, Fadden, Johnson, Leggatt, & Shankar, 2007; Table 9.2).

Family-focused services in Somerset

A comprehensive mental health service would be in a position to meet a range of family needs. Families' needs may vary along a continuum. At one end, there might be a need to talk about their experiences and have them respectfully acknowledged, as well as developing problem-solving skills and coping strategies. At the other end, these needs might extend to an interest in more complex considerations about the nature of family relationships and interactions, in the context of multi-generational family history, culture, and social position (Pearson, Burbach, & Stanbridge, 2007).

We would argue that a range of family-based approaches is required and, in Somerset, family therapists play major roles in three complementary services. Our contribution has been to develop a

Table 9.2.   Recommendations to develop sustainable Family Interventions services

---

- Ensure support for the programme of training and service development at all levels of the organisation, including the highest level of management and lead professionals.
- Agree a service development strategy to ensure an appropriate service context and the availability of sufficient resources to enable practice post training (protected time, smaller case loads, and practical support for clinicians).
- Establish robust supervision structures to ensure post-training expert clinical supervision is available.
- Use a team training approach or ensure that there is a local critical mass of trained practitioners who can support one another.
- Involve families/carers in the training programme and in the design and governance of the service.
- Appoint local service leads/champions who are responsible for the development and maintenance of the service.
- Use audit and ongoing update training to maintain quality once the service is established.
- Ensure that the service remains valued by managers and commissioners through the provision of reports, testimonials, publications, etc.

---

specialist family interventions in psychosis service to complement our existing systemic psychotherapy services, as well as a Family Liaison Service to meet the broader needs of families on entry to the mental health services.

Systemic psychotherapy is provided as one of the core approaches within the psychological therapies' service. Maintaining specialist family services requires appropriate leadership and robust supervision arrangements. Each family therapy clinic is led by a qualified, UKCP registered family therapist. A Trust-wide Systemic Psychotherapy Forum provides a quarterly opportunity to present cases, updates on clinical theory and practice, develop research/audit projects, agree best practice, policies, and procedures, and provide mutual support.

Our other specialist service reflects the strong evidence base for family work where there is psychosis. We have developed a model that integrates psycho-educational, cognitive–behavioural approaches with systemic therapy. We have successfully provided our one-year course in each of our four service areas and have established a team in each. Each team comprises six to eight staff from a range of disciplines and parts of the service. Each team member has management agreement to provide a minimum of half a day per week to the family interventions service. This structure ensures that the service is linked with the local inpatient and community teams, which enables appropriate referrals and continuity of care. In order to maintain the focus and quality of the service, the team works in pairs and meets for monthly supervision. In addition, all team members attend a study day on a quarterly basis. Further details of the service are described in Burbach and Stanbridge (2009) and Stanbridge and Burbach (2007b). Thus, both specialist services have Trust-wide, as well as team-based, supervision and support.

Whereas some families will need specialist services, we have found that the majority will require information, involvement in their relatives' care, and support (Gore & Stanbridge, 2012). In keeping with the Trust Strategy to Enhance Working Partnerships with Families and Carers, and building on the three-day training programme, we have developed best practice guidelines which promote making contact with families within twenty-four hours of admission to an inpatient unit and holding a family meeting within seven days of the admission. In order to implement these guidelines, we have developed the Family Liaison Service (Stanbridge, 2012). In this service, a systemically trained therapist is employed one day a week on each of the six adult and older people's inpatient units to work alongside ward staff and to hold meetings with families as part of the assessment/admission process. A ward champion from the inpatient team has been identified on each ward to provide the necessary organisational support and maintain team awareness. The meetings provide an opportunity to share and exchange information with the families, giving them the opportunity to talk about their expectations and experiences leading up to the admission, and to discuss the support available to families/carers both during and after the admission, including a carer's assessment (Carter, 2011; Leftwich, Carter, McIver, & Stanbridge, 2011). These meetings provide a pathway for identifying both adult and young carers at an early stage and consideration of whether a referral to other family and carer services might be appropriate, that is, carers' assessment worker, "Young Carers" project, family therapy, or family interventions in psychosis services.

The impact of adult mental health problems on children is well documented (Aldridge & Becker, 2003; Cooklin, 2010) and family liaison meetings provide an opportunity to identify any children involved and to consider their needs (Social Care Institute for Excellence, 2011). We are also exploring with colleagues in the child and safeguarding teams how we might offer further support.

The involvement of systemically trained therapists on inpatient units has been welcomed by ward staff and has led to a substantial increase in the number of family meetings held as part of the assessment and admission process. In our experience, ward staff often feel more confident in holding meetings with families when working alongside systemic psychotherapists who have experience in handling family meetings and managing interactions. Teams often find it difficult to sustain this kind of development without the additional input from specially trained staff who have credible expertise and experience in family work. It has also raised staff appreciation of what is required to meet the range of family needs and led to an increase in referrals to specialist family services and for carer assessments. In addition, data on the service appears to show an association between having a family liaison meeting and an increase in contact between all professionals and family members during the course of an admission. Although a tentative finding, it is replicated across all wards for working age adults and older people and provides a strong indication that holding family liaison meetings is associated with improved involvement of families. For a description and evaluation of the Family Liaison Service, see Stanbridge, 2012.

In addition to bringing skills in understanding and managing family interactions to family meetings, having a systemic therapist working alongside ward staff facilitates a continuity and coherence of services. The same systemic therapists who previously provided the three-day training programme in family inclusive ways of working then go on to provide ongoing supervision and support to the ward teams. They are also involved in providing the specialist family services within the Trust and are, therefore, well placed to enable appropriate referrals to family therapy and family interventions services when required.

The role of the family therapist

In mental health services in the UK, most family therapy posts have been developed in order to provide a specialist psychological therapy service. Family therapists traditionally receive referrals either follow-ing an initial assessment by another professional, or later on in the care pathway. Like other psychological therapists, a systemic psychotherapist would meet a relatively small proportion of people referred to a mental health service. Family therapists working in this way clearly provide a valuable service for these particular families, but are vulnerable to being seen as an optional, non-essential service. We would argue that it is, therefore, essential for family therapists to consider how they might contribute to meeting the needs of all the families presenting to mental health services.

Although we have a small number of designated family therapist posts in Somerset, we also have a wider number of qualified family therapists working in other professions. This allows us to ensure that all specialist family therapy and family interventions teams include a qualified family therapist to provide clinical leadership. For all four of our family therapy posts in adult services (two full-time and two part-time), the job descriptions include the provision of specialist therapy as well as collaboration with mainstream services. The family therapists contribute to the teaching on all of the three training pro-grammes. They also consult to frontline teams regarding particular cases, including offering joint assessments. For three of the four family therapists, a significant part of their role is dedicated to working with particular inpatient units to provide the family liaison service.

These expanded roles allow family therapists to bring their knowl-edge and expertise to routine services to better inform team contact with families and carers. This can, in turn, maximise the value of specialist-trained staff both to families and to mental health trusts.

Reflections

While writing this chapter, we reflected on some of the key elements involved in successfully developing a range of family-based adult services.

In Somerset, family therapy clinics have existed for over thirty years (Pottle, 1984; Procter & Pieczora, 1992). However, these services have relied on the enthusiasm of individual clinicians. In the National Health Service in the 1990s, there was an increased focus on quality assurance (DoH, 1993) and our Trust management decided to focus on psychological therapies. Family therapy was, perhaps, the least under-stood, and perceived by some as expensive due to the team approach and specialist facilities (family therapy suites with audio-visual equip-ment). This resulted in an audit of family therapy clinics in Somerset in 1996 (Burbach, Stanbridge, & Chapman, 1997). Although, at the time, clinicians felt exposed by this process, in retrospect, we feel that this audit, which highlighted both good practice and identified areas for development, contributed to securing the place of family therapy in the Trust. Interestingly, this mirrored some of the issues which concerned family therapists at that time, such as the sense of belong-ing to an under-recognised school of therapy, not having a profes-sional structure or power base, or a consensus regarding an acceptable outcome measure for family work. There were also anxieties about the cost of a multi-disciplinary team approach and a sense that other ther-apies, which had a more extensive evidence base, were more highly valued. The situation now feels very different.

It was also at this time that Mental Health Trusts were being asked about their provision of family interventions in psychosis services (DoH, 1994). Being aware of the difficulties experienced following other training projects, we put forward a proposal to develop these services in Somerset drawing on both systemic and psycho-educational approaches. We worked with Trust managers to provide a course in all four service areas in order to establish a Somerset-wide Family Interventions Service. Close working with managers was also the basis for the development of the Strategy to Enhance Working Partnerships with Carers and Families and the Family Liaison Service.

Throughout, we have tried to appreciate the needs of the organisa-tion and to provide managers with solutions that meet their goals. This has involved talking the language of service provision and keeping up to date with current national policies and guidelines. We have found that national and local inquiries, as well as complaints processes, often highlight issues of poor communication between services and fami-lies/carers. Managers are, therefore, keen to support our training and other initiatives. We routinely collect data on our family services and audit our training courses. Thus, we are in a position to respond to management requests for information and are able to contribute positively to Trust action plans. We also take all opportunities to publi-cise our work through regular reports and presentations.

Our main motivation has been to improve services for families and to promote systemic thinking across adult mental health services. It is interesting to reflect back on the sensitivity that was required to introduce systemic ideas in the context of the dominant family intervention discourse of the time. Similarly, a sensitive approach was required to introduce systemic ideas to frontline services. It was important to listen to and understand the workplace pressures and obstacles to involving families more fully. In both cases, exploring the prevailing beliefs and attitudes of staff has been a prerequisite to introducing systemic ways of thinking and practices.

Our training approach draws upon our experience of creating the potential for change in therapeutic situations. We begin by trying to understand what it is like for individual staff and clinical teams to be carrying out their respective roles. We then discuss where they feel they are in terms of working in partnership with families and carers and where they would like to see themselves in the future. We follow this by thinking about how they could get to where they would like to be, what steps they might take, and over what timescale. An important part of the discussion concerns the obstacles or difficulties that might get in the way of their achieving their aims. Having agreed on a plan, we then return after an agreed period to see how they have got on, in terms of both successes and failures, what is still required, and whether we can be of further help.

We have found it really beneficial to involve families in our training initiatives, as this can be a powerful way of challenging unhelpful attitudes (Stanbridge & Burbach, 2007b). Partnerships with families have also informed the way in which we have designed our services. For example, the development of the Families and Carers Steering Group was a way of bringing together carers, charitable organisations, managers, and clinicians to promote family-inclusive ways of working across services in a co-ordinated way. Like Reimers and Treacher (1995), who examined family therapy from a "user" perspective, we have actively sought feedback from families (Gore & Stanbridge, 2012; Stanbridge, Burbach, Lucas, & Carter, 2003) and visited young carers' groups in order to develop "user-friendly" family services. Feedback we have received from families has often emphasised their need for information, involvement with services, and a wish to be heard. For example:

"Having information about the service as it was all completely new to me."

"It has been so helpful to have some support. To know that we are not on our own with our problems."

"It was extremely helpful to compare my direct experience of (relative's name) condition with others who have a professional understanding of the situation."

Family members also value the opportunity to be seen together as a family. For example:

"Sharing our experiences with all family members present " and having

"Open discussions in a safe and supportive environment."

Regularly receiving this kind of feedback from families has helped us feel we are on the right track and has spurred us on to continue to develop family-based services.

In our own ways, on a personal level, we have both been drawn to a systemic approach due to a particular awareness of issues of power and discrimination. Systemic psychotherapy is an approach that privileges cultural and socio-political contexts and, in adult mental health services, provides a framework to challenge narrow, overly pathologising discourses. Addressing issues of empowerment is arguably central to the context and processes of any therapeutic encounter. Dominant discourses around illness often subjugate other discourses, such as those concerned with resourcefulness, coping, courage, or the impact of relationships. However, family therapy is particularly sensitive to, and competent in, working with social difference and imbalances of power, with the "graces" (Burnham, 2012) being central to clinical practice.

Besides being motivated by having a "just cause", our determination to develop family-based services over the past decade and a half would not have been sustained without working partnerships over the years—our own, as well as the partnerships we have created with other colleagues. These partnerships have helped us to maintain our optimism and perseverance over a period of time. Although we have collaborated on joint projects, we have also developed systemic approaches in other areas. Frank has developed systemically orientated assertive outreach (Burbach, Carter, Carter, & Carter, 2007) and early interventions in psychosis services (Burbach, Fadden, & Smith, 2010; Burbach, Grinter, & Bues, 2009). Roger was appointed to the first systemic psychotherapy post in adult services and, as head of systemic psychotherapy, was subsequently able to create other designated family therapy posts. As part of this role, he led the development of the Trust's Strategy to Enhance Working Partnerships with Carers and Families and ensured that family therapists, in addition to their specialist role, became integrated with frontline services. Clearly, it has been helpful that we have both been employed in the Trust over many years and have been in positions that enabled us to influence policy and service provision. However, in our Trust, as in others, there is still some way to go before all people who use services and their families feel that their needs have been met.

We hope that our story provides the reader with ideas that will encourage the establishment or further development of family therapy and systemic approaches in adult mental health services. Although we have summarised these in Table 9.2, our main recommendation is to adopt a therapeutic approach to service development, paying careful attention to the organisational and policy contexts, making relationships with key supporters, and setting small, achievable, low-cost goals. Success should be a cause for celebration and be built on. Above all else, however, persevere!

References

AFT (2011). Summary of family interventions recommended and reviewed in NICE guidelines (updated 2011). Accessed at: www.aft.org.uk.

Age Concern (2007). Improving services and support for older people with mental health problems. The second report from the UK Inquiry into Mental Health and Well-Being in Later Life. Accessed at: www.ageconcern.org.uk

Aldridge, J., & Becker, S. (2003). *Children Caring for Parents with Mental Illness: Perspectives of Young Carers, Parents and Professionals*. Bristol: Policy Press.

Bailey, R., Burbach, F. R., & Lea, S. (2003). The ability of staff trained in family interventions to implement the approach in routine clinical practice. *Journal of Mental Health, 12*: 131–141.

Barnardo's (2008). Family minded: supporting children in families affected by mental illness. Accessed at: www.barnados.org.uk.

Brooker, C. (2001). A decade of evidence-based training for work with people with serious mental health problems: progress in the development of psychosocial interventions. *Journal of Mental Health, 10*(1): 17–31.

Burbach, F., & Stanbridge, R. (2009). Setting up a Family Interventions (FI) service: a UK case study. In: F. Lobban & C. Barrowclough (Eds.), *A Casebook of Family Interventions for Psychosis* (pp. 287–307). Oxford: Wiley-Blackwell.

Burbach, F., Stanbridge, R., & Chapman, H. (1997). Family Therapy Service Clinical Audit (unpublished report). Somerset: Avalon NHS Trust.

Burbach, F. R., & Stanbridge, R. I. (1998). A family intervention in psychosis service integrating the systemic and family management approaches. *Journal of Family Therapy, 20*: 311–325.

Burbach, F. R., & Stanbridge, R. I. (2006). Somerset's family interventions in psychosis service: an update. *Journal of Family Therapy, 28*: 39–57.

Burbach, F. R., & Stanbridge, R. I. (2008). Training to develop family-inclusive routine practice and specialist family interventions in Somerset. *Journal of Mental Health Training, Education and Practice, 3*(2): 23–31.

Burbach, F. R., Carter, J., Carter, J., & Carter, M. (2007). Assertive outreach and family work. In: R. Velleman, E. Davis, G. Smith, & M. Drage (Eds.), *Changing Outcomes in Psychosis: Collaborative Cases from Practitioners, Users and Carers* (pp. 80–97). Oxford: Blackwell.

Burbach, F. R., Donnelly, M., & Stanbridge, R. I. (2002). Service development through multidisciplinary and multi-agency partnerships. *Mental Health Review, 7*(3): 27–30.

Burbach, F. R., Fadden, G., & Smith, J. (2010). Family interventions for first episode psychosis. In: P. French, M. Read, J. Smith, M. Rayne, & D. Shiers (Eds.), *Promoting Recovery in Early Psychosis* (pp. 210–225). Chichester: Wiley-Blackwell.

Burbach, F. R., Grinter, D. J., & Bues, S. E. A. (2009). The Somerset team for early psychosis. *Early Intervention in Psychiatry, 3*: 231–235.

Burnham, J. (2012). Developments in Social GRRRAAACCEEESSS: visible–invisible and voiced–unvoiced. In: I.-B. Krause (Ed.), *Culture and Reflexivity in Systemic Psychotherapy: Mutual Perspectives* (pp. 139–162). London: Karnac.

Cabinet Office (2008). *Think Family: Improving the Life Chances of Families at Risk*. London. Cabinet Office: Social Exclusion Task Force.

Carr, A. (2009). The effectiveness of family therapy and systemic interventions for adult focused problems. *Journal of Family Therapy, 31*: 46–74.

Carter, K. (2011). Family liaison in an adult acute inpatient ward. *Mental Health Practice, 14*(8): 24–27.

Cooklin, A. (2010). 'Living upside down': being a young carer of a parent with mental illness. *Advances in Psychiatric Treatment, 16*: 141–146.

Cuipers, P. (2005). Depressive disorders in caregivers of dementia patients: a systematic review. *Aging & Mental Health, 9*(4): 325–330.

Department of Health (1993). *Clinical Audit: Meeting and Improving Standards in Health Care.* London: HMSO.

Department of Health (1994). *Mental Illness Key Area Handbook.* London: Department of Health.

Department of Health (1999). *The National Service Framework for Mental Health. Modern Standards and Service Models.* London: Department of Health.

Department of Health (2002). *Developing Services for Carers and Families of People with Mental Illness.* London: Department of Health.

Fadden, G. (1997). Implementation of family interventions in routine clinical practice following training programmes: a major cause for concern. *Journal of Mental Health, 6*(6): 599–612.

Fadden, G. (2006). Training and disseminating family interventions for schizophrenia: developing family intervention skills with multidisciplinary groups. *Journal of Family Therapy, 28*: 23–38.

Farhall, J. (2000). *Families in Partnership with Mental Health Services: Evaluation of the Get Together F.A.S.T. Initiative.* Melbourne, Australia: La Trobe University.

Froggatt, D., Fadden, G., Johnson, D. L., Leggatt, M., & Shankar, R. (Eds.) (2007). *Families as Partners in Mental Health Care: A Guidebook for Implementing Family Work.* Toronto, Canada: World Fellowship for Schizophrenia and Allied Disorders.

Gore, S., & Stanbridge, R. I. (2012). Families' views on the Family Liaison Service on mental health wards in Somerset. *Context, 121*: 25–32.

Haun, M. W., Kordy, H., Ochs, M., Zwack, J., & Schweitzer, J. (2013). Family systems psychiatry in an acute inpatient setting: the implementation and sustainability 5 years after its introduction. *Journal of Family Therapy, 35*: 159–175.

Kuipers, E., & Bebbington, P. (2005). Research on burden and coping strategies in families with people with mental disorders: problems and perspectives. In: N. Sartorius, J. Leff, J. J. Lopez-Ibor, M. Maj, &

A. Okasha (Eds.), *Families and Mental Disorder: From Burden to Empowerment* (pp. 217–234). Chichester, UK: John Wiley.

Leftwich, S., Carter, K., McIver, C., & Stanbridge, R. (2011). Facing the family: The Family Liaison Service in Somerset – three case examples. *Context, 114*: 40–44.

National Institute for Clinical Excellence (NICE) (2002). *Management of Schizophrenia in Primary and Secondary Care*. London: National Institute of Clinical Excellence.

NICE (2004a). *Eating Disorders: Core Interventions in the Treatment and Management of Anorexia Nervosa, Bulimia Nervosa and Related Eating Disorders*. London: National Institute of Clinical Excellence.

NICE (2004b). *Depression: Management of Depression in Primary and Secondary Care*. London: National Institute of Clinical Excellence.

Pearson, D., Burbach, F., & Stanbridge, R. (2007). Meeting the needs of families living with psychosis: implications for services. *Context, 93*: 9–12.

Pharoah, F. M., Mari, J. J., Rathbone, J., & Wong, W. (2010). *Family Intervention for Schizophrenia (Update). The Cochrane Library, 11*. Chichester: John Wiley.

Pinfold, V., Farmer, P., Rapaport, J., Bellringer, S., Huxley, P., Murray, J., Banerjee, S., Slade, M., Kuipers, E., Bhugra, D., & Waitere, S. (2004). *Positive and Inclusive? Effective Ways for Professionals to Involve Carers in Information Sharing*. London: National Co-ordinating Centre for NHS Service Delivery and Organisation R and D (NCCSDO).

Pottle, S. (1984). Developing a network-oriented service for elderly people and their carers. In: A. Treacher & J. Carpenter (Eds.), *Using Family Therapy* (pp. 149–165) Oxford: Blackwell.

Procter, H. G., & Pieczora, R. (1992). A family-oriented community mental health centre. In A. Treacher & J. Carpenter (Eds.), *Using Family Therapy in the 90s* (pp. 131–144). Blackwell: Oxford.

Reimers, S., & Treacher, A. (1995). *Introducing User-friendly Family Therapy*. London: Routledge.

Rethink (2003). Who cares? The experiences of mental health carers accessing services and information. Accessed at: www.rethink.org.

Shepherd, G., Murray, A., & Muijen, M. (1994). *Relative Values: The Differing Views of Users, Family Carers and Professionals on Services for People with Schizophrenia in the Community*. London: Sainsbury Centre.

Singleton, N., Aye Maung, N., Cowie, A., Sparks, J., Bumpstead, R., & Meltzer, H. (2002). *The Mental Health of Carers*. London: Stationery Office.

Social Care Institute for Excellence (2011). Think child, think parent, think family; a guide to parental mental health and child welfare. Accessed at: www.scie.org.uk.

Stacey, G., & Rayner, L. (2008). Introducing skills for psychosocial interventions into undergraduate mental health nurse education. *Journal of Mental Health Training, Education and Practice, 3*(2): 42–51.

Stanbridge, R. (2012). Including families and carers: an evaluation of the Family Liaison Service on inpatient psychiatric wards in Somerset, UK. *Mental Health Review Journal, 17*(2): 70–80.

Stanbridge, R., & Burbach, F. (2007b). Involving carers Part 1: Including carers in staff training and service development in Somerset, UK. In: D. Froggatt, G. Fadden, D. L. Johnson, M. Leggatt, & R. Shankar (Eds.), *Families as Partners in Mental Health Care: A Guidebook for Implementing Family Work* (pp. 50–65). Toronto, Canada: Worldwide Fellowship for Schizophrenia and Allied Disorders.

Stanbridge, R. I., & Burbach, F. B. (2004). Enhancing working partnerships with carers and families: a strategy and associated training programme. *Mental Health Review, 9*(4): 32–37.

Stanbridge, R. I., & Burbach, F. B. (2007a). Developing family-inclusive mainstream mental health services. *Journal of Family Therapy, 29*: 21–43.

Stanbridge, R. I., Burbach, F. R., & Leftwich, S. H. (2009). Establishing family-inclusive acute inpatient mental health services: a staff training programme in Somerset. *Journal of Family Therapy, 31*: 233–249.

Stanbridge, R. I., Burbach, F. R., Lucas, A. S., & Carter, K. (2003). A study of families' satisfaction with a family interventions in psychosis service in Somerset. *Journal of Family Therapy, 25*: 181–204.

Stanbridge, R. I., Burbach, F. R., Rapsey, E. H. S., Leftwich, S., & McIver, C. C. (2013). Improving partnerships with families and carers in in-patient mental health services for older people: a staff training programme and family liaison service. *Journal of Family Therapy, 35*: 176–197.

Stratton, P. (2011). The evidence base of systemic family and couples therapy. Association of Family Therapy. Accessed at: www.aft.org.uk.

The Schizophrenia Commission (2012). *The Abandoned Illness: A Report from the Schizophrenia Commission.* London: Rethink Mental Illness.

Worthington, A., & Rooney, P. (2010). *The Triangle of Care. Carers Included: A Guide to Best Practice in Acute Mental Health Care.* National Mental Health Development Unit and Princess Royal Trust for Carers. Accessed on 14 December 2010 at: www.carers.org.

CHAPTER TEN

The significance of dialogue to wellbeing: learning from social constructionist couple therapy

Taiwo Afuape

Introduction

I shall start by briefly describing my cultural background as a backdrop to my interest in the relational nature of self, before exploring how couple therapy informed by social constructionist and liberation psychology ideas has shaped my understanding of the dialogical nature of wellbeing. I will focus on social constructionist couple therapy rather than systemic therapy in general, first because couple therapy is less commonly explored when discussing critical approaches to mental health, and second, I hope this focus will demonstrate the relationship between dialogue and wellbeing in a tangible way that people can relate to in place of abstract philosophical ideas that seem far removed from everyday reality.

Couple work is a useful focus given the intrinsic association with intimacy. According to Langan and Davidson (2010) intimacy is a discourse based on taken-for-granted, ideological assumptions that change over time and are affected by the cultural contexts they inhabit. These assumptions are not right or wrong *per se*, but shape how we view the couple, our ideas about what is important in intimate relationships, and our behaviour in such relationships. The plethora of love stories dominant in the minority world present, almost exclusively, heterosexual, romantic intimacy as a desired end goal for every adult. This is based on an ideal that promotes romance—that is, heterosexual romance—as a tool for individual salvation rather than intimacy as an ongoing, diverse, and collective activity resulting in wellbeing. I define European and North American culture as minority world culture and those of Africa, Asia, the Far East, the Middle East and South America as majority world cultures, since Europeans and the cultures they have created represent a small minority when viewed on a global scale.

Although I write about the mental health system, my focus is on wellbeing rather than mental health for the following reasons.

- Moving towards wellbeing is a preference common to us all. This concept binds and links us—rather than dividing people into healthy and unhealthy, service providers and service users, clinicians and patients—and locates clients within a sphere of normality.
- Wellbeing refers to all aspects of health and is not just confined to cognitive, rational, and intrapsychic experience, and, therefore, better addresses the relational nature of self.

As a Black British-born Nigerian, my parents' cultural framework is rooted in community and spirituality, based on the pursuit of balance, interconnection, and harmony, as opposed to rationality, mastery, and control. Everything in nature is understood to rely on everything outside itself for its reality and meaning. This manifested itself in an emphasis in my upbringing on the self-as-actor, above the self-as-thinker promoted in the minority world (Holdstock, 2000). Despite my British acculturation, the widespread emphasis in British culture on the self-sufficient thinking self does not make complete sense to me. This focus is particularly prominent in the adult mental health system and is demonstrated by the use of psychiatric diagnoses that reduce people and their distress to internal mental experience. This location of distress within the minds of individuals parallels a growing alienation from relational, social, and political concerns. The mental health system is still largely based on an expert stance that views mental health difficulties as discoverable "things" existing in the individual.

In recent years, social constructionism has been instrumental in forming a robust critique of the tendency within the mental health field to disconnect individuals from their context. Social construction-ism views reality, experience, and knowledge as constructed between people in relationship and context. It argues that the self is not a possession of the individual, but a product of social interchange (Gergen & Gergen, 1988). From a social constructionist perspective, language creates realities as opposed to discovering them, which means that "mental health problems", diagnoses, and associated concepts can be viewed as social constructions.

Social constructionist approaches to couple therapy

Co-ordinated management of meaning

Co-ordinated management of meaning (CMM), developed by Pearce and Cronen (1980), is a social constructionist theory of how meanings and actions emerge in context. CMM is based on the notion that the processes of living always involve communication, in which we co-construct social realities with each other. Pearce and Cronen described *coherence* as the ways in which we interpret the world and our experi-ences; *co-ordination* as the ways we interact with the world and each other, and *mystery* as the aspects of life not under rational control or thought, as there is more to life than we think we know in the imme-diate moment (Pearce & Cronen, 1980). This process necessitates both making meaning *and* co-ordinating our actions with others. Pearce (2007) argued that both should be considered equally important; however, we tend to either focus on co-ordinating our actions at the expense of making meaning, or we attempt to make meaning without co-ordinating our actions. If individual actions and experience cannot be considered totally autonomous, but rather "ultimate destinations" originating in relational and social dynamics (Foucault, 2000), then wellbeing happens in the interaction between people, rather than inside an individual.

For each couple, there is a context in which the stories of their lives are formed and understood. Social constructionist couple therapy attempts to encourage relational understanding, by reflecting on how multiple levels of context (Figure 10.1) influences the interactions of

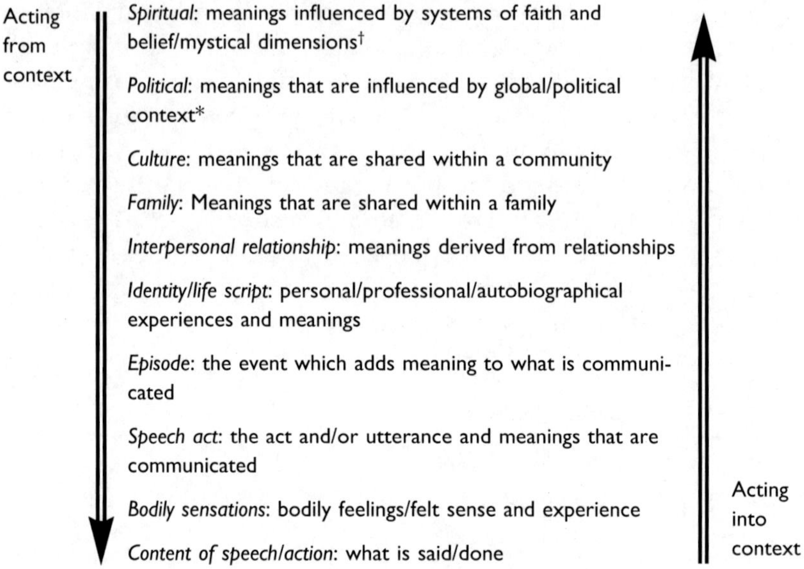

Acting from context	*Spiritual*: meanings influenced by systems of faith and belief/mystical dimensions[†]
	Political: meanings that are influenced by global/political context[*]
	Culture: meanings that are shared within a community
	Family: Meanings that are shared within a family
	Interpersonal relationship: meanings derived from relationships
	Identity/life script: personal/professional/autobiographical experiences and meanings
	Episode: the event which adds meaning to what is communicated
	Speech act: the act and/or utterance and meanings that are communicated
	Bodily sensations: bodily feelings/felt sense and experience
	Content of speech/action: what is said/done

Acting into context

Figure 10. 1.   CMM multiple levels of context
(adapted from Cronen and Pearce, 1985).

* Addition made by Nimisha Patel, November 2005, personal communication.
† Addition made by Karen Partridge, May 2007, personal communication.

the couple as well as our interactions with them. Reflecting on social GRRAACCEEESS,[1] for example, illuminates the ways in which the contexts of gender, class, sexuality, or skin colour are powerful contributors to the plot of our lives. There is also a continual focus on power, and abuse of power (e.g., domestic violence) is viewed in its social, cultural, and political context. There is recognition that therapists, as part of the system, bring preconceived ideas into therapy that greatly influences their interactions with couples.

Narrative approaches

Stories or narratives are central to an understanding of social constructionist ways of working, as *narrative* acts as a useful metaphor for human experience. Our attempts to make meaning forms the plot of a story (Morgan, 2000), and there are many stories about our lives and relationships occurring simultaneously. When we reduce and simplify all the complexities and contradictions of life into expert understanding about others, we engage in what narrative therapists call "thin description". Thin description allows little space for people to articulate their own particular meanings and the contexts in which they occur (Morgan, 2000).

Narrative therapy seeks to be a respectful, non-blaming approach to supporting people's wellbeing, based on viewing people as the experts in their own lives. There are many possible directions that any conversation can take and the client plays a significant part in determining the directions that are taken (Morgan, 2000).

Dialogue as co-ordination

Couple therapy can create a space for acute listening to each other's experiences and feelings. However, dialogue can be seen as more than a cognitive exchange of ideas, as it also contains non-rational elements associated with mystery, coherence, and co-ordination, and socio-political elements associated with liberation. CMM and narrative therapy view dialogue as the type of interaction between people that enables them to go on together.

In mainstream mental health services, conversation has traditionally been viewed as a necessary conduit for exchanging information between therapist and client and, therefore, secondary to "treatment" (Lock & Strong, 2010). However, as Friedman (1993) argues, talk is not a neutral tool used to get the real work done; rather, talk, and how we do this talk, is of primary importance to well-being.

Liberation psychology

Liberation can be thought of as opening up possibilities that we originally did not have, towards our preferences for living. Liberation is suppressed when dialogue is suppressed, with one party imposing their will, needs, or views on another. Liberation psychology locates individuals in context and directly addresses oppression. Liberation theorists, such as Martín-Baró (1996), Freire (1973), and Du Bois (Du Bois, 1994), argued that wellbeing was achieved through social transformation, which Freire argued was only possible if we combine reflection and action, as reflection without action is empty (mere verbalism) and action without reflection is action for the sake of action (activism) (Freire, 1973).

Dialogue as liberation from final conclusions and domination

Liberation is what happens in the space between people in dialogue rather than self-achieved or what one person does for another (Freire, 1973). From a liberation psychology perspective, clients are subjects, not objects, in conversation, such that social and interpersonal transformation happens *with* the oppressed rather than *for* them (Freire, 1973). We cannot enter into genuine dialogue if we are captivated by various forms of "knowing already" (Riikonen, 1999). It is important to go beyond the standard positions we take in order to truly engage in dialogue. Rather than replacing ideas, we seek to extend them, because there is an understanding that making meaning and co-ordinating with others is infinite and ongoing. We do not just attempt to move away from final conclusions, we understand more and more that there are no final conclusions, as it is impossible to have an unchanging, all-embracing, and complete world view. Rather than making better counter arguments that reinforce our world view, dialogue attempts to open up "space for diversity, for otherness, for other forms of life" (Falzon, 1998, p. 3).

Some implications for practice

Social constructionist couple therapists often work with a reflecting team of two or more colleagues, who either remain in the room throughout the session, or can be invited in from behind a one-way screen from time to time to share their ideas (Andersen, 1987, 1991, 1992). This team listens to and observes the content and process of the session, based on the idea that being in an observer position opens up the possibility of being able to see and understand new things (Andersen, 1993).

Coherence, co-ordination, and mystery

When working with couples, it would not make sense to focus purely on meaning-making with one or other of the couple without reflecting on co-ordination, yet we often do so when trying to understand mental health difficulties. The term *co-ordination* calls our attention to the fact that whatever we experience does not stand alone, but shapes and is shaped by the interpretations and actions of other people.

Darryl and Sade felt that their different approaches to tackling problems led to conflict in their relationship. Darryl said that he tended to want to talk about things and see different sides of an argument, whereas Sade described herself as more "impulsive", responding in the moment and challenging any experiences of harm or invalidation. Sade talked about "falling out with herself" (rather than "depression", the term used by her doctor) because she was not the person she thought she should be. She talked about carrying around "the burden of shame" and the power of feeling "you are a bad person in the eyes of your lover".

We explored their families of origin, social GRRAACCEEESS, and levels of context that included experiences of oppression in their lives outside the relationship. We also explored how their different responses at times led to them working well together, as well as what happened when they clashed. Sade described "depression" as a "shorthand" for all these interacting issues.

Darryl and Sade were able to see each other's differences as a resource to draw on and this allowed them to move into different positions: for example, Sade began to notice when she was reflective and Darryl started to bring Sade to mind when he needed to find ways of defending what was most meaningful and important to him to facilitate changes in his environment.

Deep was a twenty-nine-year-old Anglo-Indian male inpatient on a psychiatric ward with a diagnosis of schizophrenia. He was referred by his psychiatrist, Dr Manor, for therapy to "understand and manage his anger". He was frequently excluded from activities and medicated in response to the threat he was perceived to be.

We asked if we could meet with Deep and Dr Manor together for the initial session. We asked if we could start by talking with Deep about this issue and inviting his referrer to listen, as I had met Dr Manor previously but not Deep. Deep talked about experiences of racism, exclusion, abuse, and invalidation that had occurred all his life.

We explored the relationships in Deep's life that were supportive, respectful, and loving, and who he wanted to become as a result of these relationships. Deep talked about his younger siblings and his old youth worker, with respect to his desire to become a youth worker himself in order to "connect with people" and "mentor young people".

The reflecting team reflected that Deep's anger seemed to represent the ways in which he protested his experiences of harm from others and wondered if other people would act differently in response to his anger if they understood it that way. They commented that Deep wanted both to protest harm and connect to people around him, and that this was a tricky dilemma many people faced. They wondered what Deep might need to do to help those around him see the *protest* in his actions as well as his *desire for connection*. I turned to Dr Manor and asked him what struck him, and he reflected that he was struck by Deep's desire to get on with others and be a role model for young people. I wondered if Deep's old youth worker might know something about how to protest wrongs while maintaining connections and being a role model.

As a result of these dialogues, Deep decided he would ask his brother to track down their old youth worker and invite him to the next session, with Dr Manor to talk about this dilemma further.

In both situations, the team and I, together with the clients and significant people within their system, reflected on:

- actions as part of a multi-person process, which involves responding to and eliciting responses from other people, creating the social world we live in and shaping our experience of wellbeing;
- there being more to meaning than we can ever fully know; therefore co-ordinating with others to make meaning is more about exploring a mystery than solving a puzzle;
- the importance of treating all ideas, and not just those of the client, as incomplete, unfinished, influenced by context, and fluid;
- the need to be curious about other people's stories and how they develop in relationship and context.

We used questions such as:

- How does this (social GRRAACCEEESS, level of context) influence your interaction?
- How has the way you conceptualised your relationship influenced your perception of each other?

- Where have you seen these practices before? Who first introduced you to, or what situations first exposed you to, these ways of relating? What contexts are most likely to reinforce these ways of relating?
- Who else is likely to hold these views and how influential are they in your life?
- If you were to challenge these ideas or ways of acting, from where would you experience most pressure to conform? Where would you receive support?
- In what ways are you already resisting these ideas and practices?

Existing within the in-between

Given the sometimes tentative nature of couple work and the possibility that the couple might not want to stay together, it is important to be able to entertain many different possibilities and adapt to the fluid nature of moving towards preferences. The effective joining skills that might be used in individual therapy can backfire when working with a couple if we are not able to multiply engage with different stories, experiences, and views at the same time. This often means being able to exist in the in-between-ness of experience and hold tensions, because no single story can be free of ambiguity or contradiction, or can encapsulate all the contingencies of life (Morgan, 2000).

In my work with couples, I have found it helpful to develop bridging concepts that make sense of, and join the space between, two positions or perspectives emerging in the therapeutic space. Ziarek (2000) suggests that therapists pay attention to "the interval rather than the opposites, and to transformative opening rather than negation" (Ziarek, 2000, p. 134). This might look like:

- moving from *either/or* to *both/and* descriptions of multiple realities;
- developing relational language in describing problems, rather than talking in ways that reinforce the view of the problem as residing in one person or one end of an oppositional divide;
- reflecting on what is being created in the relationship and the impact of power and difference;

- being transparent in a way that suggests that I have opinions and perspectives that are open to challenge in co-creating with the client.

Ron and Peter were concerned that when they wanted to make important decisions, they ended up arguing, which caused them both immense distress. Ron was concerned that he was contributing to his partner's mental health difficulties. He talked about being responsive to Peter when he talked to him, using his body to communicate that he was listening, but described Peter as "unresponsive"; for example, Peter often looked "into thin air" as Ron talked to him, or had his arms folded as though he did not want to listen, which made Ron angry. The more angry Ron became, the more Peter withdrew. Peter explained that he regarded himself as a very sensitive and responsive person, but that he often felt stressed and low in mood as a result of bullying at work, which triggered memories of rejection by his family. I asked about times when they both felt that they responded well to each other and they described being relaxed and communicating well when on holiday.

I asked, if we were to entertain the idea that they were *both* being responsive in the difficult moments they describe, what ideas they had about what Ron was responding to? From this exploration emerged the notion that at these times they were being responsive to different things, so that Ron might be responsive to a desire to connect with Peter and Peter might be responsive to an experience that happened in the past or outside their relationship.

We talked about the impact of stress on their ability to respond "from the same context" and the ways in which they could bring more of the experience of being on holiday into their everyday lives—for example, they were more tactile on holiday and Peter described needing loving *bodily* contact when his body was responding to difficult experiences outside of their relationship.

Sumata was concerned that she was a pessimistic person and that this had a negative effect on her relationship with her boyfriend, Luca, who was "hopeful". The reflecting team commented that hope and hopelessness were not as opposite as we might assume, and that the two lived side by side, and inside each other. They reflected on the power of the word "hope" and all its associations to make people feel as though it does not figure in their lives.

Sumata and I explored how opposing positions can fix people into static identities, which reduce curiosity. In response to inviting Sumata to be more curious about what she called, "pessimism", she commented that if she were to rate their relationship on a Likert scale, her "low" score would represent her determination to strive to make their relationship better. A high score would be a negative score for Sumata, as it would imply that there was no need to keep striving. For Sumata, striving was commitment and commitment was "a close relative of hope".

Sumata described times when she felt that she was "going back to square one" and how this made her fear that she was "not moving forward". To map how the feeling of regression and the experience of moving forward could co-exist coherently, I drew a spiral alongside a straight line to highlight the difference between understanding progress in a way that incorporates backwards as well as forward movement (often the reality), compared with understanding progress as linear progressive development (often the fantasy).

Developing relational understanding

The use of reflecting processes (where one of the individuals in a couple sits with the lead therapist while their partner sits with the reflecting team, or I talk with one in front of the other) can encourage the couple to see each other differently. Reflecting processes can be useful with any system member, whether they are part of the client's intimate or professional network. This type of observer position might support individuals to challenge taken-for-granted assumptions they have about the other and about their relationship.

Jeni was a single parent diagnosed with bipolar affective disorder and her six-year-old son had been taken into foster care in order to give Jeni space to "iron out" the chaotic nature of her life. She was referred to a psychologist by her social worker, Simon, who was concerned that Jeni was still agitated and low in mood. In therapy with the psychologist, Jeni was able to talk about multiple stresses— financial worries, difficult relationships with her family, and job stress—which, although she was getting support for these difficulties, were having an impact on her life.

In therapy, Jeni talked about the parts of her that were functioning well and her developing ability to form supportive relationships where she was able to connect to her resources. However, she would shut down when she met Simon, whose job it was to assess her ability to care for herself and her son.

We explored what her social worker was seeing that meant that he believed Jeni was still not functioning very well, as well as what the reflecting team and I were seeing that her social worker was not, which had us reflecting on her resources.

We discussed what Jeni wanted her social worker to know about her and invited him to a session to sit in the reflecting team. Jeni and I started the session by exploring what Jeni wanted Simon to listen out for, as well hopes for what difference this might make to their relationship, his assessment, and her wellbeing. After the session, Jeni and I invited Simon back to be interviewed by me about what difference it made to him to hear aspects of Jeni's life that he had not heard before. Jeni was then invited to reflect with the reflecting team about what it was like for her to hear her social worker's positive response to her reflections about her life.

Reflecting on taken-for-granted assumptions

Dialogue often involves reflecting on the ways in which experiences that seem to be largely governed by the wishes and motivations of the individual or couple are influenced by the external cultural and social world. For example, we might explore where we get our ideas about what intimacy or sex is. Dominant discourses emphasise the importance of developing intimacy in romantic relationships, but rarely question what intimacy is or consider alternatives to how it might be understood or experienced. There are couples who view their relationship as intimate and are in non-monogamous relationships, or have group sex with other partners, or are not always living in close physical proximity to each other. These couples challenge mainstream assumptions about the prerequisites for intimacy. There are other couples who meet dominant cultural expectations (for example, married heterosexual couples) who describe their relationship as not intimate.

Debunking the idea that intimacy is achievable only in monogamous romantic relationships means being open to other experiences of intimacy that often exist (for example, friendships, support groups, spiritual communities), where more than two individuals can come together and create intimacy. Understanding intimacy as dialogue means viewing intimate interactions as ongoing activities occurring when people "share or co-create meaning and are able to coordinate their actions to reflect their mutual meaning-making" (Weingarten, 1991, p. 287).

Implications for understanding wellbeing

Social constructionist couple therapy has taught me that there is an important reciprocal relationship between dialogue and wellbeing. Yet, couple therapy tends only to be viewed as an attempt to improve romantic relationships rather than offering insights into the nature of wellbeing itself. In the adult mental health field, wellbeing is rarely viewed as "a joint achievement of professionals and clients", or a product of dialogue (Riikonen, 1999, pp. 142–143). Instead, current understandings of wellbeing present the client and the "non-professional" as not competent and the professional as knower.

The importance of dialogue has not yet penetrated into the adult mental health system as profoundly as paradigms of "self-help", which for years have preached that individuals are responsible for their own wellbeing. The growing popularity of cognitive behaviour therapy and aspects of positive psychology have further reinforced this notion. A focus on dialogue might make us ask different questions about well-being. For instance, is distress the result of experiences of disconnection (abuse, violence, prejudice, materialism, isolation, individualism) that do not fit our true interconnected nature? If so, what practices strengthen genuinely dialogical elements in our interaction and in our societies? What types of experiences of self are we shaping when we engage in different types of talk and how do we know what the other person's preferences are? How do we co-ordinate our preferences?

A dialogical approach also means acknowledging, validating, and supporting everyday, non-specialist dialogical activities, often under-valued in the mental health system, that help to create and sustain wellbeing.

Niki was referred to the adolescent mental health team for psycho-logical intervention to manage her "antisocial behaviour". Niki spoke to me on the phone and explained that she did not want to, and would not, come to see me because she was not mad and did not need "mental help". She said that she had not been involved in any anti-social behaviour for the past four months. I asked what Niki was doing that she was finding helpful. Niki talked about her love of music (in particular Grime and UK hip-hop) and how she often wrote and performed lyrics (spitting) about her life experiences for spitting[2] battles where she made up lyrics on the spot in response to another person's improvised rap. Niki said that this helped her understand herself and her experiences better, gave her a sense of community, and energised her. She talked about getting "new ideas" from the experiences and views of other people in her network. Niki agreed to let me visit her at the community music studio she attended, to learn more from her about her creative ways of addressing the difficulties in her life, so that I could better help other young people who did not want to use mental health services.

Social constructionist couple therapy does not just offer impor-tant insights into the relational nature of wellness, but also provides creative approaches to addressing distress. Given our relational nature, some form of intimacy seems to be central to our wellbeing. If we stop valorising romantic intimacy over other forms, we might refocus the mental health system from changing what is worst in the individual to promoting and supporting what is best between us.

This perspective suggests that the solution to distress is a relational revolution or renaissance that does not view dialogue as secondary to social or psychological interventions, but central to how we define wellbeing. We might then be better able to move beyond merely redescribing what already exists—such as using systemic ideas to formulate why people develop mental health difficulties—to radically changing our ways of understanding each other and, thereby, enabling *new* forms of social life to come into existence.

"[D]ialogue cannot exist . . . in the absence of a profound love for the world and for people. . . . Love is at the same time the foundation of dialogue and dialogue itself" (Freire, 2004, p. 89).

Dedication

I would like to dedicate this chapter to Lynne Hestletine and the late Barnett Pearce, to whom I feel enormous gratitude. Barnett's compassion and ethical commitment lives on beyond him and Lynne continues to offer me invaluable insights in supervision.

Notes

1. The social GRRAACCEEESS (Afuape, 2011) is my extension of Roper-Hall's (1998) social GRACES acronym reminding us to reflect on Gender, Religion, Age, Ability, Class/caste, Culture, Colour (skin), Ethnicity, Education, Economics, Sexuality, Spirituality.
2. Grime is a style of UK music influenced by hip-hop, speed garage, dub step, and drum 'n' bass. Spitting is a UK word for rapping.

References

Afuape, T. (2011). *Power, Resistance and Liberation in Therapy with Survivors of Trauma: To Have our Hearts Broken*. London: Routledge.

Andersen, T. (1987). The reflecting team: dialogue and meta-dialogue in clinical work. *Family Process*, 26(4): 415–428.

Andersen, T. (1991). *The Reflecting Team: Dialogues and Dialogues about the Dialogues*. New York: Norton.

Andersen, T. (1992). Reflections on reflecting with families. In: S. McNamee & K. J. Gergen (Eds.), *Therapy as Social Construction* (pp. 54–68). Thousand Oaks, CA: Sage.

Andersen, T. (1993). See and hear, and be seen and heard. In: S. Friedman (Ed.), *The New Language of Change: Constructive Collaboration in Psychotherapy* (pp. 303–322). New York: Guilford Press.

Cronen, V. E., & Pearce, W. B. (1985). Towards an explanation of how the Milan method works: an invitation to a systemic epistemology and the evolution of family systems. In: D. Campbell & R. Draper (Eds.), *Applications of Systemic Family Therapy: The Milan Approach* (pp. 69–84). London: Grune and Stratton.

Du Bois, W. E. B. (1994). *The Souls of Black Folks*. New York: Dover.

Falzon, C. (1998). *Foucault and Social Dialogue: Beyond Fragmentation*. London: Routledge.

Foucault, M. (2000). *Essential Works of Foucault 1954–1984, Volume III: Power*. New York: New Press.

Freire, P. (1973). *Pedagogy of the Oppressed*. New York: Seabury Press.

Freire, P. (2004). *Pedagogy of Hope: Reliving Pedagogy of the Oppressed*. New York: Continuum International.

Friedman, S. (1993). *The Reflecting Team in Action: Collaborative Practice in Family Therapy*. New York: Guilford Press.

Gergen, K. J., & Gergen, M. M. (1988). Narrative and the self as relationship. In: L. Berkowitz (Ed.), *Advances in Experimental Social Psychology* (pp. 17–56). New York: Academic Press.

Holdstock, L. T. (2000). *Re-examining Psychology: Critical Perspectives and African Insights*. London: Routledge.

Langan, D., & Davidson, D. (2010). Rethinking intimate questions: intimacy as discourse. In: N. Mandell & A. Duffy (Eds.), *Canadian Families: Diversity, Conflict and Change* (4th edn.) (pp. 117–143). Toronto: Nelson and Thompson.

Lock, A., & Strong, T. (2010). *Social Constructionism: Sources and Stirrings in Theory and Practice*. Cambridge: Cambridge University Press.

Martín-Baró, I. (1996). *Writings for a Liberation Psychology*. New York: Harvard University Press.

Morgan, A. (2000). *What is Narrative Therapy? An Easy to Read Introduction*. Adelaide, Australia: Dulwich Centre.

Partridge, K. (2007). Personal communication.

Patel, N. (2005). Personal communication.

Pearce, W. B. (2007). *Making Social Worlds: A Communication Perspective*. Oxford: Blackwell.

Pearce, W. B., & Cronen, V. E. (1980). *Communication, Action and Meaning: The Creation of Social Realities*. New York: Praeger.

Riikonen, E. (1999). Inspiring dialogues and relational responsibility. In: S. McNamee & K. J. Gergen (Eds.), *Relational Responsibility: Resources for Sustainable Dialogue* (pp. 139–150). London: Sage.

Roper-Hall, A. (1998). Working systemically with older people and their families who have 'come to grief'. In: P. Sutcliffe, G. Tufnell & U. Cornish (Eds.), *Working with the Dying and Bereaved: Systemic Approaches to Therapeutic Work* (pp. 177–206). London: Macmillan.

Weingarten, K. (1991). The discourses of intimacy: adding a social constructionist and feminist view. *Family Process, 30*(3): 285–305.

Ziarek, K. (2000). Proximities: Irigaray and Heidegger on difference. *Continental Philosophy Review, 33*(2): 133–158.

PART II

PRIVILEGING THE VOICE OF THE CLIENT AND THERAPIST

Narrative therapy with children of parents experiencing mental health difficulties*

Ruth Pluznick and Natasha Kis-Sines

E very culture has its own stories about what it means to be a "good parent". In Canada, this includes a parent who has the resources to look after children in a consistently nurturing manner, a parent who will put the needs of her children before her or his own needs, and a parent who can meet the challenges of parenting in a variety of different circumstances. The portrayal of "good parent" excludes parents who love their children but have difficulties of their own that sometimes get in the way of meeting their children's needs. These parents are often judged harshly in our society and their different experiences of "mother" and "father" are misrepresented, diminished, or dismissed. Sometimes, their children are removed from their care. There are many parents "on the margins" who face these circumstances; included in this group are parents who experience mental health difficulties. In Canada, 12.1% of all children under the age of twelve lives with a parent who has been given at least one psychiatric diagnosis in the previous twelve months (Bassani, Padoin, Phillipp, & Veldhuizen, 2009).

---

* Parts of this paper were previously published in *Context, 108*: 40–46 and *International Journal of Narrative Therapy & Community Work*, 2008(4): 15–26.

Discourses about parents experiencing mental health challenges often implicitly carry stories about their children. Some of the dominant ideas about children in these families include concerns that these are "children at risk" (Beardslee, Versage, & Gladstone, 1998; Hall 2004), that they are burdened by extra responsibilities, that their needs are being sacrificed for those of parents (Chase, 1999). Universal claims about childhood, in which "childhood is usually idealized as a time of little responsibility, innocence and being carefree" (Gladstone, Boydell, & McKeever, 2006) are embedded in developmental theories of "normal child development". Evaluations of the lives of children growing up with parents with mental health difficulties against these normative ideas invites "pathologising diagnosis, such as the child is being robbed or his/her childhood and predictions of dire circumstances" (White & Morgan, 2006, p. 131). Further, "work by children, especially caregiving activities for parents and siblings is often interpreted as part of the same moral universe as child abuse" (Newman, quoted in Gladstone, Boydell, & McKeever, 2006).

The concept of resilience offers some optimism, but is problematic when it is constructed as an attribute of "extraordinary children". By implication, other children could be seen as passive recipients in their journeys through life or, worse, as "victims" of events beyond their control. In a review by Masten (2001) of current research findings, he suggests an alternative perspective: "the ordinariness of resilience is a common rather than an extraordinary characteristic in the process of human adaptive development" (as quoted in Gladstone, Boydell, & McKeever, 2006). Is it then possible, from this suggestion, to imagine that "resilience" is implicated in the acquisition by ordinary children of the skills and knowledge that arise in response to unique or everyday circumstances of living? From this perspective, all children possess resilience.

Conclusions drawn by Gladstone, Boydell, and McKeever, after an extensive review of research with respect to families with a parent who is experiencing mental health difficulties, make visible the absence of the voices of children in these studies. The authors state,

> researchers usually position children as objects rather than participants in the process. Moreover, their experiences are often represented by proxy; the perceptions of parents, teachers and health care providers standing in for those of children themselves. A recent body

of literature suggests that the concerns and needs expressed by children may be very different from adults. (2006, pp. 2546–2547)

An understanding of these young people as having skills to express their views might provide researchers and therapists, and perhaps the general public, with alternative accounts of life in these families.

Creating a platform for voices of children of parents with mental health challenges

In 2006, the Dulwich Centre in Adelaide, Australia invited narrative practitioners around the world to participate in a project intended to gather stories about growing up with a parent facing mental health difficulties. Specifically, the Dulwich Centre was seeking stories to counter the dominant problem-saturated accounts of lives in these families. The invitation from the project stated:

> We aim to gather stories that relate to the experience of children whose parents or caregivers have or had serious mental health difficulties. The project is seeking stories that not only richly acknowledge the difficulties faced, but also the skills and knowledge of children in these situations and the many different facets of the relationships between parents and child. We are interested in including examples of the ways in which parents with serious mental health concerns continue to love and cherish their children. (Russell, 2006, p. 59)

We are daughters of mothers who experienced mental health difficulties. We are also social workers committed to practices of social justice. In our work with young people, we witnessed the impacts of deficit-dominated storylines for families with mental health challenges, and we were concerned about the contributions of these storylines to decisions that led to children being placed in foster or group homes. We decided to bring the "gathering stories" project to our centre and to introduce it to the young people and families who had already identified "parental mental health" as a concern. In so doing, we hoped to provide opportunities for participants to develop alternative and preferred storylines for their lives and relationships. We were confident that stories that captured both the struggles and the "possibilities" for life, despite difficulties, would also inspire new ways of thinking about, and working with, these families (White, 2002). On a more personal note, we believed the gathering stories project offered the two of us a way to honour the experience of our own mothers.

An invitation to young people and parents

We began with teenagers who were already involved in counselling at our centre. We soon found ourselves curious as well about the perspectives of parents, and invited them to join the project. (The first parents to offer their stories were mothers (see Cheryl White, 2008 for considerations of gender and mental health).) We were transparent about our intentions:

- we were hoping to learn more about life in families where a parent has mental health difficulties, *both* the challenges they face *and* also the skills and knowledge, people, and things that sustain them;
- we were interested in discovering stories of love and connection;
- we were wondering if a more "balanced" account of their lives circulated among other parents and professionals might be influential in reducing stigma.

A narrative approach to work with young people with a parent experiencing mental health challenges

Our work is guided by the narrative ideas and practices of Michael White and David Epston (White & Epston, 1990). We begin with the assumption that experiences in life are given meaning by the stories we tell and the stories we hear (White & Epston, 1990). For example, a parent experiencing mental health difficulties might be described as a "problem" for the family. "The doctor praised my father for looking after my mother 'with all her problems'." Narrative therapists are guided by the belief that no single story can capture all of a person's experience; there will always be alternative storylines waiting to be discovered. A young woman tells us, "My mother had problems, yes, but she was also my mother who I could sit around and talk with, who

I could tell all about my day, who I could rely on when things were bad at school . . ."

When listening to stories of parents and young people, we are interested in the effects of stories on lives and relationships as well as the possibilities for alternative and preferred storylines. In expanding the repertoire of available storylines, new options for identity, relationships, and action becomes available.

Who names the problem?

In narrative therapy, the question of "who names the problem" has always been significant. Michael White (2007) spoke of the importance of "experience near" description of events to invite practitioners to pay attention to the ways in which people give meaning to their experiences. Who has "naming rights" is particularly relevant for parents experiencing mental health difficulties, because medical discourse is privileged and compelling (Vassallo, 2002; White, 2005).

Veronica: The psychiatrist met with me for twenty minutes and diagnosed me with "generalised anxiety". He recommended medication. How could he give me a diagnosis after twenty minutes?

R & N: What name would you give the problem?

Veronica: Living with a man who abused me.

Or, as one young woman, Ilona, told us, "The doctor called my Mum's troubles 'psychosis' and wanted to give her medication, but we're First Nations and I think her problem is trauma from colonisation." For families with a parent experiencing mental health challenges, a diagnosis can obscure the social context of problems.

A diagnosis is also problematic when it becomes an identity. One mother, who was diagnosed with bipolar reported, "When I was given the diagnosis of bipolar by the psychiatrist, my family began to see everything I said or did through that lens." For most people, the diagnosis is accompanied by stigma. A mother of two teenagers said, "I was diagnosed with depression. I'd never tell my children this, because I believe they'd think less of themselves or me. And if the school knew, they'd treat my children differently."

There are some families and parents who find diagnosis helpful, as an antidote to fear and isolation. The name helps them to give meaning to confusing thoughts and actions and links them to others with the same label. In these circumstances, we ask ourselves, "Can a label be non-pathologising?" We use the narrative practice of externalisation to separate the person's identity from the problem/ diagnosis, and to undermine the development of single storied experiences of life and relationships.

Naming the problem makes it possible to begin an externalising conversation.

Externalisation

The narrative practice of externalisation is central to our work in this initiative. Externalisation involves turning an adjective, "I'm a *depressed* mother" into a noun, "I am experiencing *depression*". In this way, externalisation separates the person's identity from the problem (White & Epston, 1990). The mother is not the problem, the problem is depression. It is then possible to look at the effects: "the depression has got me thinking I'm not a good parent", or "the depression saps my energy and it's difficult for me to keep up with everything that needs to be done for my children." Externalising also creates space to explore and develop storylines about "life outside the problem": "despite the presence of depression in my life, I'm an advocate for my children and they get the programmes and services they need".

In our work in this project, we are continually reminded by the young people, as well as by parents, how meaningful it is to remember it is the "mental health difficulties", not Mum or Dad, that bring challenging experiences to their lives. As one young person told us, "I was sometimes embarrassed by my mother's behaviour, but I was never embarrassed of her. I knew it wasn't her fault. Knowing this helped me. I was still sometimes upset, but I also wanted to do things to make life easier for her."

Some examples of externalising questions in our conversations with young people and parents include the following.

- Effects of the problem
  For parents:

What is the name you would give your difficulties?

What effect does this have on your relationships with friends and family?

Does it ever have you saying or doing things you might not otherwise say or do?

For young people:

How do you understand your mum/dad's difficulties? What name do you give this?

Does it get in the way of your relationship with your mum/dad?

How does it affect other relationships in the family?

Does it have any effects on your school life? Your friendships?

- Skills and knowledge for getting through difficult times (Russell, 2006, Denborough, 2006)

  Who or what sustains you during the difficult times?

  Are there skills you have developed to lessen or minimise harm or to address your unique predicaments?

  What are some of the particular understandings or learnings you have gained about life through your experience of having/being a parent with mental health challenges?

- Life apart from the problem

  What do you most value about your relationship with your children (or for young people, "your mum or dad")?

  Do you have stories about the good or fun times with your children/your mum or dad?

  Who supports you as a parent? What do they most appreciate about you as a mother/father?

The effects of living with mental health difficulties

In our conversations with young people and parents, we usually begin with an enquiry about the effects of living with mental health difficulties. Young people are more likely to tell us the difficulties first, and then we find openings to stories of love and care. With the parents, perhaps because of the shame and blame they experience, interviews frequently begin by talking about their love and care for their children. When their skills and knowledge are acknowledged, it is easier to talk about the difficulties they face as parents.

None the less, there is remarkable agreement between young people and parents on the effects of mental health difficulties on their lives and relationships. Here are some of the responses to the question, "What are some of the challenges you've experienced?"

Young people's experiences

- Confusion about what was happening to parent.
- Believing it was our fault, that we had done something to bring distress.
- Sadness or anger at the distress of parents or their behaviour.
- Fearfulness, not knowing what to expect (good mood or bad mood).
- Trying hard to please, calm, or cheer up parent.
- Having to protect parent from shame or blame.
- Living with poor decision making and priorities of parents during troubled times.
- Hearing things about parent that are negative or judgemental.
- Feeling different from other young people or their families.
- Not inviting friends home because parent might be acting badly.
- Not attending school regularly or arriving late.
- Not having parent who can help with schoolwork, or who participates in extracurricular events of children.
- Living with effects of parent's medication: over-medicated or under-medicated.
- Not included in meetings with doctors, so perspective not influential.
- Sometimes dealing with parent's drug or alcohol use and the troubles this can bring families.
- When there is violence in the family, how to get help without having to be removed from home.
- Living through the added stress of parent caught up with police/court/hospitals and the injustices that parents experience.
- The experience of loneliness when parent is hospitalised.
- Being assigned responsibilities and decisions that are more than we can handle.
- Needs of young people overtaken by parent's needs.
- Loss of image of parent as "hero".

In our conversations with parents, they shared their perspective of the effects of a mental health difficulty on lives and relationships with their children. All of the parents expressed regret that it had interfered with their efforts to become the parent they wanted to be. For some, depression made its presence felt and brought apathy with it; during these times, it was difficult to get themselves going in the morning and get their children to school on time, to look after the practical details of everyday life, and to participate in activities with children. For others, anxiety kept them from participating in their children's lives in ways that were meaningful to them. For some, mood swings were a challenge to manage, and parents were aware that this was also difficult for their children.

Sometimes, alcohol and drugs seemed to help, but then became a source of conflict and troubles within families. There were times when the difficulties caused parents to say and do things they would not have otherwise done, and they are aware that this might have been hurtful or embarrassing for other family members. For others, memory itself is a problem, and events that were significant to friends or family went unacknowledged. At times, their own troubles fully occupied parents, and the needs of their children or partners were not easy to think about or respond to. Marital conflict or divorce was a reality for many. Most of the parents had times of unemployment or underemployment, and this contributed to financial hardship and sometimes a reliance on welfare.

Stigma was a problem for both parents and children. It got in the way of opportunities in life, had an impact on relationships with significant others at home and in the community, and invited family members to think that their difference from others meant they were "less than". Here are some of the questions we learnt to ask parents and young people.

- What are some of the dominant ideas you had to face about families with a parent experiencing mental health difficulties?
- Did you ever feel that people had trouble seeing you (your mother/father) as a person apart from mental health challenges? Is there a story that illustrates this?
- If you overheard or witnessed unfavourable beliefs, what impact did this have on you?
- How do you think that these experiences shaped your responses to your (your parents') difficulties?

Double listening

It was not our intention to minimise the significance of the difficulties experienced by young people or parents, yet, while they were speaking about their challenges, we were listening for clues for openings to other storylines. This is a narrative practice known as "double listening" (Denborough, 2006, 2008, 2010; Denborough, Freedman, & White, 2008; White, 2005, 2007). Double listening acknowledges hardship and its effects on lives and relationships while also opening space for the particular skills and understandings, people, and things that allow young people and parents to navigate their lives through troubles. As a result, a totalising problem-dominated storyline of life, relationships, and identity is contradicted.

The narrative practice of double listening provides many pathways to new storylines: noticing skills and knowledge for getting through difficult times, discovering unique outcomes, and making visible what is "absent, but implicit" in the lives and relationships of young people and parents.

Skills and knowledge for getting through difficult times

Three questions from the "gathering stories" project (Russell, 2006) were particularly helpful for making visible the skills and knowledge of young people growing up in families with a parent experiencing mental health challenges.

- During some of the more difficult or complex times, were there certain things or people that sustained you? People or pets or toys you turned to? Were there certain things you did that brought you comfort?
- Were there any particular skills you developed to care for other members of your family, or skills to lessen or minimise harm, or to address your unique predicaments?
- Do you think you have gained particular understandings or learnings about life through your experience of having a parent with mental health issues? Can you describe some of these learnings and understandings?

All the young people named at least one person who had helped them in troubled times. They received comfort and support (and, many said, "a sense of normality") from siblings, the other parent, grandparents, aunts and uncles, friends, and teachers. Many had pets who provided comfort and "unconditional love". Art, music, films, and books that "offered escape or better understandings of what we were going through" sustained many of these young people and helped to shape dreams for future lives.

There were many stories of times when their own actions had made life better for themselves or others. This was particularly true for young people who looked after their siblings. They valued their roles as care-givers, particularly when it was acknowledged as a contribution. Other skills that were named were skills of advocacy, skills of thinking "outside the box", skills of understanding complexities, skills of independence, skills to "escape the world", skills of creating sanctuary from troubles, skills of staying connected to the parent during difficult times, skills of staying connected to other people in my life, "just living" skills, skills of "staying true to what's important", skills for helping others, and skills for fun-making.

There were also many learnings about life for these young people, and most of them felt they would be able to use them in the future to face other tough times in life. The learnings included the knowledge that life is multi-storied: a relationship can be a source of frustration, anger, or sadness and still be loving; that there are good times as well as bad times in life; that it is important to recognise small moments of happiness as well as big ones; that "new doors" can open for families even when someone is taken into care; that "difference" doesn't have to be "deficit"; that kindness, compassion, and fairness are treasured values. These learnings were often traced to significant people in their lives, including the parent with the mental health challenges. Many of the young people also attributed their commitments to social justice and possible careers as professional helpers to their experiences of growing up in these unique circumstances.

We were also interested in learning more about the skills and knowledge of parents facing mental health challenges. When parents experience themselves as defined by their troubles, they can lose sight of what they know and do to help their children succeed in life. Yet, collectively, their acts of parenting suggest a world of knowledge and skills. A different storyline emerges with respect to the love and care in these families. For example, one of our parents tells us about a history of depression and the ways it has robbed her of meaningful engagement in life. "What keeps you going in difficult times?" we ask. "My daughter," she says. "Even during difficult times I held on to the hope that I can make a difference in my daughter's life. I tell myself, if I can't do much, I can at least do something." A conversation then opens about the "something" she is able to do for her daughter. Every parent has something they are able to do for their children, despite difficulties.

Making visible (and giving significance to) what parents are able to do for their children, despite challenges, provides a different focus for their relationship with their children.

The social relational context for the development of skills

Skills are not simply individual, independent responses to problems in living. These responses have been shaped by the relationships of history, by culture, and by family or community tradition (Denborough, 2008; White, 2004). For example, many young people trace their skills of looking after others to the value placed on care-giving by (and their experiences with) either or both parents or other family members. In this sense, making visible the skills of young people has also offered openings to new storylines for families, their hopes and dreams, principles and commitments. Serena's story provides an illustration.

Serena is one of four siblings who were placed in foster homes by child protection services. Serena believes that "negligence" was the name given to the complaint. During the court hearing, Serena heard that the house was "unfit" for children, there was not enough food, and her mother did not spend enough time with Serena and her siblings. Serena adds, "my mum had to work two jobs to provide for all of us."

Despite continuous involvement with court and social agencies, Serena's mother found strategies for staying connected to her children. When she was restricted to supervised weekly visits with her children at a local child protection agency, she turned the visits into meaningful family events by bringing their favourite food for dinner and games they enjoyed playing together. Serena has stories she likes to share which suggest that her mother is making contributions to her life, albeit in ways that are largely unrecognised by others and not documented in court records. Still, the separation from her mum is stressful for both mother and children.

When we ask Serena about the people in her life who have been helpful during this time of separation from her mum, one of the people she names is a teacher. After a good discussion of the ways he has contributed positively to her life this past year, we ask her what he most admires about her . . .

> Serena: I think he loves my people skills. I'll talk to anyone. If you are quiet in the room, I'll be beside you, I'll strike up a conversation. I like everyone to be comfortable and I will go out of my way to talk to someone or even just say 'hi'. If there is a grade nine student who is shy or quiet, the teacher knows he can bring me over to them and I will help them to talk.
>
> R & N: Where did you learn these people skills?
>
> Serena: We have big family barbecues and dinners. My mum would tell us to bring our friends and their families and let the neighbours know they're invited. If you were just walking down the street and passed our barbecue, you are coming to it, because my mum will not let you get away without having at least one piece of chicken. So definitely I got this from my mum.

Serena then goes on to connect her family's "people skills" with a principle of life: "nobody is a stranger", by which she means "no one should be circled out of a group". Serena gives us further examples of the way this principle guides her actions at school and in life.

Her mother's contribution to Serena's life is made visible in the telling of this story, and while it does not render invalid the concerns about neglect, it can challenge a single problem-dominated storyline about "neglected children" and their parents. Serena's life is joined with her mother's life "around shared and precious themes in ways that significantly thicken the counterplots of their existence" (White, 2007).

As narrative therapists, we are always on the lookout for these untold stories, as they inform us of possibilities for new conclusions about life, relationships, and identity.

Documenting skills and knowledge for getting through difficult times

Young people and parents often take for granted what they know and can do to get through difficult times; they show surprise when their skills and wisdom are acknowledged. As one young woman told us, "I didn't know how much I knew!" Michael White calls this "standing in different territory" with respect to our troubles. A context is created for the experience of personal agency (White, 2005).

With this in mind, we introduced young people and their families to the idea of creating documents (Denborough, 2006; Epston, 1999). Using their own descriptions of challenges they faced and how they had responded, we discovered and named learnings and skills of life and wrote them up in documents for them to take home and/or share with other families and professionals (Pluznick & Kis-Sines, 2008) In our experience, these documents invite new identity conclusions (White, 1999). For example, AJ is a young man who once questioned whether or not he had a future. Yet, when AJ reviews the document of what he knows and can do to get through difficult times, it is clear that he is starting to think differently about himself. We ask AJ, "If this were an account of another young person's skills and knowledge, what would you think of that person?" He tells us, "He'd be my hero!" When we asked why this person might be his hero, AJ replies, "That's a person who can do anything in life."

The documents are both platform for individual stories *and*, collectively, an alternative account of what is possible in the lives and relationships of all young people and parents in these circumstances.

Other paths to a double-storied account of life and relationships.

The discovery and documentation of what parents and children know and do, despite difficulties, is one way we are able to develop multiple (and hopeful) storylines for families where a parent is facing mental health challenges. Other pathways to new storylines are made possible through the narrative practice of listening for "unique outcomes" and "the absent, but implicit".

Unique outcomes

Problems never occupy 100% of a person or family's life and relationships. There are always moments when preferred responses gain precedence over the troubles. For example, a parent suffering depression overcomes the hopelessness it imposes and experiences pleasure in the achievements or company of his/her children. These "sparkling" moments (Epston & White, 1992) are also referred to as "unique outcomes", and they provide the foundation for an alternative storyline about the ways the parent/family has been able to resist being completely "under the influence" of the problem and hold on to hopes and dreams, purposes and commitments for themselves and their children.

> *Serena*: My mother was not a person who said "do this" or "do that" but we [her children] had lots of ideas about our lives and she always encouraged us. If I said, "I want to be a ballerina", or "I want to be a fireman and rescue kittens from trees", she said, "You can do this." If I said I wanted to be prime minister of Canada, she said, "You can do this." Every child has a dream; no one wants nothing for their lives. My mother never squashed our dreams (even in the most difficult times).

> *Tallie*: My mum likes to say, "We had fun, didn't we?" I think this is important to her because she always tried to make up for the difficult times in our lives. We had lots of fun times. One of them is when my mother would have us all dress up in our best clothes. Then she'd call a taxi and take us to the drive-through at McDonald's. Or she'd take us bowling at midnight. Ordinary events became something special.

When Serena says, "my mother never squashed our dreams", or Tallie says "ordinary events became something special", these are illustrations of "unique outcomes" in the storyline of children growing up with a parent experiencing mental health difficulties. They counter single-storied accounts, which focus on deficits. As unique outcomes are identified, further questions (Why is it important for your mother (or father) to help you to sustain your dreams or make ordinary events special? What does it say about their hopes and dreams for themselves as parents or for you? How does this make a difference for you/your life?, etc.) can lead to "thicker" storylines of these experiences and provide opportunities for new meanings and value for aspects of parenting/family life that might have been overlooked or taken for granted by children, parents, and service providers.

We also listen for unique outcomes in the stories of parents. For example, Lorna is lamenting the effects of depression on her relationship with her children. She sighs, and says, "I keep thinking about what a great mother I was when they were little [before the depression], we had so much fun . . ." We then ask, Can you tell us a little more about those times? and Lorna talks about Christmas parties, picnics, art projects with her children. This storyline can be further developed: "You said that you were 'a great mother' . . . what sorts of skills or wisdom did you bring to the 'job'? Who else knew you were a 'great' mother? What might she/he most appreciate about you as a mother? What do you think your daughters most appreciate?" The story of "great mother" is given more visibility and can have more influence.

The absent, but implicit

New storylines can also be hidden in a complaint. A young person might say, "Why can't my mum be 'normal'?" or a parent will say, "I'm not the parent I want to be." As narrative therapists, the concept of "absent, but implicit" guides us to be on the lookout for storylines which are suggested by complaints or expressions of anger, despair, regret, etc. By asking the question, "What does this dissatisfaction suggest about how you wanted things to be?" (White, 2007), an opportunity for an alternative story becomes available.

For example, when Drake speaks about his mother, the conversation is dominated by complaints. He says, "My mum doesn't act like other mums". He adds, "She's more like a sister than a mother." These complaints are disheartening for his mother and contribute to a sense of failure for her as a mother and for them as mother–son. Yet, the practice of looking for "absent, but implicit" helps us to see that Drake's complaints are also statements of longing. We can ask, "What do these complaints tell us about what you prefer for a mother–son relationship?" "Why is it important to you that a mother be more like a mum than a sister?" "How might this relationship make a difference for your life?" These questions help us to understand what it is that Drake wants for his life as well as for his relationship with his mother.

Further, the thinking behind "absent, but implicit" is that Drake must have some experience of "good mothering" to complain about its absence (White, 2007). A person cannot experience "loss" of something they have never had. When Drake says, "A mum should be someone who encourages you, hugs you when you're upset, and instead of telling you that you are wrong, helps you to learn from your mistakes", it is possible to ask him if there is someone in his life that has done this for him, even just a little? After some thought, he says, "My grandmother." Then, "and sometimes my mum." Asking for stories that would illustrate the times that Drake felt he had received this encouragement, comfort, and guidance from his grandmother and mother opens new conversations that would not be possible if complaints were taken at face value.

Similarly, when a parent expresses sadness or regret, "I'm not the parent I wanted to be", the practice of looking at the "absent, but implicit" opens space for storylines that might otherwise be hidden. One line of enquiry leads to a deconstruction of what it means to be a mother. Another helps us to understand this particular mother's hopes and dreams for her children as well as her preferences and commitments as a mother. "Can you say more about 'the mother you wanted to be'?" "What does it suggest about your hopes and dreams for your life and life as a mother for your children?" "What does this say you stand for as a parent?" "Who and what is this connected to?" "What actions fit with these hopes and dreams, values and commitments?" We might also enquire about times when the parent is "the mother I wanted to be": "Can you share a story of something you do for (or with) your children that is in harmony with these preferences?"

In exploring "unique outcomes" and the "absent, but implicit", multiple storylines become available rather than a single storyline of failure. This reduces experiences of shame and blame and offers possibilities for new meanings of their experiences as a family.

Additional learnings from our work with young people

Before closing the chapter, we highlight some additional learnings from our conversations with young people. Their perspectives will shape the future direction of our work.

1.   Young people want help to negotiate relationships with parents. One young woman said, "My mother had care-givers, and my dad found people who could look after me. But no one helped me and my mum with our relationship. People took over my mother's responsibilities as parent. She stopped knowing about

my life. We became strangers." This young woman spoke directly of the need to support relationships within families when a parent is experiencing mental health challenges.

2.   The support networks of families are influential in shaping the way a son or daughter understands and relates to the parent facing mental health difficulties.

 Tallie: My dad helped me, he was understanding of my mum and he cared about her. He tried to help me make sense of it. He said, "You haven't done anything wrong. It isn't your fault. It isn't your mum's fault either. She's not thinking right about things." Tallie then adds, "And my mother's family helped out. They were there for me when they recognised mum was a little overboard. They saw her as 'eccentric' or 'a misfit', but they cared about her and this made a difference for both of us because sometimes my mother got us into difficult situations and they would bail us out. They were a support for both my mum and for me."

 In our work with young people, we are increasingly aware of the need to engage the network of friends and family to promote understanding and support relationships with the parent experiencing mental health challenges. This is helpful for the children of these parents.

3.   Sometimes, parents and young people have different stories about events. While narrative therapy gives value to multiple perspectives, stories may "compete" with each other because family members commit themselves to "the truth" about what has happened.

One young woman, Kelly, is the daughter of a mother who has been hospitalised on many occasions. Kelly recounts a conversation with her mother in which it becomes clear to her (Kelly) that her mum thought she had done more for her than she had.

 Kelly: One night at dinner with friends, we were talking about school work and how someone got help with a project and I made a comment: "I wish my mum could have helped me with projects when I was little." My mum got very upset because her understanding was that she *was* helping . . .

 R & N: Why do you think your mum was upset when she heard you say you wished she'd been there to help you when you were little?

> *Kelly*:   It's just really weird because I know she did the best she could but her impression of it all was that she was there for me more than she was and that she played a bigger role in my growing up . . .
>
> *R & N*:   Is it possible that those were her intentions . . . that she wanted to be there for you as a mother at all times? That those were her hopes?
>
> Kelly: I know that she wanted to be there for me . . .

There is more congruence in Kelly's and her mother's hopes and dreams for their relationship than in the stories of what actually happened. A platform is created in which "the very real effects of their actions" (Hardy, 2005) can be juxtaposed with the intentions parents had for themselves and their children. The family is helped to challenge the certainty of "one truth", and the competing stories become doorways to new shared meanings. A further question, "Do you think depression (or anxiety, etc.) got in the way of what your mother/father wanted to do for you?" offers an opportunity to further challenge the dominant story of failure and creates space for other, more hopeful and helpful, storylines for the family to embrace.

4.   "A difference is not a deficit." This was a realisation by one of the young people we spoke to when he recounted some of his mum's "unusual" behaviours. He also reminded us that there are many reasons to celebrate being raised by parents who are "different". His sentiments were echoed by many of the other young people.
     "I used to ask my mum why she wasn't like other mums and why she couldn't just be a 'normal' mum but, looking back, if she had been a 'normal' mum, I would have missed out on all the good times I had with her."

Stepping away from expectations to be like other families opens space for new storylines about preferences for lives and relationships (Hutton, 2008; White, 2002), or in the words of Lynda, a grandparent we interviewed,

> I have been thinking about my family . . . the way we don't seem to fit in. It seems to me that there are people who just don't succeed in the world "as it's supposed to be". They cannot find their place in this

world. They get called odd, eccentric or mentally ill. But maybe it's the world "as it's supposed to be", not us, that's the problem . . .

Conclusion

The gathering stories project is intended to generate multiple storylines for young people and families with a parent experiencing mental health challenges. In expanding the repertoire of available storylines, we hope to challenge single storylines shaped by troubles and offer new options for identities, relationships, and lives. As one young person said, "No one should be defined by their bad days." There are always other stories waiting to be "brought out of the shadows" (White, 2007).

Acknowledgements

We want to thank the young people who shared their stories in hopes for a "better world" for families like their own. Their commitment to make a contribution to the lives of others energises our work. Special thanks to Tallie, Serena, AJ, Madeline, Drake, Ilona, Kelly and Lorna, K, V, and to Lynda, a grandparent, for helping us to discover what Jane Hutton calls "the perfection of imperfection", or what is possible when we step away from expectations of being a "normal family".

References

Bassani, D. G., Padoin, C. V., Phillipp, D., & Veldhuizen, S. (2009). Estimating the number of children exposed to parental psychiatric disorders through a national health survey. *Child and Adolescent Psychiatry and Mental Health, 3*: Article 6.

Beardslee, W. R., Versage, E. M., & Gladstone T. R. G. (1998). Children of affectively ill parents: a review of the past 10 years. *Journal of American Academy of Child and Adolescent Psychiatry, 37*: 1134–1141.

Chase, N. D. (1999). *Burdened Children: Theory, Research, and Treatment of Parentification*. Thousand Oaks, CA: Sage.

Denborough, D. (2006). A framework for receiving and documenting testimonies of trauma. In: D. Denborough (Ed.), *Trauma: Narrative*

Responses to Traumatic Experience (pp. 115–130). Adelaide, Australia: Dulwich Centre.

Denborough, D. (2008). *Collective Narrative Practice. In Responding to Individuals, Groups, and Communities Who Have Experienced Trauma.* Adelaide, Australia: Dulwich Centre.

Denborough, D. (2010). *Working with Memory in the Shadow of Genocide: The Narrative Practices of Ibuka Trauma Counsellors.* Adelaide, Australia: Dulwich Centre.

Denborough, D., Freedman J., & White, C. (2008). *Strengthening Resistance: The Use of Narrative Practices in Working with Genocide Survivors.* Adelaide, Australia: Dulwich Centre.

Epston, D. (1999). Co-research: the making of an alternative knowledge. In: *Narrative Therapy and Community Work: A Conference Collection.* Adelaide, Australia: Dulwich Centre.

Epston, D., & White, M. (1992). *Experience, Contradiction, Narrative and Imagination.* Adelaide, Australia: Dulwich Centre.

Gladstone, B. M., Boydell, K. M., & McKeever, P. (2006). Recasting research into children's experiences of parental mental illness: beyond risk and resilience. *Social Science and Medicine, 62*(10): 2540–2550.

Hall, A. (2004). Parental psychiatric disorder and the developing child. In: M. Gopfert, J. Webster, & M. Seeman (Eds.), *Parental Psychiatric Disorder: Distressed Parents and their* Families (pp. 22–49). Cambridge: Cambridge University Press.

Hardy, K. (2005). An interview on multiculturalism and psychotherapy. Accessed at www.psychotherapy.net/interview/kenneth-hardy.

Hutton, J. (2008). Turning the spotlight back on the normalizing gaze. *International Journal of Narrative Therapy and Community work, 1*: 3–15.

Masten, A. S. (2001). Ordinary magic: resilience processes in development. *American Psychologist, 56*: 227–238.

Pluznick, R., & Kis-Sines, N. (2008). Growing up with parents with mental health difficulties. *International Journal of Narrative Therapy & Community Work, 4*: 15–26.

Russell, S. (2006). Gathering stories about growing up with a parent with mental health difficulties. *International Journal of Narrative Therapy and Community Work, 3*: 59–67.

Vassallo, T. (2002). Narrative group therapy with seriously mentally ill: a case study. *Australian and New Zealand Journal of Family Therapy, 19(1).* Accessed 24 November 2012 at: www.narrativeapproaches.com.

White, C. (2008). Children, parents and mental health. *International Journal of Narrative Therapy & Community Work, 4*: 3–14.

White, M. (1999). Migration of identity map in narrative therapy. Three-day training workshop. Toronto, Brief Therapy Training Centres.

White, M. (2002). Addressing personal failure. *International Journal of Narrative Therapy and Community Work*, 3: 33–76.

White, M. (2004). Working with people who are suffering the consequences of multiple trauma: a narrative perspective. *International Journal of Narrative Therapy and Community Work*, 1: 45–76.

White, M. (2005). Children, trauma and subordinate storyline development. *International Journal of Narrative Therapy and Community Work*, 3 & 4: 10–21.

White, M. (2007). *Maps of Narrative Practice*. New York: W. W. Norton.

White, M., & Epston, D. (1990). *Narrative Means to Therapeutic Ends*. New York: W. W. Norton.

White, M., & Morgan, A. (2006). *Narrative Therapy with Children and their Families*. Adelaide, Australia: Dulwich Centre.

CHAPTER TWELVE

Hearing Voices: creating theatre from stories told by mental health service users

Clare Summerskill

*H*earing Voices is the title of a play that I wrote, based entirely on interviews given to me by a number of people that I met while I was a patient on a secure psychiatric ward in 2006. The script consists of interview extracts combined with my own account of that stay. After writing the play, I secured Arts Council funding to produce a rehearsed play-reading at The Cochrane in London, and then, the following year, to take it on a tour to theatres around the country. I performed in the production, as myself, along-side members of my theatre company, Artemis.

From university, where I studied history for my first degree, I went on to drama school and then into acting. I worked in community theatre, repertory, the West End, and on television. Nowadays, I perform as a lesbian stand-up comedienne on the comedy circuit and I regularly tour my own one-woman shows.

I have appeared in several plays that I have written for my theatre company, many of which have been based entirely on people's stories and memories. This method of writing is known as "verbatim theatre" and consists of interviewing a number of people about a particular subject or theme, recording their memories, transcribing those interviews, and then writing up a play from that material, where there is nothing in the script that has not been said by one of the contributors. The play is then presented to audiences who are often composed of the kind of people who had given the stories for the play.

When creating a piece of verbatim theatre, the interviewing procedure is one of the very first stages. At that point, there is a thin line separating the two processes of simply gathering oral history and interviewing someone about their life stories in order for that material to be transcribed for, and included in, a theatre production. Oral history has previously been regarded by some as the poor relation to more traditional forms of historical documentation. Nowadays, however, it is championed by many marginalised, excluded, and oppressed groups as a way of recording their previously unheard voices and as providing a means by which a diverse society can reach and document memories and stories from many of its citizens. Because of this, there is a close connection between oral history and the voices of those from the non-hegemonic classes. This is why the telling of the stories of people who have experienced mental health issues is so very important. Those with mental health issues live on the margins of our society and, consequently, their voices are seldom heard and their stories seldom told.

Paget (1987), who first coined the term "verbatim theatre", argued that both oral history and verbatim theatre "are operating in and seeking to extend the space left by the 'official' recording and reporting media". Recent high profile examples of verbatim theatre are *The Tribunal Plays* at the Tricycle Theatre in London, which used official transcripts of judicial proceedings of the Stephen Lawrence case and Britain's involvement in the Iraq war. For me, creating a piece of verbatim theatre about the experiences of mental health service users, whose stories of poor treatment are often either denied or ignored by the NHS, untold in most of the media, and unknown among many members of the general public, is my way of contributing to this form of journalistic drama. One of the main differences between me and many other playwrights who work in this field is that I was writing about what I had witnessed first-hand.

A few years ago, after the ending of a long-term relationship, I had a breakdown. Over the following years, it became clear that I was suffering from a form of post traumatic stress syndrome. When it all started, because I had tours and gigs booked up, I did not actually stop work until I was feeling violently suicidal. At that point, I found out about a place in north London called Maytree, which called itself a "sanctuary for the suicidal". It was free and you could stay there for up to four nights. I found it to be a very caring and safe environment, but at the end of the week I had to go home. I was still feeling suicidal and I knew that I would not be safe on my own, so I then did one of the hardest things I have ever done in my life: I took myself along to the emergency clinic of a psychiatric hospital and was admitted. That was in 2004.

I was there for a week and it was an absolutely vile and terrifying experience. I was put on suicide watch, medicated, and confined on a locked ward, but, even though I was feeling suicidal, I was constantly encouraged to go back home because the nurses made it quite clear that they saw me as taking up a much needed bed. The food was inedible and there was no heating. Many of the other patients were quite frightening to be around, let alone to be sleeping in close proximity to, on a mixed ward, as it was then. So, even though I was still clearly quite unwell, I managed to get myself out of there, went back to work (as I had a tour booked that I could not cancel), and continued somehow for another two years to work and live with that level of depression, self-harm, and suicidal ideation.

After a successful, but personally very stressful, national tour of a play that I had written and performed with members of my theatre company in 2006, I spent a few days tying up the production accounts, and then I decided, with as much of a clear head as I could muster, to kill myself. This is the opening monologue from the play *Hearing Voices* about that particular time:

CLARE: For two years I had been feeling suicidal and I was exhausted. I had been living in a world with no joy, no hope and my only thoughts were about how to stop all this pain and end my life.

I went to Paris on my own for a holiday, hoping that the beauty of that city and the contents of its galleries and museums might somehow calm my troubled mind. But you know that Van Gogh painting? The one of his room with a bed and a wicker chair and the perspective's at a slant? That one? Well there I was, looking at it in the Musée D'Orsay, when the objects in the picture started sort of coming out at me, like it was 3D. And at that moment I understood that the painter had clearly been mad and I could now see that madness in his work and amongst the bright and vivid colours I could also see his pain.

Then I looked at some of the other Van Goghs and they all seemed to be coming away from the wall, calling for my attention and I began to freak, because it was like hallucinating, and it was then that I knew what this all meant . . . that I was maybe going where he had been.

Over the next few weeks things went from bad to worse until one morning I made an appointment with my GP and asked for some sleeping pills. Then I went back home and I took the whole packet. I remember running out of water, there were so many pills to swallow and having to fill the glass up again and then I sat down on my bed, thinking, "I've finally had the courage to do it. Peace at long last!"

That done, I laid me down to die and I remember that bit being wonderful.

I was so tired, so low, so empty of any kind of hope that things could ever improve and it was such a relief to stop struggling and to finally give up the fight. I could feel myself slipping into a seductive state of unconsciousness when, completely on the spur of the moment, I decided to call my therapist.

I didn't think of it as a cry for help, I thought it was too late for that, I just wanted to explain to her what I had done and why and to say sorry that I didn't have the strength to keep battling on. But my therapist was out and I got the answer phone.

But the reason I'm still here to tell my tale is because she phoned me back a few hours later, got no reply, because by then I was unconscious, and she then called the police who sent the fire brigade round to my flat to break in and rescue me.

But I knew nothing about all that. A day and a half later I vaguely remember being at a general hospital and I was then transferred to a secure psychiatric ward at another hospital where I stayed for two months.

During my time there, I met some other patients with whom I became friends. They all had incredible stories about their own personal experiences and, when I was discharged, I decided to ask them if I could interview them about their lives. Looking back on that time, I can now see that I was still quite ill myself but, none the less, I had this compulsion to keep in touch with them since, in the back of my mind, I knew that their stories could somehow make an amazing piece of theatre. With hindsight, I think that I was an example of someone who, although suffering from severe mental health problems, had an ability to "pass", in that, except for being hospitalised for two and a half months over a period of around seven years, I managed to carry on my work so that many people did not actually realise quite how ill I was. Over a period of a couple of years, I would go out in the evening and perform shows and gigs and then, as soon as I came home, I would start thinking about how I could kill myself.

Two of the friends I made in hospital were Alison and Mary, who are both schizophrenics but used to hold down full-time jobs in local government and teaching, respectively. I also met a wonderful young woman called Eilis, who had been hospitalised twenty-two times in five years after taking overdoses. I got to know Tony, who is a lovely, kind, young Hindu man who self-harms to the point of endangering his life. Another fabulous character I met while I was in there was a woman called Deb.

Of the good friends that I made during my stay in hospital, four out of six of us were gay or bisexual. It was probably not a coincidence that we became close, as we were undoubtedly drawn together by this similarity. One day I would be interested in writing about how gay men and lesbians are treated in the psychiatric system, first because, as far as I know, this is a relatively unresearched area, and second, because my own experience in hospital demonstrated that most, if not all, of the nurses on the ward strongly disapproved of our sexual orientation. I am one of the most "out" people I know, but even I was at certain times scared of letting the staff know that I was a lesbian. Of course, they might well have guessed, but I felt that if I revealed it directly or talked about it, I might suffer from their discrimination at a point where my life could literally depend on their help.

A few months after we had all left the hospital, though some of the contributors were to return there again, I had several transcribed interviews in my possession and I decided to try to weave them together into some sort of a play. As I began to work with the material in the interviews, it struck me that these were stories that I was pretty sure not many other people had ever heard. Personally, I had never met either a psychiatrist or a psychiatric nurse who actually wanted to listen to anything about my own personal history. In fact, they almost flinched if you began talking about anything personal or why you might be feeling depressed or suicidal.

My own experience on a locked ward was that the nurses were cold-hearted and quite uninterested in the patients unless there were actual suicide attempts happening during their shift—only then would they move into action. They seemed to have quite a punitive attitude towards self-harm. One nurse told us that anyone who said they wanted to self-harm was "attention-seeking" and others said that they thought suicide was "against God's will". I believe that this cold, slightly cruel way of behaving towards the patients reinforces and reactivates deep-rooted feelings of neglect, trauma, abandonment, and abuse experienced in our early lives, thereby increasing our current mental distress.

Both times that I was hospitalised, there was no talking therapy offered. I was never once asked by a member of staff why I felt suicidal, why I had tried to kill myself, why I had a constant tremor that was nothing to do with medication, why my legs seemed to give way and I would collapse on the floor when I was distressed, or why I had the need to self-harm so often. Patients were confined and medicated and that was all. Twice a week, you got to see a psychiatrist who asked you what your mood was: "High or low?" They would look down at your notes for a few minutes and then decide whether your medication should be changed. Then you were shown out of the room. So, if you ever have a friend, a partner, or a relative who is mentally unwell and they end up in hospital, please do not make the mistake of thinking what I would have thought before I had the experiences I had, that "They're being taken care of now by professionals, at least they're in the right place." Personally, I can't think of a worse place to be for someone who is ill.

In between acting jobs, I myself had worked for many years on and off as a care assistant for Mencap and I felt that I had some understanding about what it means to do a shift, do a handover, to be a carer. So, it is probably the case that a part of me was summing up the nurses' work from a professional point of view as well as from a patient's perspective.

When I asked my fellow patients if, when they had been in hospital, anyone had ever asked them about how they were feeling, the answer was always the same, "No." For that reason alone, I decided to tell their stories myself so that people could know that behind every "mental health service user" (as we are called) there is a story, a past, and often a disturbed and abusive one. This might be a little controversial, but I believe that people do not just one day become mad, suicidal, or chronically depressed. I think that something, or a number of things, in their own life experience have probably brought them to that terrifying place. I decided that my play was to be entitled *Hearing Voices* because no one in hospital had ever wanted to hear ours and I was trying somehow to redress this.

Originally, I had intended the play to be based entirely on the interviews I had had with the patients on the ward with whom I had become friends. But, at an early stage in the writing process, I had a colleague look over what I had worked on so far and she was insistent that an audience would be interested in why I had been in hospital myself. I eventually gave in to her argument, and that is how my own story, in some detail (I must say, far more than I originally intended), became part of the play. However, by the time I had included a few of my own stories of life on the ward, I realised that the piece was now looking a little bleak. All our stories about being in hospital were showing the nurses, the consultants, and the entire psychiatric system in quite a grim light. I could not change my memories of what had happened to me in there, and neither could I change the opinions of my fellow contributors, but I decided the way I could try to lift the piece a bit and make it a little more hopeful was to offer some examples of what I considered to be "best practice". I then sought out some people who also operate professionally in the area of mental health, but in a kinder and more humane and understanding way than was offered by the nurses and consultants that I had encountered.

So, I included extracts from four interviews with people I call the "alternative professionals" who, I believe, look at mental distress in a more effective and intelligent way than that demonstrated to me by my own experience within the psychiatric system. One of these contributors is a woman called Paddy Bazeley, who was a founding director of Maytree. She talks about how it is possible to work successfully with, and alleviate the pain of, very distressed people in a kind, supportive, listening, non-judgemental, non-medically driven environment. When she saw the final version of the play she stated, "I set up

Maytree because of people saying what Clare is saying and dying because the fear of hospital is so great."

She says about Maytree that "We wanted to get a balance of the place being safe in a physical sense that would reflect the safety we were offering in the psychological and emotional sense. Because suicidal people have a fear of actually falling apart."

There are also extracts from an interview with Dr Rufus May, who is a clinical psychologist. He believes, by his own example, that people who have been given diagnoses like schizophrenia are able to live full and active lives if they get the right support. He further believes that people given such diagnoses do not need to rely on neuroleptic drugs, which most clinicians insist on people taking for the long term. This is an extract from Dr Rufus May's interview:

> *Rufus:*   I just see terms like schizophrenia or bipolar disorder as diag-
> noses, labels really. Whenever you put someone on a drug all
> you're doing is suppressing the experience. In a holistic
> approach, the argument is that the illness is a release of toxins
> from the body, so acute illness is a way of the body attempting
> to release toxins. It's a way of the body trying to survive. But
> medical models try to battle with the illness and treat it. If they
> can't treat it, then they suppress the symptoms, but something
> else then comes along that's just as difficult to manage. It might
> be apathy and hopelessness or it might be that a person puts
> on weight and develops diabetes and a heart condition. These
> are all very common effects of being on long-term psychiatric
> medication.
>
> Madness is a creative way of dealing with pain. Brutalising
> someone does not help them. We need to listen deeply to people
> in crisis and we need to question the idea that chemical changes
> are the main cause of emotional changes. If Arsenal loses to
> Tottenham, I will experience a deep sinking feeling. This will
> probably be reflected by chemical changes in my brain, but they
> did not cause this. Football players did, combined with my
> attachment to Arsenal!
>
> I would argue that medicalising and numbing our pain does not
> help. It mystifies its meaning in our lives and ignores the social
> and psychological avenues to making our lives more fulfilling.

In the play, we had one of the actors playing the part of Dr Rufus May and we had him giving some of his views between extracts of an interview with a fellow patient, Deb, who has been diagnosed as being bipolar. In this way, I hoped to combine both the theory and the reality of issues surrounding a severe mental health condition. Deb is an amazing and very intelligent woman. She is a singer and a song-writer and a mother of five. This is an extract from her interview:

> *Deb*:   When I went on the Lithium they said it would decrease my episode, but they didn't tell me that if I didn't take the Lithium then my episodes would get worse than they ever had. Like, I get seriously ill. Whereas before I might have been a "Crazy nut nut lady", now I'm getting really ill.
>
> There was one time I went to go up to Brixton with nothing on but a sleeping bag, looked like a bloomin' caterpillar! Jumped up on a bus, dropped me sleeping bag. Then the police took me home and my boyfriend, David, who I live with, he looked after me until I got better.

Deb followed the development of the play very closely, joining in the after-show discussion at the rehearsed play reading and posting her own review of the production on YouTube. The review was very positive and also quite moving, but there was one section of it that I thought was incredibly powerful and highly significant. She said,

> "Clare Summerskill's play has opened my eyes because the treatment Clare perceived as wrong, inhumane, unjust, uncalled for, I had been accepting that as the norm because I was a bad naughty bipolar person I felt I deserved it because I was hyper-manic."

I think this is an interesting point, that people in our society who suffer from any form of mental distress often think that they should not be in the state that they are, that they are somehow not strong enough to manage as well as other people seem to be doing. This is not the case with those who suffer from physical illnesses, which generates sympathy from the public, family, and nurses alike. You are allowed time off work, flowers are sent to you in hospital, and sympathy is the standard reaction to news of anyone's poor health. But society's stigma around people suffering from mental illness means that someone like Deb will, at some deeper level, feel that when she is hospitalised she is somehow deserving of being treated in an uncaring way by the staff.

Deb's feedback about the play was invaluable to me, as, of course, was all the feedback I got, but particularly the feedback that I received from other people in mental distress and those who had spent time in a psychiatric hospital. I wanted to see if my experiences reflected their own. I am sorry to say that all around the country, in every town and city where this play was performed, other service users told me and the cast, either in person or on the feedback forms that they filled in after each show, that their treatment in the psychiatric system had been very similar to mine.

Another "alternative professional" whom I interviewed for the play was Pam Blackwood, who had been Head of Operations with Samaritans between 2003 and 2009 and was a member of the Guideline Development Group for the 2005 NICE report on Self-Harm. She has her own views on the treatment given by psychiatric nurses to those who self-harm on hospital wards.

Pam: I think one of the difficulties is that nursing is about medicine and you might choose to specialise in psychiatry but, in a way, it's still about treating people with medicine and making them better and that's the reward of the job. But if there is somebody who is a revolving door patient, and people who self-harm often are, there's a sense of impotence for some people who think, "my skills aren't helping you and therefore I feel bad". But for other people I actually think there may be something punitive and, I really wouldn't want to generalise, but if a nurse feels that self-harm isn't a mental illness and therefore "you shouldn't be here because you're taking up a bed from somebody with schizophrenia" who "I know I can do something for", then that's the thought process that actually gets them to be punitive in some way.

I also perceived a slight difference of attitude from the staff towards those of us whom they viewed as having "medically treatable" psychiatric conditions and those of us who were suicidal, self-harmers, or both. I believe that such people need, first and foremost, a calm and healing environment in which to begin to recover, which the wards I have stayed on did not provide. Violent and non-violent patients were placed together and I witnessed patients bringing in crack cocaine, trying to sell it to other patients, and smoking it in their rooms. There were daily thefts of personal belongings from our rooms, which was very distressing for us, and the staff would do absolutely nothing to try and stop them. People who are feeling mentally fragile need to experience a feeling of safe containment, which was certainly not provided, and they require compassionate nursing and caring and attentive listeners. I believe that these important and necessary changes could quite easily be implemented by the psychiatric system at little extra financial cost. The option of talking therapy should, of course, also be provided for patients.

In my own view, the difficulty for nurses and consultants is twofold: first, it appears that they are trained to believe that they have to think of a patient with mental health issues as somehow being "other", someone they cannot relate to or empathise with. This will inevitably lessen their ability to regard us as fellow human beings, which will, in turn, result in us being treated as less than human rather than just as ill. Second, if the staff are actually encouraged to listen to the details of the emotional pain that someone is in, then they might have to hear about the systemic abuse that goes on within our society which has caused these now mentally traumatised people to be at the place they have reached. And that is something they do not want to hear about and which the psychiatric system will actually go to great lengths to avoid, to such an extent that they will continue the funding of highly expensive, but not always effective, drugs and provide prison-like wards run by people who act more as guards than nurses. But this reflects the general thinking of the society we live in. To blame the victim rather than the abuse excuses people from determining where the cruelty is actually coming from in the first place, or looking at any effective means of tackling its existence and the underlying causes.

Over the course of my researching this play, writing it, and finally touring in it as an actress, I have learnt quite a lot about some of the current issues surrounding mental healthcare in our society. One crucial learning curve for me emerged when we presented the rehearsed play-reading of the piece to an audience of nearly three hundred at The Cochrane in London. I realised that night that not only was the play addressing an already explosive area of debate, the role and efficacy of psychiatry in our society, but that there appeared to be a divide between people working in the NHS and those working in other areas of mental health. It seems pretty obvious now, with hindsight, that anyone working within the NHS psychiatric system would have found what I was writing about and dramatising on stage to be uncomfortable viewing, to say the least. But I had not expected that, during the question and answer session following the rehearsed play-reading, certain audience members would essentially suggest that I might have distorted the truth of how I had been treated during my stays on hospital wards.

After the play-reading, I got up on to the stage and was joined by the other cast members and two of my contributor ex-patient friends, Tony and Deb. One audience member said, quite forcefully, that she just could not believe that there had not been any nice nurses on the ward. I told her that that was, unfortunately, the case during my stay and both Tony and Deb backed me up, saying, "No, Clare's right; there really weren't any."

Then it was suggested by another audience member that perhaps I should have put one in the play to balance things out. To which I replied, "But this is a piece of theatre based on interviews, with my own personal story woven around them. Everything said in the play is something that has been said in an interview or from my diary. If I made up characters and storylines, I couldn't call it verbatim theatre."

But on she went: "But if you did have a nice nurse in the play, we could more readily listen to the bad examples of treatment that you show."

And Deb, bless her, popped up again with "But didn't you hear what we said? There weren't any nice nurses."

And Tony agreed.

This particular subject of debate had quite an impact on me. It was becoming clear that some people who worked in mental health clearly found it easier to acknowledge instances of bad practice only if they could be shown examples of good practice as well. Including extracts in the play from my so-called "alternative professionals" did not seem to have solved this problem either. So, after the play-reading, I had to decide whether I should portray things as they actually had been in real life, as testified not only by me but by the other contributors, or whether I should somehow alter the truth of the story to make it more credible to some of the audience who doubted the veracity of what they were hearing. I did not want to upset people, and neither did I want to be called a liar, but I still felt I could not and should not alter the truth, my truth, our truth about what happened to us. I felt that if I started doing that for dramatic purposes, it was a slippery slope to making the whole piece fiction, which would, therefore, detract from the power of the production, which was that it was all taken from patients' own personal testimonies. Finally, a full grant was secured from the Arts Council for a five-week tour of the play, which was then later made into a DVD version from which there are now extracts on YouTube, so that those in mental distress, and any other interested people, can see them for free now that the play is no longer touring.

The world of the mental health service user, especially the time spent behind locked doors on a psychiatric ward, is quite a hidden and comparatively neglected area of social concern and surveillance. There is still a high degree of stigma, of shame and social exclusion around anyone who admits to struggling with mental illness and they will often experience discrimination. I hope this play allows the voices of a few mental health service users to be heard in a clear, rational, and dramatically powerful manner. I hope that it enables the audience to witness, from dramatised first-hand accounts, what actually goes on in psychiatric wards and to gain a greater understanding of, and perhaps a little more empathy for, the people who end up in such places as patients.

Ideally, I would like to think that this piece challenges the accepted belief that medication and confinement, although possibly needed in some cases, are the only ways to look after patients in mental distress. I hope the result is an engaging story of a group of friends which shows our personal histories and our particular experiences and needs in a system which is there to help and protect us, but which very often appears to fail us completely in this regard.

References

To find more information about the play *Hearing Voices*, as well as the published script and DVD version of the play, visit: www.hearingvoicesplay.co.uk; www.claresummerksill.co.uk

Paget, D. (1987). Verbatim theatre: oral history and documentary techniques. *New Theatre Quarterly*, 3(12): 326.
Summerskill, C. (2012). *Hearing Voices*. London: Tollington Press.

CHAPTER THIRTEEN

Beyond the spoken word

Gail Simon

Silence in therapy

S ilence, as we might know from our own experiences, can be beautiful, welcoming, terrifying, confusing, grounding—so many things. But a therapist's reading of a silence might not tell us whether it is a desirable and friendly silence for people or whether people want help with talking in general or about something in particular.

My training in psychoanalytic therapy and my experience of having psychoanalytic therapy taught me about the uses of just sitting with people without feeling a responsibility to populate the space between us with a wordy attempt to understand and process through questions, answers, and reflections. On the other hand, I think back with horror to other times in my therapeutic career when I might have contributed to unnecessary discomfort for some people by not creating additional choices with them. The move in systemic therapy towards dialogical and collaborative relationships in therapy brings me great relief. A reflexive, appreciative, and learning stance in therapy opens space for therapists and the clients to negotiate rewarding and creative ways of communicating together. This is a better ethical and practical fit for me. It opens up possibilities to get alongside people in their silence and find useful and fitting ways of being together.

The spoken word is not everyone's first or preferred language. In this chapter, I share some examples of how people coming to therapy and I have experimented and found ways of talking without being so dependent on talking aloud. In addition, I show how I have tried to get over some of the insidious narratives in our profession which privilege "aloud talk" as the optimum medium for a successful therapeutic outcome, and the use of therapeutic techniques over spontaneous responsiveness (Shotter & Katz, 1998; Vedeler, 2011) in therapeutic relationships.

In the following story, Susan and I work out how to co-ordinate in the silence. Despite what I said about being prepared for silences and not being in a rush to talk and understand, I can sometimes feel a discomfort which reflects my need to set a context for silences. If talking exchanges are not available in therapy, it creates a dilemma for the collaborative practitioner. How can I avoid imposing my agenda or my way of talking on people coming for therapy without them offering me guidance? The reflexive rescuer in me needs to know the extent of her responsibilities, to establish that the "call" button is working, and that people know how to use it.

Susan and I try to work out how to talk

Months go by. We sit in silence most of the time, but it is a silence which is far from quiet. Susan's discomfort is apparent. She looks pained when I ask questions and does not answer. Well, not in any way which I can make sense of. I just see-hear-feel her pain. There is an appearance of stillness in the room, but I feel we are both busy. I try many things—including not trying things. I come up with all kinds of questions and suggestions. Perhaps just one or two each session. These attempts to open communication feel as if I am making things more difficult, which means there are still long periods of silence. I have absolutely no idea how to navigate these meetings. I am not sure whose job it is to steer. I ask context setting questions and questions about talk.

"Would you like me to ask you questions?"

"Is this a comfortable silence or one you'd like us to get rid of?"

"What makes you more comfortable when we are together? Is it for me to imagine quietly to myself what you might be thinking? Or for me to imagine aloud to you what you might be thinking and for you to give me signs if I am on the right track or not?"

"Am I talking too much? Or too little?"

But I am in a bind. Susan cannot answer me. And I cannot interpret what signs there might be, such as blinks, her appearing more tense, and so on. Sometimes, I just try to sink into a mellow frame of mind and let the silence be kindly and exude an acceptance that this is part of the therapeutic process. Other times, I feel I am sitting opposite someone trapped by a lack of openings and that the therapy is torture to her. At these times, I try to talk, reflect aloud, share my wonderings, share stories, ask about safe topics and immerse myself in the experience of one word answers. At other times, I allow myself to feel lost. And with her.

I am often struck by the effort she is making to get to the appointments. There is the long journey, the fares, not being able to ask for a seat on the train if she feels unwell, the difficulty of managing her feelings and the stuff in her head when she is here, and the challenge of communicating with me. I have the feeling she has invested a lot in coming to therapy. I just do not know what.

One of the turning points in our work together comes when I refocus from seeing Susan as stuck, as unable to speak, and start to share with her my noticing about how much thinking she appears to be doing. I say to her that she seems to be doing a lot of talking with me and with herself in her head. Susan nods vigorously and then appears to collapse into the chair with what comes over to me as relief. She starts to breathe with her whole body. It is only now that I realise how much of her energy is going into holding something so tightly that her body has been rigid. Months later, Susan tells me, "I was ready to explode with the thoughts I was having. In my mind, I was shouting. I needed you to know that I did have things to say. I would sit there imagining myself talking to you. I was telling you things. Lots of things. But you couldn't hear me."

I still catch myself at times positioning myself as a kindly facilitator, focused on helping Susan overcome her "disabilities", and things quickly start to feel stuck. So, I shift to noticing her determination, her courage, her pensiveness, and her sense of humour, her achievements throughout her childhood, her education, her relationships, and her career. When I reposition myself to foreground her abilities, communication becomes easier between us. I see and appreciate her attempts to communicate and we find ways of going forward.

Silence as response

My experience of working with people who use silence in therapy is that they have often experienced trauma that has, one way or another, had an impact on voluntary and involuntary choices about speaking. Lang, in his chapter on silence in therapy with holocaust survivors (1995), gives some examples of what silence might mean and reasons people might have for maintaining silence about terrible experiences.

> In psychotherapy, talking is cure; silence is usually associated with defensiveness, resistance, negativism, and denial. The positive aspects of silence are often overlooked. The sufferer might experience silence as strength and courage. Silence can be a mark of respect. To remember, we stand together in silence; in silence we pray to honour the dead. As one survivor said, "When they walked into the gas chambers they were silent. Those who watched them watched in silence. The whole world remained silent. To talk about it now in order to gain personal relief is to desecrate their memory". Silent suffering and guilt is often a testimonial—a memorial to those who have perished (Lang, 1995, p. 22).

Living with silence is often a strategy for survival. What might this mean for how we can communicate in the therapeutic relationship?

Stepping into and out of binds

During the second year of our therapy together, Nona found ways of letting me know some of what had happened to her as a child. She did not talk aloud about it. She had been instructed as a child not to tell anyone about the violence she experienced or something very bad would happen to her. She felt sure that her survival owed a good deal to her not speaking out about these events. She had developed skills at hiding her pain and masking her fear so others would not put her at risk by asking about her distress. When a teacher she liked did ask, she was too scared to answer truthfully. Nona was certain the abuser would be believed over her and that her life would be further at risk. The abuse continued for several more years.

Somehow, I knew that my invitations to communicate had to be soft and tempered to offer real choice. I did not want inadvertently to become allied either with instructive, abusive, or kindly attentive persons who might unwittingly enhance risk. Any asking I did brought forth more evasion and more masking. But, over time, somehow we made it safe enough for her to speak with looks and gestures. Any aloud talk I did in relation to this was unpredictable in consequence. Sometimes, my aloud talk made her jump and seemed to create disturbance, not relief. At other times, she appeared very relieved. I tried to follow her communications, but I had to do this without apparently acting on all my observations. Her privacy was an important and necessary protection and to acknowledge everything, or just anything, she said or felt might have created an unbearable amount of exposure. We muddled along. Or perhaps we were attempting to co-ordinate like the improvisations of jazz musicians, following each other, elaborating but not overpowering each other's unique contribution, not staying too long in the domains of either complementarity or symmetry (Bateson, 1972). Even though more everyday kinds of outer talk were not easy for us, we interspersed the painful talk with talk about work and home life and this seemed to create a helpful sense of relief before we decided to pick up on a difficult refrain at another point.

Silence as a relational space

Silence in therapy is not something which one person does or which exists separately from the different participants in a conversation. It takes place in the relational space between therapist and client(s). It could also be taking place in relation to others who might or might not be present, but who are significant to the stories informing the silence. Silence has a human and physical geography and a temporal quality, which are perhaps not immediately apparent or audible to a therapist. When in silence, one can forget time and it can "fly by" if one gets lost in it, with or without a companion. Silence can prolong a sense of time. It can be exciting or excruciating if waiting for someone or something to happen, but, in my experience, whatever the feelings that accompany silence between people, something still moves on and time does not stand still.

Sometimes, I have a sense of ghostly presences, out of focus movements between people, indecipherable texts, muffled communications, and the massive dimensionless silence that can follow an explosion. In this space, I am lost. It is not entirely my territory. I cannot see or hear what I have not been told. I might want to reach out to find something familiar to get my bearings—such as a way of talking. As a systemic therapist, it is not difficult for me to turn to questions, histories, family trees, life maps, hopes for the future. I might search for some "facts", play with some tentative ideas, try to set a context with people in an attempt to recreate a familiar and reassuring geography of what it means to be a therapist and do therapy.

Rules of the game

At a workshop, a therapist wants to discuss a client who is not talking. This is familiar to me. It is a conversation I am hearing more and more: therapeutic concerns are becoming conflated with economic and productivity matters and therapeutic relational know-how is being diminished.

"My manager says I should close the case. She says the client is not yet ready for therapy."

"Does she turn up for appointments?" I ask.

"Oh yes, always," the therapist replies.

"Does she come on time to the appointments?"

"Oh yes. She's on time. But she doesn't really use the time."

And we get into a conversation about what using the time therapeutically might look like.

Several things are going on here. The first is that the subject of silence in mental health discourses leads us back into the modernist story of problems being located in an individual: "If *I* am willing and able to talk and the client doesn't talk, then they clearly have the problem". This thinking reflects the dominant discourse of individualised pathology as opposed to something being a social challenge for all participants in a relationship. I find it useful to nudge myself to get beyond restrictive and negating explanations for silence and use my empathic imagination to assume strength instead of weakness, to look for profundity in intent rather than confusion in action.

"If the woman you are thinking about could show you that she is getting some really important things from the time with you, how would it change how you felt when you were with her?"

"If you could develop your own criteria for being helpful with this client based on some of your favourite texts, what do you think you might come up with?"

Second, in the apparent silence and privacy of a therapeutic relationship, it turns out there are others present in the room: a watchful, monitoring voice, audible only to the therapist–employee. "How do you account for this time spent in silence as being part of an active therapeutic piece of work?" asks the watchful, panoptical eye of the internalised institution. Government-led definitions of which ways of talking count as therapy and the move towards prescribed and proscribed ways of psychotherapeutic working influence what kind of talk is allowed by and within institutions (Whitfield, 2012). Whitfield suggests that in becoming increasingly accountable to institutions over the profession of systemic therapy, the voices of practitioners become owned and shaped by the institution, as we are encouraged to speak and perform in institutionally prescribed ways within therapeutic relationships. As practitioners, Whitfield adds, we become subject to the same kinds of threats as many people coming to therapy, so resulting in professional restriction and silence (Whitfield, 2012). So one could ask:

"If you weren't feeling the presence of a value-for-money watcher, what else might you be noticing about how she is engaged in the time with you?"

"Suppose at some point in the future, this woman shows you how you were helpful to her and you write up what she says for commissioners. How would you want commissioners to learn from her experience? What kind of advocate would you want to be for people using therapy like she has done?"

Third, systemic therapists are likely to approach silence in therapy with a critical appreciation of power relations in the therapeutic relationship and, therefore, with a concern not just to take charge and do something method-led and/or formulaic. In employing relational and self-reflexivity as part of an ethical and practical stance, systemic therapists will ask themselves, "What else could I be doing?" However, institutional watchfulness, coupled with the nervous reflexivity that sitting in silence might provoke, can lead to a use of systemic techniques and questions without a critique of power in therapeutic relationships. This reminds me of earlier attempts in systemic practice to develop a reproducible method with associated techniques. Seikkula points out that

> Therapists no longer attempt to control dialogue by their questions or interventions. Therapists must instead constantly adapt to the utterances of the clients in order for the dialogue to take on life, since the dialogue itself generates new meanings. (Seikkula, 2003, p. 89)

"What kind of strengths and vulnerabilities do you need to work with people who invite you into an unfamiliar therapeutic space?"

"If you were to reposition her use of therapy as a way of doing therapy, what learning opportunities might there be for you and the rest of the systemic therapy community?"

Silence as dialogue

It was the activist and pioneer, Bertha Pappenheim, who coined the term "the talking cure" as a description of psychoanalysis following her therapy with Breuer, a colleague of Sigmund Freud (1895d). Since this time, most of the psychotherapies have been structured to be dependent on outer talk and it is common practice to regard therapeutic success as partly dependent on talking aloud about difficult matters.

The idea of "silence" usually refers to outer silence in a shared physical space. Silence does not exist on its own. Bateson's idea about the difference that makes a difference (Bateson, 1972) makes me think that something called "silence" only comes into being when contrasted to something else, for example, the sound of people talking, and that "talking" only comes into the realm of language as a result of people wanting to name a difference between one thing and another.

Silence is often far from silent to the people involved in it. Silence stops being silent the moment one acknowledges it as silence and starts to listen to it. I am not sure how it would be possible to experience silence in inner dialogue. It is the conversation in inner dialogue that debates how to go on in outer talk. Silence in outer dialogue might not, in itself, cause any discomfort. The noisy inner dialogue about how to respond to silence in outer dialogue might create some strain for therapist and client(s). Some voices in inner dialogue and the narratives they are connecting with might feel a bigger sense of entitlement to make themselves heard than other voices. They might attempt to push conversational participants towards a particular story of what good therapy requires in the way of outer talk. For example, in moments of anxiety during silences, with the voice of a worried referrer in mind, or in response to a person's distress, I will act with manualised thinking and do something I have done before which has worked. And sometimes it works again. More often it does not. And then I have to manage my intolerance of discomfort or turn down the volume on the voice of the referrer's worried request for me to *do* something and, instead, do that other kind of something in which I surrender to the "not knowing" and allow the map to unfold between us rather than follow prescribed ways of working.

"The therapeutic relationship" of outer conversation

This positions both clients and therapists as conversational respondents belonging to the visible and audible arena of outer talk. But, of course, there are other relational therapeutic spaces. There are the worlds of inner dialogue for all parties which run parallel to the outer dialogue and which shape and are themselves shaped in the movements between *and in* inner and outer dialogue. *Thinking* is popularly considered to be a silent activity—something which happens in the apparently soundproof enclosure *in one's own head*. Thinking is made up of thoughts. And, in this cognitive understanding of the relationship between speaking and thinking, thoughts inform the acts of speech. Some have described thought as monologue (Vygotsky, 1934) but I have come to think of monologue *not* as a thing in itself, as if existing outside a relational context. I understand monologue less as a fixed thing but more as a relational response, subject "thought" as an isolated, definable, fixed thing in the brain, to Bateson's idea of mind as meaning-making activities in the fluid social spaces between people and their environment. In post-positivist, relational construc-tionism (McNamee & Hosking, 2012), we can understand thinking in a relational way as inner conversation between different voices, each with their own relationships with various narratives (Simon, 2012a)

"Silence, like talking, is interactive" (Lang, 1995).

The emphasis on outer expressions, on utterance (Bakhtin, 1986) distracts us from a parallel activity of *gutterance* (Whitfield & Simon, 2008) that precedes the expression of any utterance. Gutterance refers to inner movements that precede, accompany, and follow any outer talk. It is activated by the narratives living within the body, which control whether talk stays "inner" or makes it into outer talk. Gutteral responses from the bodies of conversational participants or witnesses to conversations make themselves heard before more recognisable inner dialogue kicks in and before any outer utterance. In my rela-tional restorying of "thought", I hear the inner dialogue discussing the body's message and deciding how to respond inwardly and outwardly. This conversation influences the shape of outer talk. Systemic therapist and supervisor Anne Hedvig Vedeler develops the work of John Shotter and Mikhail Bakhtin in her detailed account of the relationship between embodied knowing, inner dialogue, and joint outer movement with clients and supervisees (Vedeler, 2004, 2011).

I could easily slip into describing Susan (above) as sitting in silence or "thinking" things to herself. I could also say that she was experiencing, as I was at the same time, much activity in inner dialogue. From her later descriptions, these were not single isolated thoughts, but a busy and noisy exchange of conversational responses to different voices, each with its own suggestions and anticipation of possible consequences of these articulations, both inner and antici-pated outer articulations.

While it is sometimes difficult to attribute these monological sounding voices and their narratives to a *particular* relationship or event, conversing with the concerns behind the narrative *as if it were a person with an opinion*, allows for conversation to develop and we find a way of going on in conversation. I hear more talk within systemic practice inviting reflexivity about the quality of the silence and about how to co-mission an appropriate response to it. I have been consid-ering all utterances (Bakhtin, 1986)—inner and outer, audible and inaudible, understandable or not—as a form of dialogue, but with different intentions based on a person's narratives about probable social consequences.

Reading and writing as therapeutic dialogue

Maitland, in her *A Book of Silence* (2008), discusses the problems of the *Oxford English Dictionary*'s definitions of silence and applies them to writing reading material and reading writing.

> If you take the first OED definition and understand silence as an absence of *language* then simply there is and can be no silence on a printed page, because it is made up entirely of language. If, on the other hand, you take the second definition, that silence is an absence of sound, then written language is silent, because whatever else it does, a printed page of text does not make any sound. (Maitland, 2008, p. 146)

The page of writing "in itself" makes no sound, despite being full of language. It needs a reader to render the words into soundfulness and enter the writing into a relational arena in which words can be heard and experienced and meaning can come into being. The writer needs a reader for their writing to be heard and to have a chance of being understood, really heard with "mind" and "body".

Somehow, despite minimal outer talk in our time together, Ben lets me know how painful it is to speak about the dislocation he feels in the UK. "Home" no longer exists and, in any case, is loaded with unrepeatable memories. In the silences with Ben's pain, I somehow know that any attempts on my part to attempt to understand or enquire could be too clumsy and dilute or fracture something rich and precious. This gutterance phase is followed by a lot of inner talk for me, in which I hear some of the many reasons which are stopping me from speaking. Something important, both strong and vulnerable, has surfaced, and it feels to me as if we have something left exposed and out in the open. I ask Ben if I can read something. Well, read someone. And I invite in to our conversation the voice of another therapist, Maxwell Mudarikiri. I read aloud Mudarikiri's feelings on returning "home" to Zimbabwe.

> In my reflections on my experiences, I realised how much I missed the people, relationships, practices and environment that I had grown up

with in Zimbabwe. The different aspects of life that had gained special significance and meaning seemed less accessible living in London. At the same time the strife and trouble happening there created added pressure in how to be an enfranchised Zimbabwean in white Britain. All these are not always public conversations; they are private conversations (of course with an internal audience) which here I am calling, musings. (Mudarikiri, 2002, p. 6)

We hear some of these musings together. They speak volumes to my client about things I could never know about. Ben is very moved. So am I. After this, aloud talk comes into the conversation. Ben speaks about his sense of not feeling at home anywhere and grounds his experience in a community of dislocated others who know something of how he feels. I do not need to speak. Ben can see I have understood something. I have already used my voice to hear Mudarikiri in our conversation. Now it is my turn to be silent.

By my inviting the voice of Mudarikiri into our conversational space, another conversation is foregrounded over the therapist–client relationship. I could just have given Ben the text to read on his own, but then we would probably not have had that experience of both being moved and seeing the other moved. We did not talk about it. It just happened. And then other things happened. Our conversation progressed. It was as if Ben had told me those things himself.

With Susan, she writes and then passes me the notepad. Sometimes, I read her words "silent", but often aloud, and then I hand her back the notepad. On occasions, I share my thoughts on her writing with her and she goes on to write more. In the following episode, I write back on the notepad after a period of my reading her writing aloud.

Susan writes, "I guess I am just 'talking' about mum because she is on my mind."

Gail writes,"Why the quotes?" I draw an arrow pointing to "talking".

Susan writes,"Am I talking or writing—perhaps communicating, expressing myself and asking questions."

I look up and say, "I feel I hear your voice when I read aloud what you have written."

Susan nods vigorously and writes, "Sounds like me."

I have found it useful to borrow from Burnham's practice of "lending someone his imagination" in thinking about lending someone your voice or, indeed, borrowing their voice with which to speak (Burnham, 2003).

Susan has taught me much about the use of writing as a first or preferred language in therapy, but there are sometimes binds we create for and with each other.

After weeks of trying out different ways of being in mostly silent conversation with each other, I noticed her looking at my clipboard. She was looking at it very intently, as if she was trying to tell me something. Eventually, I thought to ask her if she would like to write what she was thinking or feeling. Susan suddenly twitched violently. It looked as if she was about to leap out of the chair and grab the clipboard. But she stopped herself. I pushed the clipboard across the floor to her. "Use it if you want. Ignore it if you prefer." Again, Susan started as if to pick it up, hesitated, and then bent down and picked it up. For a moment she looked relieved, but then the frozenness returned. She looked anxiously around. She did not have a pen, but she could not ask for one. This was an example of the speechless bind in which she was living: a pen would have enabled her to ask for a pen. I got her one. And then Susan transformed in front of my eyes. I saw the tension fall away. She looked relieved, animated, and ready to get going. Her demeanour showed confidence and thoughtfulness. And so it came to pass that Susan brought writing to each session and my clipboard started to travel beyond my lap and between us. She wrote, handed it to me. I read and handed it back. She wrote some more. I do not think either of us could have imagined back then that one day Susan would arrive, take something from her bag, and say, "I've brought you a present." Susan can be quite ironic. It was not for me. It was a bright pink clipboard for other people coming to therapy to use. My facilitation was needed even less. Now Susan used her own clipboard.

People who need or want to use an alternative language through which to communicate need to speak in the dominant language to get to speak in their preferred language. For example, when I go to Norway, I avoid some confusion and feel it is respectful to start with the question "*Snakker du engelsk?*" (Do you speak English?), but the answer cannot be too complicated and I cannot carry on the conversation in Norwegian because I cannot speak that language. My foray into the host or dominant language is simply a way of opening up the possibility of continuing together in a common language. As it happens, most Norwegian people whom I meet do speak English. And, fortunately, most therapists can both read and write. However, many therapists still question whether they should be accepting and reading written communications, poems, journal entries, and so on from and by people with whom they are working. And I remember this from my own therapy when I handed things I had so carefully written to my therapist, only to be asked to "tell her about it" instead. This is a practice I still hear time and time again from therapists. They ask people to either read it aloud to them or tell them about it. I spoke with some of my doctoral colleagues about the problem of trying to describe in spontaneous spoken language things which were intricately crafted in and for written language over a much longer period of time than can be hoped for in swift conversation. A doctoral colleague said, "It took me so long to choose my words, to put them in this order or that—until it felt right, like that was what I intended it to say. But I didn't always know what I wanted to say until I started writing. And then things happened. And I couldn't hope to speak such complexity with any fluency. Or even accuracy. It is written for readers. Some things are not for casual conversation. When I try to say them, I become speechless."

> Writing in some respects requires more trust and openness than words—in writing the words can not be erased—they are in front of you and I feel sometimes have more meaning than the spoken word. Sometimes perhaps more feeling too—poetry—sometimes just reading poetry evokes as much or more meaning. (Susan, quoted in Simon, 2012b)

"I wish I never had to speak again," said one rather tired colleague soon after getting her doctorate. "They should just call me Dr Silence. Dr Silence. That would be nice. Then I can just listen and I won't have to talk. People can just read my papers."

Summary

By inventing our own ways of communicating with those people with whom we are working, we can create opportunities for overcoming isolating and limiting effects of compulsory speech practices expected in mainstream psychotherapy. Professional expectations that people will tell them what has been going on, and why they have come to this point in their lives might inadvertently bring forth shame and a sense of inadequacy. It can echo a person's earlier experience of coercive and restrictive demands and result in paralysis. By creating alternative approaches for articulating, sharing, and responding to accounts of experiences, we open up the possibility for the production of witness-able, respond-able-to accounts (Andersen, 1997; Anderson, 1997; White & Denborough, 2005). I am reminded of John Shotter's idea that "if our ways of talking are constrained in any way—if, for instance, only certain ways of talking are considered legitimate and not others—then our understanding, and apparently our experience of ourselves, will be constrained also" (Shotter, 1989, p. 141).

When Susan says, "I was ready to explode with the thoughts I was having. In my mind, I was shouting. I needed you to know that I did have things to say. I would sit there imagining myself talking to you. I was telling you things. Lots of things. But you couldn't hear me", Shotter can offer some support for Susan's experience.

> I act not simply 'out of' my own plans and desires, unrestricted by the social circumstances of my performances, but in some sense also 'in to' the opportunities offered to me to act, or else my attempts to communicate will fail or be sanctioned in some way. (Shotter, 1989, p. 144)

Language, in whatever form, has its limits. Attempts to use language that result in a feeling of inadequacy are opportunities for alternative ways of being in relation (Vedeler, 2004) and not for attributing stories of deficit and inadequacy to participants in the conversational process. However, feelings of inadequacy—for clients and therapists—might be an important part of a therapeutic process and wordlessness, feeling there is nothing one can do but be in a conversation somehow might reflect something more important than attempting a narration of events and feelings.

Gergen has said, "If you change the activities you change the language" (Gergen & Gergen, 2007). There is a reflexive relationship between the two. One changes the other. Silence is never "just silence". Neither is it without sound or without language, or even without speakers. Silence can be a busy, interactive, news-ful space. It is also a co-created space with, potentially, a range of relational possi-bilities. Systemic therapists, psychotherapists, and counsellors work-ing within other approaches face ethical and practical challenges in a changing, resource-led landscape of mental health provision whose industry standards prescribe fixed ways of working with individual persons as the prescribed site for treatment. It seems that different media and different activities allow us to find new ways of going on in conversation, in relationship with each other. Negotiating changes in activities introduces a shift in the balance of power and in the means of negotiating what will count as useful and productive thera-peutic practice. When I made the shift from thinking of Susan as someone who struggled with communication to seeing her as a writer, as someone who can communicate well, there was a transformation in our relationship. The movement in our activities creates the condi-tions for us to foreground *mutual abilities* over *individualised struggles*.

References

Andersen, T. (1997). Researching client–therapist relationships: a collabo-rative study for informing therapy. *Journal of Systemic Therapies*, 16(2): 125–133.

Anderson, H. (1997). *Conversation, Language and Possibilities: A Postmodern Approach to Therapy*. New York: Basic Books.

Bakhtin, M. (1986). *Speech Genres and Other Late Essays*, C. Emerson & M. Holquist (Eds.), V. W. McGee (Trans.). Austin, TX: University of Texas Press, 2007.

Bateson, G. (1972). *Steps to an Ecology of Mind*. London: Paladin.

Burnham, J. (2003). Systemic questions workshop, Harrogate, Yorkshire.

Freud, S. (1895d). *Studies in Hysteria*. S.E., 2. London: Hogarth.

Gergen, K. J., & Gergen, M. (2007). Positive aging workshop, Kensington Consultation Centre, London.

Lang, M. (1995). Silence: therapy with Holocaust survivors and their families. Draft from *Resilience: Stories of a Family Therapist*, M. Lang & T. Lang (Eds.). Melbourne: Reed Books.

Maitland, S. (2008). *A Book of Silence*. London: Granta.

McNamee, S., & Hosking, D. M. (2012). *Research and Social Change: A Relational Constructionist Approach*. London: Routledge.

Mudarikiri, M. M. (2002). Spiritual disgruntlement. *Human Systems: The Journal of Systemic Consultation and Management*, 13(1): 5–14.

Seikkula, J. (2003). Dialogue is the change: understanding psychotherapy as a semiotic process of Bakhtin, Voloshinov and Vygotsky. *Human Systems: The Journal of Systemic Consultation and Management, 14*(2): 83–94.

Shotter, J. (1989). Social accountability and the social construction of '*you*'. In: K. Gergen & J. Shotter (Eds.), *Texts of Identity*. London: Sage.

Shotter, J., & Katz, A. (1998). 'Living moments' in dialogical exchanges. *Human Systems: Journal of Systemic Consultation and Management, 9*: 81–93.

Simon, G. (2012a). Relational ethnography: writing and reading in and about research relationships. *Forum Qualitative Sozialforschung/Forum: Qualitative Social Research*. http://nbn-resolving.de/urn:nbn:de:0114-fqs130147. Accessed 30 November 2012.

Simon, G. (2012b). Writing as talk. *International Journal of Collaborative Practices,   3*. http://ijcp.files.wordpress.com/2012/06/simon_final_english-witing-as-talk_new.pdf. Acessed 20 July 2012.

Vedeler, A. H. (2004). Do you hear me? About therapeutic listening creating space for voices to emerge and to be heard. MSc Dissertation in Systemic Therapy. KCC International & University of Luton. www.taosinstitute.net/Websites/taos/Images/ResourcesNoteworthy/dissert_Vedeler.pdf. Accessed 26 April 2009.

Vedeler, A. H. (2011). Dialogical practices: diving in the poetic mo(ve)ment. Exploring 'supervision' and 'therapy'. Doctoral Dissertation, Department of Applied Social Studies, University of Bedfordshire, http://hdl.handle.net/10547/223011. Accessed 3 March 2012.

Vygotsky, L. S. (1934). *Thinking and Speech. The Collected Works of L. S. Vygotsky*. New York: Plenum, 1987.

White, C., & Denborough, D. (2005). *A Community of Ideas: Behind the Scenes*. Adelaide, Australia: Dulwich Centre.

Whitfield, G. (2012). Personal communication. 1 March.

Whitfield, G., & Simon, G. (2008). Personal communication, 10 June.

CHAPTER FOURTEEN

Voices from the frontline: "keeping on keeping on"— what matters to staff working in adult mental health services?

Iona Cook

> "The miracle is not to fly in the air, or to walk on the water, but to walk on the earth"
>
> (Chinese proverb)

Introduction

The question "what matters to staff who work in adult mental health services?" evolved in the process of the research I carried out for my MSc dissertation in Systemic Psychotherapy (Cook, unpublished, 2010) In this chapter, I reflect on the process of research interviews with two members of staff within a Community Mental Health Team (CMHT) and through their voices, I aim to consider some of the overarching themes of what is important to staff on the frontline and what keeps them going over time.

Community Mental Health Teams are interdisciplinary teams, usually comprising social workers, community psychiatric nurses, psychiatrists, support workers, psychologists, and sometimes psychotherapists of different disciplines. CMHTs came into being as a result of the mass closure of the old asylums and institutions in the late 1980s and early 1990s and are, according to Peck (1999), the most common model for community services for people with severe and enduring mental illness in the UK.

My political, personal, and professional context

I am a white, able-bodied, married Scottish woman of thirty-six. As a child, I was very aware of the poverty and desperation present within the West of Scotland in the 1980s. This was caused in part by the destruction of communities by Thatcherism. The Thatcher government closed down the centres of industry in Scotland without any further investment or consideration of the impact on the people who lived there. The structures of employment and social cohesion were taken away without anything to replace them. These communities had a long history of being based round industry, which provided employment and a sense of identity to many people as well as some financial stability to families. It was not uncommon for generation after generation to work in the shipyards or in mining. Many of these areas now have families where generation after generation have experienced unemployment, poverty, and, often, drug and alcohol abuse. This sense of deprivation is central to my consciousness and still haunts my thinking today.

At the moment, all services that care for those who are struggling with desperate aspects of life are facing violent cuts and their clients more deprivations. The searing pain of this knowledge is at the heart of my deep and ferocious need to write something. In adult mental health services, as I explore in more depth later, social exclusion, vulnerability, working with people's experiences of alienation, poverty, and deep distress are the bread and butter of everyday life. Therefore, it feels timely that in these desperate times for staff, service users, and carers alike I attempt to represent the voices of my research participants—two workers on the front line in a community mental health service in England.

The seeds of the research reported here were sown one day within the CMHT where I used to work. I was in our duty office into which referrals come. Reading through people's multiple experiences of intensely difficult life events, social exclusion, pain, and trauma, I was aware of a sense of pain and despair within my own body. This triggered a reflection on the emotional intimacy of the work we do. At this point, I began to wonder what keeps people doing this work, which, at times, can feel quite overwhelming, hopeless, and bleak.

As I write, it is a sparkling cold day rich with beauty. In my own life, the sharp reality of vulnerability and dependence is current. I am recovering from illness. The recovery has been gruelling. The emotional and physical realities of this have forced me to think about "keeping on" and what it means to be vulnerable in a deeply personal way.

As can be seen from some of the comments I have made so far, I like to emphasise transparency and use the "I" position. Charmaz and Mitchell (1997) and Etherington (2004) argue that the use of the "I" position indicates the writer's ownership of what is constructed and, thus, this chapter reflects my ideas and experiences and does not attempt to make claims about any truths.

Conversations with participants

It was with much excitement, uncertainty, and anxiety that I approached the interviews for my research. I met Suzanna, a psychologist, and was energised and engaged by her passion for her work and her political awareness. I then met George, a community psychiatric nurse, and was incredibly moved by his commitment to his clients and to the service he works within. My heart has been touched in a lasting way by their courage and knowledge. I loved the conversations I had with them and both of them inspired and moved me deeply.

In both interviews and in the transcribing process I was struck by the way in which the words of my participants touched my own experience and generated many more questions for me. Finlay (2003) describes the process between researcher and participant as the intersubjective space where one's emotions, experiences, and values meet with those of one's participants. Finlay's assertion that the process is similar to that of the therapeutic space made complete sense to me.

Themes

A number of key themes surfaced out of my conversations with Suzanna and George and I concentrate on four in this chapter. They are professional growth, professional frustration, making a difference, and the connection between the personal and professional in working with people with mental health difficulties.

What enables professional growth?

The theme of professional growth was apparent within both interviews. Two connected but distinct aspects that enable professional growth within the work and training context seemed to emerge. The first is spacious, reflective, and rigorous supervision. By spaciousness, I am referring to an energetic deconstruction of the taken for granted and space to breathe and think. This is the opposite of rigid "slogans" and fixed ideas, which can feel oppressive at times. Suzanna, in talking about the importance of supervision and training, said of her trainees, "To see them blossom over the years is nice."

This comment set me wondering about what growth meant and how this happens for trainees. I recalled the jaggedness of my anxiety in the training context and the tough but necessary "growing pains" in contrast to the verdant images of gardens, flowers, and rich summertime evoked by the word "blossom". Maybe growth in training was both delicate and vibrant and painful and productive. When I think of Suzanna in her supervisory role, I see her as a nurturer of trainees and, like a gardener, she is patient. Her supervisory work is intricate, involved, and knowledgeable.

The other important aspect for professional growth concerns the values that are dominant within working teams. Suzanna cited one of the reasons she felt her team was a good place to work in was because it was a "teamly team" unlike a "piranha tank".

I found the idea of a team that privileges principles of collaboration and harmonious working compelling, with its implication of warmth and containment in which workers could grow. Some authors, however, perceive multi-disciplinary teams to be more what Suzanna called "a piranha tank".

One of the central preoccupations of Peck and Norman's (1999) paper, which explores different professional groups' experiences of CMHT work, highlights the issue of who has the strongest voice and who has most professional credibility. In their recommendations, Norman and Peck (1999) state that one of the problems of multi-disciplinary team working is that there is a dominant pretence that there is no hierarchy. Indeed, they write of "an overvalued allegiance to democracy". They argue that if community mental health teams are to work, there needs to be honesty about the competitiveness of different professional factions vying for power.

It is interesting to think about what ideas are influential in shaping this view. I would argue that these ideas are rooted within a discourse that privileges competition and power as fundamental truths and deems those who fail to play the competitive game as abnormal.

What factors contribute to professional frustration?

Intertwined with ideas about professional growth, inevitably, were Suzanna's and George's experiences of professional frustration, which were central to both their accounts. The pressure within the wider context of targets, "one size fits all interventions", and the rigidity of referral criteria were recurrent complaints.

Both of them used the word "blinkered" to talk about aspects of their experiences of colleagues that they also found frustrating. This is exemplified by George explaining, "They can't or won't adapt themselves to slightly different situations. OK, let's be a bit creative here, or inquisitive perhaps—let's just find out instead of just no, no, no."

I think this overly cautious, "jobsworth" attitude stems from a top-down rigidity that stunts curiosity about clients. I was acutely aware of the contrast between this stuck situation described by George and the sense of flexibility and openness to new ideas that he described when talking about creativity.

The reasons for such overly cautious attitudes are complex and I believe that organisational factors make a major contribution. David Lammy, the MP for Tottenham, talks about mental health services as a "Cinderella" service (Lammy, 2011). Lack of resources, not only financial but also those of time and space, are significant. In such a culture, where political and economic pressures drive targets, staff are put under so much pressure that they are unable to breathe and think and they risk ceasing to see their clients as people. When clients are seen as products to be fixed or made well, then there is a grave risk that some of the complexity which is at the heart of human growth will be forgotten, and this is potentially dangerous to staff and service users alike. This is particularly relevant in the context of working with clients with severe and enduring mental health difficulties, who often

live in areas of considerable social deprivation where, for all concerned, the nature of distress and social exclusion is incredibly painful
and exhausting.

Although the wish to fix things for patients and their families
comes from a place of good intention, it is not always achievable,
particularly given the complexities of mental health problems. Repper
and Perkins (2003) talk about the danger of professionals believing
that they have solutions for clients and thinking that situations are
solvable when they might not be. They also comment that this can
make both staff and clients feel they have failed. As a social work
colleague once remarked to me, one of the most damaging influences
on the self of the professional is fear of "looking like a failure".

What does it mean to make a difference?

Making a difference was a central part of what mattered to both
participants in my research. Suzanna emphasised the value, meaning,
and importance of change for her. "I suppose it's worthwhile and
meaningful when you feel that people are getting benefits from the
therapy. People are getting better. You see people being able to do
things they could not do before. Moving on with their lives—all those
kind of things make it worthwhile."

To me, these words are evidence of a professional knowledge base.
Nieboer, Moss, and Partridge (2000) explore what is meant by
"evidence-based practice". They suggest that the notion of positivist,
scientific evidence has become a gold standard dictating what is credible and legitimate in terms of what works in practice within mental
health services. They argue that this positivist dominance is connected
to a hidden political and economic agenda. I agree with their position
that finding out truths about what works in mental health services is
intrinsically problematic. In a sense, they broaden the definition of
evidence by suggesting that evidence seeking should be a collaborative process between staff and service users. They seem to advocate a
more flexible and creative way of thinking about what helps and what
works for people. This is relevant in the above description as Suzanna
witnesses multi-layered changes in clients lives. "To suddenly do
something a bit different. And it worked. It worked. It sort of cut
down the number of referrals requiring joint assessments. People in
urgent situations got seen."

Here, I see an example of how an intervention of George's made a significant difference to the service provided. On another level, I see George's passion about the importance of dealing with urgent referrals efficiently and seeing that it does make a significant difference to the numbers. Also, I would imagine that this has an impact on the experiences of service users in crisis.

The idea of small changes that mattered was important to both participants. Suzanna said, "I think more often we see people make some changes or improve some things", while George reported, "Again it is the hope that something I do makes a difference to someone, even in a minuscule way—you know—and I hope that that will continue."

In both quotes, George and Suzanna demonstrate how finely in tune they are with the needs of their clients and the complex problems and challenges experienced by many people with severe and enduring mental health problems which often make the recovery process complicated and difficult and steps forward small. It suggests something to me about Suzanna and George really having understood something of the plight of their service users. Through such hearing, listening, and witnessing, credence is given to people's real experiences of distress and poverty and, like Flaskas (2007), I believe this to be a political and ethical act. Such listening does not make the problems go away, but acknowledgement of their existence affirms people's experiences, whereas not hearing equates with the negation of people's experiences of pain and makes it easier for the wider culture to ignore them and, in so doing, ignore collective responsibility.

At the same time, issues of voice, power, and credibility are also intrinsically linked to being able to make a difference and the issue of whose voice is privileged and given wider credibility and power in terms of policy is relevant here. Our policy makers, in my opinion, are primarily white middle- to upper-class men, a view which echoes Gaines' (1992) assertion that diagnosis is constructed through a male, white, middle-class lens. The privileged position of those making the policies is, as we know, in contrast to the demography of those using mental health services, for example, the huge overrepresentation of black men within the mental health system (Lammy, 2011). Clearly, this points to an obvious gap between those who construct policy and those who are on the receiving end of it.

How does the personal influence the professional?
Working on the margins

The connection between George's professional and personal experiences and Suzanna's was striking. During our conversation on this theme, Suzanna said. "I think it is often not really taken into account . . . the kind of emotional toll of doing this kind of work."

The simplicity and compassion of her words for her clients, her colleagues, and for herself throughout our discussion were moving. I realised afresh how unsettling some interactions with people's distress can feel. Doane (2003), who writes about her own journey as a nurse, psychologist, and researcher, critiques the idea that we need to close off to suffering as researchers and professionals; instead, she advocates a position of openness to the experience and, like me, views sensitivity as a resource for workers. Despite this, Doane (2003) believes that the dominant view of reflexivity within qualitative research is that emotion needs to be somehow cut off or managed.

Flaskas (2007) writes that it is part of the deal of therapeutic work that the stories of the client will touch the stories of the mental health worker. In my opinion, it is part of what it means to be human to be touched by the experience of the other, and an acceptance and acknowledgement that the work is painful and difficult at times is necessary. However, saying this still remains something of a taboo, so that in the research interview with Suzanna, I was deeply curious about her experiences, but aware that I was reticent about asking too much about them. On reflection, I realised I did not want her to feel exposed and, by the same token, did not want to expose myself, given that her experience mirrored mine in terms of how affected I often feel by my clients' experiences. I felt ashamed in the research not only of how affected I can feel by clients' experiences, but also by how moved and emotional I felt in the room with both participants. On one level, I knew this was a resource. However, there was a strong sense for me that how I felt was somehow the wrong way for a researcher to feel. I felt that I should somehow be more "objective" and distant from the experience. I started to look for some explanations for this strong emotional response.

Kavner and McNab (2005), in their exploration of shame within the therapeutic relationship, describe shame as follows: "Shame can link to anxiety, through internalizing the contempt of others, or depression—the feeling of failure, inadequacy, not being loved or successful enough" (p. 143).

Flaskas (2005), in describing therapeutic failure and impasse, suggests that feeling stuck with clients can lead to feelings of shame and blame which are anti-therapeutic. She describes different theoretical takes on managing impasse and, thus, shame. For me, the most useful idea is curiosity (Cecchin, 1987), one of the cornerstones of systemic psychotherapy.

Another major theme around shame that arose in this project was the impact of working with social exclusion. Suzanna and George both spoke movingly about the stigma associated with living on the margins of society, particularly for those with a severe and enduring mental illness, and the impact this has on them as workers.

Suzanna said,

"There are a lot of psychosocial difficulties in this area and I feel strongly about giving a service to people that would not get a service otherwise. They are just . . . kind of what politicians call a kind of underclass and I feel really . . . kind of passionately that somebody should do something instead of just saying these kids are all . . . kind of hoodies and they'll never go anywhere you know. Who is doing something about it? Who is going to pick up the pieces? And I think it is often quite an important part of our role to stick with people when they are being contradictory and difficult."

Suzanna was referring to the complex matrix of difficulties often experienced by clients with severe and enduring mental health problems and living with poverty and social exclusion. An image of a worker remaining still within a churning and chaotic place came to my mind.

Her comments also made me pose the following questions. What does it mean to live as part of a society that stigmatises the "mentally distressed", yet work with people diagnosed with mental health problems every day? If people with mental health problems are so stigmatised, what does this mean for those people who work alongside them? The answers to this are complex. I would argue that professionals can also, to some extent, carry the stigma and the inevitable sense of shame themselves in their work. Neuberg, Smith, Hoffman, and Russell (1994) describe a phenomenon they name as "stigma by association". This is when staff who work in mental health services are stigmatised as a result of working with people who experience mental distress. Neuberg and colleagues also comment on the cost to people of being labelled "abnormal" or deviant.

In a sense, the stigma experienced by staff and, of course, to a much greater extent by clients themselves, represents the internalising of the wider projections of a society that struggles for many reasons with difficult emotions about people defined as having mental health problems (Kavner & McNab, 2005), as well as fearing that which is deemed "different" or unusual (Repper & Perkins, 2003). Furthermore Repper and Perkins (2003) contend that a distancing and a further stigmatising of clients can occur as a way of staff trying to deny their own internalised shame. This polarisation of "us" and "them" might offer some explanation of why, at times, service users are not treated as well as they should be. This fits with Flaskas (2007), who states that "despair, anger, shame and blame often trigger anti-therapeutic sequences" (p. 31). It would seem, therefore, imperative to think about lessening shame as a necessary step forward for the wellbeing of staff and clients.

How might this happen? Kavner and McNab's argument that combating shame is, in part, to do with staff being prepared to be exposed fits for me. They are very sensitive to the difficulties and pain of doing this, but at the same time strongly argue that in order to be therapeutic we do need to be transparent and authentic. This has affected my experience of managing shame and I have discovered that just the act of thinking about shame and naming it to oneself and others can be helpful, since shame thrives on secrecy and the hidden. I have also concluded that I might need to be braver in asking about and thinking in an open way about how I might marginalise or shame other colleagues as well as clients.

What keeps us going?

Having reviewed some of George's and Suzanna's key preoccupations in their work in CMHTs, I shall now conclude by giving some thought to what maintains any of us who work in teams with similar challenges.

During the process of redrafting this chapter, one of the suggestions of the editors was that I have a stronger voice within the text. I have tried to do this, but I am aware that finding my voice has not been easy. I was scared of ranting, of sounding too aggressive, of worrying about whether I sounded too passionate, too political. In reflecting on the roots of this, I realised that it is in part to do with making myself vulnerable to an unknown audience. In Gilligan's book (1982) on the psychological development of women, she talks about girls losing their voices in adolescence in order to gain social approval within a wider patriarchal society and being encouraged to see the world through a male lens. Is the current NHS love affair with randomised control trials and formulaic practice to do with gaining a kind of academic approval that is defined by a white male lens? Like our clients within mental health services, if we step out of this discourse do we not run the risk ourselves of being labelled as some- how academically not credible and wacky? Will we, too, be seen as "mad"? Taking the risk to speak out and join our voices as a collective is one way we can keep going together. We must continue to ask ques- tions and challenge assumptions about dominant ways of doing things in the NHS.

In an increasingly financially restricted NHS, what are the impli- cations for clients whose recovery journey is a complex one? I worry that the more interest there is in "results", the more pressure there will be on clients and staff alike. What does living in a political climate that seems to further belittle and humiliate the poor mean for people who have mental health problems and also often carry the additional stigma of poverty? Stigma and shame about not being able to get "well" could be compounded for clients and staff and such shame further impede their "recovery".

Like Repper and Perkins (2003), I feel passionately that the voice of the service user needs to be represented and integrated at all levels of the system in formal research, in policy, and in our day-to- day practice in finding out what is helpful to clients. More papers need to be written by service users and a wider and richer debate needs to develop. In hard times, marginalised voices need to shout loudly, and I believe hearing these voices more would be helpful in maintaining our energies and commitment to the work.

For me, the most abiding aspect of Suzanna and George's accounts was the holding of hope and the doing of hope (Weingarten, 2007) every day in work that at times can feel gruelling and hopeless. It is my view that the voices of pain that are intertwined in Suzanna's and

George's accounts can also be the voices of hope. Hope and hopeless-ness, as Flaskas avers (2007), are relevant to all therapeutic work. Weingarten (2007) and Repper and Perkins (2003) all talk about the importance of us as workers "doing hope" with our clients and the devastation that can ensue when staff lose hope and imply to clients, however subtly, that things are hopeless.

At a personal level, I know that what has sustained me through my recent period of ill health has been the huge and precious support of family, friends, professional helpers, and colleagues who, with their patience and containment, have enabled me to "do hope".

The question of how people keep on going as workers is particu-larly significant at a time when the NHS is experiencing devastating cuts and a deeply uncertain future. I feel overwhelmed by terror and a kind of voiceless rage when I think about the possibility of things becoming harder and even more unjust for users of mental health services. I notice in the current talk about the NHS reforms that very little is said about mental health services. Sometimes, the impossibil-ity of having any influence on an organisation as large as the NHS, embedded as it is in a powerful political discourse, seems great, but at other times, I shift to a more hopeful position, believing that indi-viduals can and do have an impact and reminding myself that tireless campaigning by marginalised groups has always changed things and continues to do so.

One of the things I have learnt from George and Suzanna is that no matter what is happening in the wider context, it is important to hold on to the micro level, one-to-one experience within the collective one, and to remember the many times I have seen at first hand the difference that can be made by the therapeutic relationship between clients and professionals from all disciplines. In my view, that is some-thing to celebrate and keep stitched within my heart.

I keep going because I will not do anything else, as I believe it is right to do so. I believe that I belong to something bigger than myself (McGoldrick & Hines, 2007). I do believe there is such a thing as soci-ety and I think social change always involves pain. I hold on to the community of voices of the many people from my personal and pro-fessional life who have taught me so much about humanity and humility throughout my career. I long for a world where there is appreciation of diverse voices. I turn to the cyclical nature of the seasons and the organic nature of life for comfort. It is clichéd but true that after the bitter frost and grey of winter, there are always buds of new life that make way for the green of springtime. I wish to conclude with the words of Weingarten (2007), who says "Hope depends on pathways thinking to an achievable goal, whether that goal breaks our heart or not" (p. 17).

References

Cecchin, G. (1987). Hypothesizing, circularity and neutrality revisited: an invitation to curiosity. *Family Process, 26*: 405–413.

Charmaz, K., & Mitchell, R. G. (1997). The myth of silent authorship: self, substance and style in ethnographic writing. In: R. Hertz (Ed.), *Reflexivity and Voice* (pp. 193–215). London: Sage.

Cook, I. (2010). "Keeping on keeping on." What matters to people working in adult community mental health services? Unpublished research dissertation for MSc in Systemic Psychotherapy, KCC, London.

Doane, G. (2003). Reflexivity as presence: a journey of self-inquiry. In: L. Finlay & B. Gough (Eds.), *Reflexivity: A Practical Guide for Researchers in Health and Social Sciences* (pp. 93–102). Oxford: Blackwell.

Etherington, K. (2004). *Becoming a Reflexive Researcher: Using our Selves in Research.* London: Jessica Kingsley.

Finlay, L. (2003). The reflexive journey: mapping multiple routes. In: L. Finlay & B. Gough (Eds.), *A Practical Guide for Researchers in Health and Social Sciences* (pp. 3–20). Oxford: Blackwell.

Flaskas, C. (2005). Sticky situations, therapy mess: on impasse and the therapist's position. In: C. Flaskas, B. Mason, & A. Perlesz (Eds.), *The Space Between: Experience, Context, and Process in the Therapeutic Relationship* (pp. 111–125). London: Karnac.

Flaskas, C. (2007). The balance of hope and hopelessness. In: C. Flaskas, I. McCarthy, & J. Sheehan (Eds.), *Hope and Despair in Narrative and Family Therapy: Adversity, Forgiveness and Reconciliation* (pp. 24–35). London: Routledge.

Gaines, A. D. (1992). From DSM-IV to DSM III-R: voices of self, mastery and the other: a cultural constructivist reading of US psychiatric classification. *Social Science and Medicine, 35*(1): 3–24.

Gilligan, C. (1982). *In a Different Voice: Psychological Theory and Women's Development.* Cambridge, MA: Harvard University Press.

Kavner, E., & McNab, S. (2005). Shame and the therapeutic relationship. In: C. Flaskas, B. Mason, & A. Perlesz (Eds.), *The Space Between:*

Experience, Context, and Process in the Therapeutic Relationship (pp. 141–155). London: Karnac.

Lammy, D. (2011). Personal communication. UKCP Black Men on the Couch Event, Tottenham, London.

McGoldrick, M., & Hines, P. M. (2007). Hope: the far side of despair. In: C. Flaskas, I. McCarthy, & J. Sheehan (Eds.), *Hope and Despair in Narrative and Family Therapy: Adversity, Forgiveness and Reconciliation* (pp. 51–62). London: Routledge.

Neuberg, S. L., Smith, D. M., Hoffman, J. C., & Russell, F. J. (1994). When we observe stigamtised and "normal" individuals interacting: stigma by association. *Personality and Social Psychology Bulletin, 30*: 196–209.

Nieboer, R., Moss, D., & Partridge, K. (2000). A great servant but a poor master: a critical look at the rhetoric of evidence-based practice. *Clinical Psychology Forum, 136*: 17–19.

Norman, I. J., & Peck, E. (1999). Working together in adult community mental health services: an interprofessional dialogue. *Journal of Mental Health, 8*(3): 217–230.

Peck, E. (1999). Introduction to special section on community mental health teams. *Journal of Mental Health, 8*(3): 215–216.

Peck, E., & Norman, I. J. (1999). Working together in adult community mental health services: exploring inter-professional role relations. *Journal of Mental Health, 8*(3): 231–243.

Repper, J., & Perkins, R. (2003). *Social Inclusion and Recovery: A Model for Mental Health Practice*. Edinburgh: Balliere Tindall.

Weingarten, K. (2007). Hope in a time of global despair. In: C. Flaskas, I. McCarthy, & J. Sheehan (Eds.), *Hope and Despair in Narrative and Family Therapy: Adversity, Forgiveness and Reconciliation* (pp. 13–23). London: Routledge.

Reflections from trainee therapists

Shona Reed-Purvis and Paul Flecknoe

W e worked for eighteen months in specialist psychological services in an adult mental health (AMH) context as part of the MSc in Systemic Psychotherapy that we studied together at the Tavistock Clinic in London. We wanted to share, in conversation together, some of our thoughts about this experience.

Shona: I was wondering, Paul, what your reaction was when you heard you were going to be in an AMH placement?

Paul: I was pleased because this related well to my context at the time, working as a clinical psychologist with adults experiencing distressing psychoses. However, I was less familiar with thinking about their problems systemically and I felt that AMH would be a valuable context to develop my systemic skills. While I would have also welcomed the opportunity to work in a CAMHS [Child and Adolescent Mental Health Service] setting, one of my concerns on starting the course was that the training might tend to be a bit CAMHS-centric, so I welcomed the AMH opportunity.

Shona: I agree, I was also excited, and felt lucky to be going into an adult placement; it was unusual and I was already working in a

CAMHS setting. But, unlike you, I had never worked in such a setting before, so I was concerned that without a professional psychiatric training I would have little to offer. I remember being very pleased that we were going to work as a consulting pair, I felt very unconfident and thought I would be helped by your expertise.

Paul: How did you find the actual experience compared to your hopes and expectations?

Shona: I learnt so much, both about myself and the power of systemic ideas to challenge some of the stigmatisation of mental illness. I found the context of adult mental health quite upsetting at times. We heard stories where people's illnesses were still treated solely in a conventional pharmacological way, where issues of race, gender, and disability seemed to skew treatment and attitudes. I learnt how this sometimes left people feeling abused by the system. I also heard from community mental health teams and GPs who were frustrated by chronic illnesses, and how this constrained them and what the system would then offer. I saw the effects of labelling people with illness: how that constructed the lenses through which all behaviour was then viewed. Again and again, systemic ideas were a powerful antidote to this.

Paul: One thing that struck me in working with the broader family is how the whole mental health system is so fragmented, and the care is driven by the pathologising of one or more family members. Often, this led to the need to try to liaise with different types of services and across age boundaries. Sometimes, it felt as if being a family therapist gave you a unique overview, as one of the few professionals who might have a picture of how the family was connected to different aspects of the system.

Shona: Tell me a bit more about how it was working as a family therapist having worked in an AMH context as a psychologist?

Paul: Starting the placement meant juggling a sense of uncertainty with familiarity. I was familiar with the systems, language, and types of dilemmas common in an AMH setting. It also felt familiar to try to consider other kinds of explanations and discourses to make sense of what is often understood as an "illness" residing inside a person. However, I was less familiar with thinking about this systemically, and many of my psychological explanations were still intrapsychic. I remember, in an early session working with all three generations of a family, being drawn towards wanting to ask in detail about a father's obsessional behaviours, rather than engage the family more broadly.

Shona: Yes, I found it liberating to work systemically, and being able to move away from seeing the patient or the illness as the problem. It felt a privilege to be able to think and work where meanings about illness, and the consequences of significant illnesses, could be explored (Campbell, Draper, & Huffington, 1991). I felt the rewarding nature of family therapy, where small changes were making significant improvements in people's lives.

Some of the challenges were often the mirror image of the opportunities.

The context of AMH invites us to think only of the patient and not of the whole family, and often in the clinic we thought about the way partners and children had been less involved, thought about or included by the wider system. By thinking and working with the family, unexpected benefits emerged. Symptoms reduced as meanings changed between couples, where patterns of behaviour that had been influenced by attitudes to illness shifted.

Paul: For me, it was starting to see members of the family other than the adults. Working with children again, as well as adolescents and grandparents, were all challenges to me, which required some reconnecting with skills last practised during my clinical training over ten years ago. When we began to think about the needs of a whole family, it sometimes became overwhelming to try to work out what needed to be the focus of the ongoing therapy. This led to rich discussions in our supervision group about how first the AMH context and second the "referred person" should be seen as additional contextual influences that required careful attention in our work. It was interesting to consider this, especially in comparison to other contexts, such as CAMHS, where the work is perhaps, at some level, seen as being in the service of the referred child, even if the focus of the work is with parents or other family members.

Shona: That's a really interesting point, because it makes me think that the work *was* in the service of the family, as that is what was best for the "adult patient". Sometimes, in CAMHS, I agree, family therapy is clearly undertaken in the service of the child, and this can sometimes lead to seeing the parents as being the problem.

I was wondering what you felt you had learnt about yourself and your practice in AMH and family therapy?

Paul: A challenge for me was developing my personal style, and working alongside someone who was very different from me, who used themselves more in the therapy, helped me to start to explore my style. Until this point, I had been more influenced by the sense of needing to maintain a "professional" stance in clinical psychology and in an NHS AMH setting. Offering more transparency to families, and bringing my personal self more into the work alongside my professional self, was a key development for me as the placement developed. I am pleased to say I have found this reasonably easy to transfer back to my work setting.

Shona: I think it affected me more on a personal level, as a woman developing my own confidence and voice in relation to you as a psychiatric professional. Sometimes, when we worked with couples, this had powerful resonances in the therapeutic work and led to some really useful discussions and development of my role (Real, 1990).

Shona: Having worked in adult and children's services, it seems the family is more fully understood in the domain of children. When children are facing mental distress, it is often in the context of needing support at a life-cycle change and is often an early intervention. In the adult mental health setting, it was far more about long-term ill health and "stuckness" in the family system. This experience was a very positive opportunity to think differently about adults in families and to work closely with you and your different and refreshing perspective from adult mental health.

Paul: I think, when I started in the placement, I was already aware of and interested in the relationship between family issues and the kinds of difficulties people presented with in AMH. Having completed the placement, it seems impossible to ignore the family when trying to understand people's struggles with mental health problems. Since this is such a rare commodity in AMH, I feel in a unique, privileged, but sometimes frustrating, position in trying to promote systemic and family-orientated perspectives in this area.

References

Campbell, D., Draper, R., & Huffington, C. (1991). *Second Thoughts on the Theory and Practice of the Milan Approach to Family Therapy.* London: Karnac.

Real, T. (1990). The therapeutic use of self in constructionist/systemic therapy. *Family Process, 29*(3): 255–272.

The Moving on Group

Jo and Kevin

W e have been having a very difficult time with our son: it is really affecting my health and both of us are at our wits end. I apologise for not being able to write much, but my thoughts are all over the place and [it is] difficult to concentrate on anything really. Here are a few thoughts . . .

How do you keep going when, as a parent, you are presented with very difficult behaviours, unpredictability, irrational thinking, then, a few minutes or hours later, a distraught person who is so sorry for the behaviours and appears rational for a while, and then, as if a wand has been waved, the cycle starts all over again. This cycle happens throughout any one day, every day. You start to lose trust in your loved one because the behaviours can be so unpredictable and concerning. You can't be in the house on your own with them or go out with them or do anything with them. What do you do when despite all your efforts over a long period of years nothing seems to work to help your young person in their desperate struggles? When you do not really have a diagnosis, where do you go to find specialist help? The terrible feeling that you are letting the person down because you just do not know what to do next. How do you come to terms with this when you realise that you cannot go on living this heartbreaking journey?

31 October 2011

What makes the A Ward a model for others to follow?

The A Ward has made a significant difference to our son's and our lives. How? By meeting the needs of our son and by including us, his family. The ward has a mission statement and detailed points of how they will work towards it. A lot of places have mission statements, but it is often hard to match up the words with the actions. However, the A statement is straightforward and written in plain language, as are the detailed points to fulfil the statement. For example,

- developing a therapeutic relationship with patients and significant others;
- working in partnership with patients and carers;
- sharing ideas, anxieties, hopes, fears,and the identified vision for a service that we are proud to belong to;
- enabling our patients to develop methods of coping with their illness and managing risks.

These points are inclusive and very important to patients and carers. There are many examples that we, as parents and carers, could give for each of the points above. For instance, we have been welcomed and encouraged to participate in our son's journey towards recovery and to consider our own recovery from the extreme stresses that his illness and inadequate mental health services have had on our emotional and physical health prior to our son being admitted. Staff have positively welcomed our input, and we in turn have welcomed their suggestions. Their professional approach, leadership, and teamwork have been outstanding. As carers, we can ring any time or visit, reassured that a member of staff can speak to us with authority and confidence about our son and his care.

We know that staff work towards enabling patients to help themselves by offering them a high percentage of time and quality nursing to meet patients' individual needs. Our son has benefited so much from their input. Staff offered us hope when we had none, support and time to talk in more depth. Families are listened to and included in the care of their loved ones. This approach is crucial to parents and carers, as it is us who will eventually have the responsibility of the day-to-day support of a loved one with enduring mental health difficulties. The A Ward has successfully translated words into actions; staff demonstrate this on a daily basis. The leadership cannot be over-estimated, as it has created a professional team approach and a caring environment which works for staff, patients, and families together, which makes such a difference to those of us seriously affected by severe mental health. In our opinion, the A Ward, at this present time, is a model that other mental health services could follow.

June 2012

Aaltonen, J., 132–133, 141, 146
abuse, 11, 68, 72, 76, 106, 153, 193, 199,
    209, 232, 237, 245, 274
  alcohol, 11, 260
  child, 206
  drug, 11
  of power, 190
  racial, 11
  sexual, xxvi
  systemic, 237
ACT Mental Health Consumers
    Network & Dulwich Centre, 79
AFT, 169, 182
Afuape, T., 12–13, 18, 201
Age Concern, 168
Alakare, B., 133, 146
Alanen, Y., 132, 141
Aldridge, J., 176
American Psychiatric Association, 5,
    113, 154
Amias, D., xxxviii
Andersen, T., 47, 49, 140, 142, 192, 255
Anderson, H., 9, 16–17, 47, 49, 255
Andrews, B., 90
anger, xxxi, 33, 56–57, 99, 104–105, 113,
    118–119, 134, 168, 193–194, 196,
    212, 215, 220, 268
anxiety, xxx, 26, 28, 46, 52–54, 60–61,
    120, 134, 144, 156–157, 163, 179,
    213, 223, 249, 253, 261–262, 266,
    280

anticipatory, 54
chronic, 54
debilitating, 152
disorders, 169
extreme, xxxiii
generalised, 209
-laden, xxiii
-provoking, 54
severe, 53, 154
Arcelloni, T., 117
Arnkil, T. E., 44, 145
Atukunda, J., 68
Aye Maung, N., 169

Bailey, R., 173
Bakhtin, M., xvi, 140–141, 250
Banerjee, S., 168
Barley, D. E., 57
Barnardo's, 168
Barnes, R. K., 36
Bassani, D. G., 205
Bateson, G., xxv, 46, 109–110, 245,
    248–249
Beardslee, W. R., 206
Bebbington, P., 169
Becker, S., 176
behaviour(al), xxv, xxxi, 7, 10, 47, 50,
    58, 112, 117, 119, 135, 174, 187, 210,
    212, 232, 274, 279
  aggressive, 53
  antisocial, 199–200

challenging, xxx, 51
cognitive-, xliii, 19, 46, 155, 175,
    199
difficult, 134, 279
obsessional, 275
overt, 102
patterns of, 275
psychotic, 145, 147
regressive, 141
rules of, 145
social, 11
story, xxv
symptomatic, 52, 117
unusual, 223
violent, 53
Bellringer, S., 168
Beltz, J., 115
Bentall, R. P., 9
Berger, M. M., 110
Berkowitz, R., 116
Bertrando, P., xlii, 115, 117, 121–122
Bhugra, D., 168
Bianco, V., 60
Biomed Childhood Depression
    Research Project, 50, 60
Birley, J. L. T., 110–111
Bland, J., 54
Blashfield, R. K., 7
Borden, A., 151
Boydell, K. M., 206
Boyle, M., 9, 12
Bressi, C., 115
Brewin, C. R., 90
Brigitte, 72, 79
Broderick, C. B., 109–110
Brooker, C., 171
Brown, G. W., 110–111
Buddhism, xlv, 26, 29, 35, 38
Bues, S. E. A., 182
Bullimore, P., 72, 83
Bumpstead, R., 169
Burbach, F. B., xliii, 46, 172–173, 176,
    180
Burbach, F. R., xliii, 46, 173–174, 176,
    179, 182
Burnham, J., 12, 181, 253
Burns, T., xxiv
Butzlaff, R. L., 111
Byrne, D., 75

Cabinet Office, 169
Camberwell Family Interview, 111
Campbell, D., 50, 275
Campbell, P., 9
Campbell, W., 12–13
Cardullo, B., 33
Carlat, D., 156
Carr, A., 18, 169
Carter, Jane, 182
Carter, John, 182
Carter, K., 176, 180
Carter, M., 182
case studies
    Addie, 152–164
    AJ, 218, 224
    Alan, xxxiv–xxxv, 44, 49, 56–58
    Alma, 51–52
    Anita, 143–145
    Dorothy, 54
    Drake, 220–221, 224
    George, 261, 263, 265–270
    Jeni, 197–198
    Jim, 43–44, 48–49, 56–59
    Jo, xxxiv, 279–280
    John, xxxiv, xxxvi, 48
    Kelly, 222–224
    Kevin, xxxiv, 279–280
    Leanna, xli, xlii, 87, 89–96, 98–99, 102,
        104–106
    Liz, xxxiv–xxxv
    Lorna, 219–220
    Louise, xxix, xxxi, xl
    Lynda, 223–224
    Lynne, xxxiv, xxxvi
    Nona, 244–245
    Pauline, 53–54
    Rob, xxix–xxxi, xl
    Serena, 216–217, 219, 224
    Simon, 197–198
    Susan, 242–243, 250, 252–256
    Suzanna, 261–262, 264–267,
        269–270
    Tallie, 219, 222
    Terenzi family, 115, 117, 119
    Veronica, 209
Castillo, H., 11
Cazzullo, C. L., 115
Cecchin, G., 48–49, 267
Chapman, H., 179

Charmaz, K., 261
Chase, N. D., 206
Chesler, P., 68
Child and Adolescent Mental Health
    Services (CAMHS), xxvii, xxxviii,
    273–275
Chodron, P., 36, 40
Clerici, M., 115
Coates, L., 88
Combs, G., 12, 14, 151
community mental health team
    (CMHT), xxiv, 6, 50–51, 57,
    259–260, 262–263, 268, 274
Cook, I., xliv, 60, 259
Cooklin, A., 176, 259
Corstens, D., 13
Coulter, J., 10
Cowie, A., 169
Craib, I., 26–27
Cromby, J., 6, 16
Cronen, V. E., xxxix, 50, 189–190
Cuipers, P., 169
Cullberg, J., 147
Dallos, R., 18
Danet, B., 91
Das, V., 69
Davidson, D., 187
Davies, E., 18
de Certeau, M., 91
de Haan, L., 147
Denborough, D., xli, 12, 14, 68–69, 71,
    75, 77, 211, 214, 216, 218, 255
Department of Health (DoH), 169, 172,
    178–179
depression, xxiii–xxiv, xxxvii, 8, 15, 26,
    30, 46, 50, 54, 60–62, 119, 134, 145,
    157–158, 160–163, 169, 193,
    209–210, 213, 215, 218–219, 223,
    229, 232
  chronic, 233
  clinical, 89, 91
  psychotic, 54
de Valda, M., 83
de Valda, S., 71–72, 75, 77, 83
development(al), 9, 74, 114
  child, xxxviii, 206
  dimension, 96
  fantasy, 36
  human adaptive, 206

journey, 35
of family relationships, 114
of mental illness, 112
progressive, 197
psychological, 269
theory, 206
Dillon, J., 7, 13
Dingemans, P., 147
disorder, 7, 169 *see also*: anxiety
  adjustment, 14
  bipolar, xxxi, 48, 197, 234
  eating, 141, 169
  mental, 90
  mood, 169
  obsessive-compulsive, xxxiii, 155
  panic, 8
  personality, 11
  psychiatric, 113, 115
Divac, A., 12
Division of Clinical Psychology, 18
Dixon, L., 46
Doane, G., 266
Doane, J. A., 112
Dohrenwend, B. S., 111
Donnelly, M., 173
Draper, R., 275
Du Bois, W. E. B., 191
Dulwich Centre, xliii, 67, 69, 79, 83, 207

Eagleton, T., 91
Eberlein-Vries, R., 116
Edkins, J., 83
Eeson, J., 5, 9, 14–15
Eichenbaum, L., xxxix
Eliot, T. S., 25, 30, 35, 37
emotion(al), xxviii, xli–xlii, 35, 57,
    59–60, 91, 105, 109–114, 117–119,
    121–122, 152, 261, 266
  attitude, 111–112
  attractors, 118, 121–122
  challenges, 156
  changes, 234
  climate, 111, 121
  content, 121
  difficult, 268
  elements, 113
  exchange, 111, 117
  expressed (EE), xlii, 46, 109–117,
    119–122

family, 121
flatness, 118
flux, 112
health, 280
heartfelt, xliv
influences, 16
interaction, xlii, 118, 121
intimacy, 261
involvement, xxxiv
level, 56–57
life, xlii, 118
loaded, 140
needs, 168
negative, 112
over-involvement, 111
pain, 237
problem, 157
processes, 118
reality, 261
resource, 161
response, 266
self-reflexivity, xlii
sense, 234
stance, 122
state, 118
support, 154, 168
system, 115
talk, 57
toll, 266
tone, 121
Engel, G. L., 113
Epston, D., 9, 13, 68–69, 71, 75, 151, 208, 210, 218–219
Eriksson, M., 44
Escher, S., 13, 68
Esteva, G., 83
Etherington, K., 261

Fadden, G., 171, 174, 182
Falloon, I. R. H., 111
Farhall, J., 174
Farma, T., 115
Farmer, P., 168
Feingold, D., 112
Fernando, S., 10
Filipas, H. H., 90
Finlay, L., 261
Finnish National Schizophrenia Project, 132

Flaskas, C., 60, 265–268, 270
formulation, 18, 31, 112
Foucault, M., 151, 189
Freedman, J., 12, 14, 151, 214
Freeman, J., 151
Freeman, W., 111
Freire, P., 191–192, 200
French, J., 5, 9, 14–15
Freud, S., 83, 248
Friedman, S., 191
Friis, S., 137, 146
Froggatt, D., 174
Fry, S., 33–34
Fuller, K., 7
Furedi, F., 7

Gaete, J., 5, 9, 14–15
Gaines, A. D., 265
Georgaca, E., 6
Gergen, K. J., 7, 9, 16, 47, 141, 189, 255
Gergen, M., 189, 255
Gilligan, C., 88, 151, 269
Gladstone, B. M., 206
Gladstone, T. R. G., 206
Gleick, J., 118
Goldberg, H., 60
Goldstein, M. J., 112
Goolishian, H. A., 9, 17, 47
Gore, S., 176, 180
Griffith, J., 15
Griffith, M. E., 15
Grinter, D. J., 182
Groenbaek, M., 50

Haarakangas, K., 133, 140, 146
Haley, J., 109
Hall, A., 206
Hamkins, S., xlii, 152, 163
Handley, R., 114
Hardy, K., 223
Harper, D. J., xl, 6, 10–14, 16, 18
Haslam, N., 18
Hassard, F., 80–81
Haun, M. W., 174
Haviland-Jones, J., xlii, 118
Healy, D., 8
Heaphy, G., 12
Herman, J. L., 68
Hines, P. M., 270

Hoffman, J. C., 60, 267–268
Hoffman, L., 9, 16, 47
Holdstock, L. T., 188
Holma, J., 133, 146
Hooley, J. M., 111
Hosking, D. M., 250
Huffington, C., 275
Hughes, T., xxxvii
Hunt, T., 81
Hutton, J., 223–224
Huxley, P., 168

Illich, I., 7
Ilyas, S., 8
Increasing Access to Psychological
    Therapies (IAPT), xxvii, 46
intervention, xxvi, 6, 19, 44, 47, 56, 112,
    122, 141, 147, 169, 248, 263, 265
  beneficial, xxxiv
  crisis, 138
  early, 55, 59, 132, 182, 276
  educational, 116
  family, 45–46, 54–55, 121, 168–170,
      173–180, 182
  helpful, 19
  medical, 147
  professional, xx
  psychological, 45, 199–200
  psychosocial, 46
  systemic, 54, 57, 174
  therapeutic, 18
Invernizzi G., 115

Jackson, D. D., 109
Jackson, V., 81
Jedlowski, P., 77
Johnson, D. L., 174
Johnstone, L., 18
Jones, S., 111
Jung, C. G., 30
Just Therapy, 12

Katz, A., 242
Kavanagh, D. J., 111
Kavner, E., 60, 266, 268
Kelly, L., 88, 222
Keränen, J., 133, 137, 146
Keropudas Hospital, Tornio, 132
Kilbride, M., 12–13

Kinderman, P., 9
Kirk, S. A., 9
Kirkuk Center for Torture Victims &
    Dulwich Centre Foundation
    International, 69, 77–79
Kis-Sines, N., xliii, 218
Klein, D., 111
Kleinman, A., 68–69, 81
Koenigsberg, H. W., 114
Kopp, S., 32
Kordy, H., 174
Kuipers, E., 168–169
Kuipers, L., 116
Kulwikowski, V., 72–74
Kutchins, H., 9

Laing, R. D., xxv, 9
Lambert, M. J., 57
Lammy, D., 263, 265
Lang, M., 244, 250
Lang, W. P., 50
Langan, D., 187
Larsen, T. K., 137, 146
Layard, R., 46
Lea, S., 173
Leff, J. P., 46, 109, 111, 114, 116
Leftwich, S. H., 173, 176
Leggatt, M., 174
Lehman, A., 46
Lehtinen, K., 132–133, 141, 146
Lehtinen, V., 133, 146
Leigh, M., 33–34
Lemert, E. M., 10
Lenior, M., 147
Lewis, B., 151
Linszen, D., 147
Little, M., 50
Lobovits, D., 151
Lock, A., 191
Lock, M., 69
London Medical Research Council, 110
Loy, D., xli, 29
Lucas, A. S., 180

Magai, C., xlii, 118
Magana-Amato, A., 112
Maisel, R., 151
Maitland, S., 251
Mancuso, J. C., 10

Manojlovic, J., xxxviii
Margalit, A., 79–80
Mari, J. J., 169
Martín-Baró, I., 191
Mason, B., 26, 32, 34, 49
Masten, A. S., 206
McCarry, N., 48
McCarthy, I., 60
McGoldrick, M., 270
McIver, C. C., 173, 176
McKeever, P., 206
McLaughlin, T., 6
McNab, S., 45, 60, 266, 268
McNamee, S., 250
Melle, I., 137, 146
Meltzer, H., 169
Mem, 72, 79
Mental Health Act, xxxi
Meriden Project, 174
Merson, S., 51
Mesterton, A., 147
Michaelson, J., 17
Midlands Psychology Group, 17
Miklowitz, D. J., 112
Mirowsky, J., 17
Mitchell, R. G., 261
Mohanty, C. T., 83
Moncrieff, J., 7–9
Morgan, A., 190–191, 195, 206
Morgan, R., 151
Morris, M., 13
Morrison, A. P., 12–13
Moss, D., xli, 32, 36, 46, 264
Moving On Group, xxxiii, xl
Mudarikiri, M. M., 251–252
Muijen, M., 168
Murray, A., 168
Murray, J., 168
Museums of Conscience, 70

National Institute for Clinical
    Excellence (NICE), 5, 46, 54,
    169
Ncube, N., 68
Neuberg, S. L., 60, 267–268
Nieboer, R., 264
Norman, I. J., 262
Nothard, S., 12–13
Nuechterlein, K. H., 112

object(ive), 10, 37, 192, 206, 229, 266
    materiality, 39
    of scrutiny, 27
    operator, 112
    position, 96
    process, 10
Ochs, M., 174
O'Neill, M., 82–83
Orbach, S., xxxix

Padoin, C. V., 205
Paget, D., 228
Palma, D. A., 12
Papadopoulos, R., 50
Pappenheim, B., 248
paranoia, 6, 101, 143–144, 157
Parker, I., 6, 13
Partridge, K., xli, 26, 48–49, 52, 55, 60,
    190, 264
Patel, N., 190
Pearce, W. B., xxxix, 189–190, 200
Pearson, D., 174
Peck, E., 260, 262
Pentecost, D., 60
Perkins, R., 264, 268–270
Pharoah, F. M., 169
Phillipp, D., 205
Pieczora, R., 178
Pilgrim, D., 10, 17
Pinfold, V., 168
Pitt, L., 12–13
Plath, S., xxxvii
Pluznick, R., xliii, 218
Pottle, S., 178
Power to Our Journeys group, 72–73,
    76, 79
Prakash, M. S., 83
Procter, H. G., 178
psychosis, xx, xxxiii, 43, 47, 61, 72, 122,
    134, 141, 145, 147, 169, 174, 209
    first-episode, 146
    service, 173, 175–176, 179, 182
    untreated, 146

Räkköläinen, V., 132, 141
Rapaport, J., 168
Rapley, M., 7
Rapsey, E. H. S., 173
Rasinkangas, A., 133, 146

Rassool, C., xli, 70, 80
Rathbone, J., 169
Rayner, L., 171
Read, J., 9, 16, 18
Real, T., 276
Reavey, P., 6, 16
Reibstein, J., 46
Reimers, S., 180
Repper, J., 264, 268–270
Rethink, 168, 172
Richardson, S. A., 111
Riikonen, E., 192, 199
Rober, P., 57, 121–122
Rogers, A. G., 10, 88
Romme, M., 13, 68, 83
Rooney, P., 168, 170
Roper-Hall, A., 201
Rose, N., 8
Rose, S., 90
Rosenhan, D. L., 9
Rowling, J. K., 28
Russell, F. J., 60, 267–268
Russell, S., 207, 211, 214
Rutter, M., 110

Sacks, O., xlvi
Sametband, I. N., 5, 9, 14–15
Sanger, M., 70, 74
Sarbin, T. R., 10
Sayce, L., 18
Scheff, T. J., 10
Schene, A., 147
schizophrenia, 6, 43, 46, 49, 54, 72,
    109–111, 115–116, 119, 132–133,
    145–147, 154, 162, 169, 193, 231,
    234, 236
Schizophrenia Commission, The, 168
Schrader, S. S., 109–110
Schweitzer, J., 174
Scott, J. C., 88
Seikkula, J., xlii, 44, 133, 137, 145–146,
    248
self, xxxviii, 13, 29, 50, 60, 187, 189, 199,
    264
  -achieved, 192
  -as-actor, 188
  -as-thinker, 188
  -care, 76
  -conscious, 98

-determined, 81
-doubt, 57, 60
harm, 229, 231–232, 236
-help, 199
-improvement, 35
-love, 81
-medication, 90
nature of, 188
non-, 29
personal, 276
professional, 276
-protection, 90
psychological, 8
-reflection, 60
-reflexivity, xlii, 57, 60, 248
sense of, 29
-serving, 18
-sufficient, 188
thinking, 188
-worth, xxx, xlii
sexual(ity), 190, 201 see also: abuse
  assault, 89, 144
  bi-, 231
  harassment, 90
  hetero-, 188, 198
  orientation, 231
  violence, 90
Shankar, R., 174
Sheehan, J., 60
Shepherd, G., 168
Sherbersky, H., 46
Shotter, J., 141, 242, 250, 255
Simon, G., 250, 254
Singleton, N., 169
Slade, M., 168
Smail, D., 26, 31, 34, 37, 39
Smith, D. E., 10
Smith, D. M., 60, 267–268
Smith, J., 174, 182
Snyder, K. S., 111–112
Social Care Institute for Excellence, 177
Social Exclusion Unit, 8
social GRRAACCEEESS, 12, 190,
    193–194, 201
Soudien, C., 70, 80
Sparks, J., 169
Speed, B., xlv, 10, 12, 16, 45, 49, 53, 61
Speed, E., 12
Spellman, D., 18

Stacey, G., 171
Stanbridge, R. I., xliii, 46, 172–174,
    176–177, 179–180
Stockell, G., 82–83
Stowell-Smith, M., 6
Strachan, A. M., 112
Stratton, P., 168
Strauss, J., 114
Strong, T., 5, 9, 14–15, 191
Sue, 72, 79
Summerskill, C., xliii, 235
Svedberg, B., 147
Szasz, T., xxv, 9

Talman, D. T., 88
Tamasese, K., 12–13, 68, 81–82
Tavistock Clinic, xliv, 273
theory, xliii, 50, 88, 235
    aetiological, 113
    basic affect, 118
    clinical, 175
    constructionist, 189
    domain, 50
    double bind, 46
    family, 113
    feminist, 151
    labelling, 10–11
    mental health, xli–xlii
    psychological, 18
    system, 118
    systemic, 47, 173
Timimi, S., 17
Todd, N., 88
Tomkins, S., 118
Tomm, K., 9
Treacher, A., 180
Trungpa, C., 29
Tuhaka, F., 12–13
Turku Psychiatric Clinic, 132
Turri, M., 51

Ullman, S. E., 90

Valetine, J., 90
Vassallo, T., 209
Vaughn, C. E., 46, 109, 111, 114
Vedeler, A. H., 242, 250, 255
Veldhuizen, S., 205
Veronika, 72, 79
Versage, E. M., 206
violence, xlii, 11, 88–91, 97, 103, 105,
    199, 212, 228, 236, 244, 253,
    see also: behaviour(al), sexual(ity)
    domestic, 52, 90, 190
    physical, 119
Voloshinov, V., 140
Vygotsky, L. S., 249

Wade, A., 88
Waitere, S., 168
Waldegrave, C., 12–13, 68, 81
Wallcraft, J., 17
Walsh, F., 114
Watters, E., 7, 68, 81–82
Weakland, J. H., 109
Weingarten, K., 199, 269, 271
Welford, M., 12–13
Wertsch, J. V., 76–77
West Midlands Psychology Group,
    17
Wevill, A. xxxvii
White, C., 214, 208, 255
White, M., 9, 13, 57, 68–69, 71–73, 75,
    79, 83, 151, 154, 206, 208–210, 214,
    216–220, 223–227
Whitehouse, L., 12
Whitfield, G., 247, 250
Whittaker, R., 156
Wing, J. K., 110–111
Wong, W., 169
World Health Organization, 5
Worthington, A., 168, 170

Ziarek, K., 195
Zwack, J., 174